"To be Anglican does not mean be[...] sort out Henry VIII's marital strife and procreative problem. To be Anglican does not mean to be white and vaguely religious. To be Anglican is not about trying to solve tense theological debates in ways that please no one and fail to address the underlying problem but will have to suffice for now. Rather, this courageous volume, ably edited by Gerald McDermott, shows that being Anglican is really about being part of the one, holy, catholic, and apostolic church. Anglicanism at its best is the marriage of the church's ancient catholic faith with the recovery of the apostolic gospel from the English Reformation. But the question is this: what will this kind of Anglicanism look like in the future? This international lineup of contributors outlines the current state of orthodox Anglicanism in its various provinces, the challenges facing Anglicanism in its various centers, and what might be the future of global Anglicanism. A fascinating read about a future fraught with challenges and buoyed by hopes."

Michael F. Bird, Academic Dean and Lecturer in Theology, Ridley College, Melbourne

"Whatever the future of orthodox Anglicanism may look like, it seems safe to suggest that it will not be monolithic. The essays in this book discuss not just the future of orthodox Anglicanism but also its identity, and on both topics the authors arrive at varying and, at times, disparate conclusions. United in opposition to what Archbishop Foley Beach calls 'neo-pagan' Anglicanism, these authors represent a broad range of traditional Anglicanism. Warm kudos to Gerald McDermott for skillfully bringing together these insightful essays from across orthodox Anglicanism."

Hans Boersma, Chair, Order of St. Benedict Servants of Christ Endowed Professorship in Ascetical Theology, Nashotah House Theological Seminary

"In *The Future of Orthodox Anglicanism* you will hear scholarly voices, perspectives from the majority world, viewpoints from ministry practitioners, and encouragement from leaders of other denominations, spoken with great conviction of the gift that Anglicanism is to the worldwide church. The writers' historical reflection and engagement with contemporary concerns serve up a feast for those new to Anglican life and for those of us who love the old ship despite its barnacles."

Rhys Bezzant, Lecturer in Christian Thought, Ridley College, Melbourne; author, *Jonathan Edwards and the Church* and *Edwards the Mentor*

"Gerald McDermott has brought together eleven essays and three responses by bishops, theologians, and church leaders from around the world, including two non-Anglicans. This varied collection provides valuable historical perspectives as well as an interesting range of opinions on the current faith and practice of the Anglican Church, coming as they do from different backgrounds, with different perspectives on the Anglican Church today and different outlooks on the future of Anglicanism. A sharp warning of the potentially suicidal effects of 'neo-pagan Anglicanism,' coupled with hopeful views from African contributors, leads McDermott to conclude that the orthodox Anglican future 'will be mostly nonwhite, led by the Global South, and devoted to Scripture.' While a book this size cannot address all major areas of contention and new developments in the global Anglican Church today, this helpful volume should provoke further thought and discussion about a subject that needs urgent prayer and active response: the future of orthodox Anglicanism."

B. A. Kwashi, Bishop of Jos, Nigeria

The Future of
Orthodox
Anglicanism

The Future of
Orthodox
Anglicanism

Edited by
Gerald R. McDermott

WHEATON, ILLINOIS

Trade paperback ISBN: 978-1-4335-6617-2
ePub ISBN: 978-1-4335-6620-2
PDF ISBN: 978-1-4335-6618-9
Mobipocket ISBN: 978-1-4335-6619-6

Library of Congress Cataloging-in-Publication Data

Names: McDermott, Gerald R. (Gerald Robert), editor.
Title: The future of Orthodox Anglicanism / edited by Gerald R. McDermott.
Description: Wheaton: Crossway, 2020. | Includes bibliographical references and index.
Identifiers: LCCN 2019025870 (print) | LCCN 2019025871 (ebook) | ISBN 9781433566172 (trade paperback) | ISBN 9781433566189 (pdf) | ISBN 9781433566196 (mobi) | ISBN 9781433566202 (epub)
Subjects: LCSH: Anglican Communion—Doctrines. | Anglican Communion—Apologetic works.
Classification: LCC BX5005 .F885 2020 (print) | LCC BX5005 (ebook) | DDC 283.01/12—dc23
LC record available at https://lccn.loc.gov/2019025870
LC ebook record available at https://lccn.loc.gov/2019025871

Crossway is a publishing ministry of Good News Publishers.

VP		29	28	27	26	25	24	23	22	21	20
15	14	13	12	11	10	9	8	7	6	5	4	3	2	1

To Julie McDermott,
the wife of an Anglican priest and mother of three Anglican boys,
who fills her home with the beauty of the Anglican way
of worshiping the triune God

CONTENTS

ACKNOWLEDGMENTS

Many hands make light work. There is wisdom in the multitude of counselors. My wife, Jean, provides the joy and help that enable me to do things like editing this book. As a zealous Anglican, she inspires and encourages me.

I am deeply grateful to Beeson Divinity School and its staff for providing space and structure for the conference that germinated this book. Dean Timothy George was not only an excellent contributor but also a source of wisdom at every point. Val Merrill made herculean efforts to ensure the success of the conference. Professor Lyle Dorsett was not only a good friend but also a source of good cheer along the way. Many thanks to Jarrod Hill, my ace student assistant, for editing and strategy.

Finally, I am grateful to Justin Taylor at Crossway for his interest in this project from my first mention of it, and his magnanimous help throughout.

Gerald R. McDermott
3 Epiphany 2019

ABBREVIATIONS

1549 BCP   "The Book of Common Prayer, 1549," in *The Book of Common Prayer: The Texts of 1549, 1559, and 1662*, ed. Brian Cummings (Oxford: Oxford University Press, 2011), 1–98.

1559 BCP   "The Book of Common Prayer, 1559," in *The Book of Common Prayer: The Texts of 1549, 1559, and 1662*, ed. Brian Cummings (Oxford: Oxford University Press, 2011), 99–181.

1662 BCP   "The Book of Common Prayer, 1662," in *The Book of Common Prayer: The Texts of 1549, 1559, and 1662*, ed. Brian Cummings (Oxford: Oxford University Press, 2011), 183–666.

1979 BCP   *The Book of Common Prayer and Administration of the Sacraments and Other Rites and Ceremonies of the Church, Together with the Psalter or Psalms of David, according to the Use of the Episcopal Church* (New York: Seabury, 1979).

LEP   Richard Hooker, *Of the Laws of Ecclesiastical Polity: A Critical Edition with Modern Spelling*, ed. Arthur Stephen McGrade, 3 vols. (Oxford: Oxford University Press, 2013).

INTRODUCTION

Why This Book?

Gerald R. McDermott

Anglicanism is the third-largest Christian communion in the world. At eighty-five million worshipers, it is growing as fast as or faster than the two larger communions, Roman Catholicism and Eastern Orthodoxy. Two aspects of that growth should be important to readers of this book. First, its new center of gravity in the Global South is predominantly orthodox, unlike its liberal parents in Canterbury and New York. Second, it is attracting more and more evangelicals who hunger for connections to the early church and its attention to mystery, sacraments, and liturgy. This is important because evangelicalism in all its varieties is growing around the world and, at 353 million self-identifying adherents, is a significant sector of worldwide Christianity.[1]

The summer of 2018 marked two pivotal events for the future of Anglicanism. The Global Anglican Future Conference (GAFCON)

---

1. Gina A. Zurlo, Todd M. Johnson, and Peter F. Crossing, "Christianity 2019: What's Missing? A Call for Further Research," *International Bulletin of Mission Research* I–II (2018): 5.

met in Jerusalem, where leaders of the orthodox core announced a sharp break with Canterbury. GAFCON leaders declared that they represented the majority of the Anglican Communion and did not need the approval of Canterbury. They proclaimed that they were retrieving the orthodox Anglican tradition by returning to the Bible as the word of God, to the Thirty-Nine Articles, and to the ecumenical creeds of the Great Tradition.[2] In July the American Episcopal Church met in Austin, Texas, where its General Convention decided that orthodox bishops could no longer keep gay marriage out of their dioceses. Another bishop must be permitted to enter the diocese to marry a same-sex couple if that couple desires it.[3] Marriage is arguably the primary biblical metaphor for God's relationship to his people, so its perversion in every diocese of the Episcopal Church means that the church has now repudiated Christian orthodoxy. It should become clear to those with eyes to see that historic Christianity has moved south with an Anglicanism deeply attached to Scripture and creeds but rejecting the ways of the grandparents in the Global North who gave it a name.

Two Questions

This book contains eleven essays by leading Anglican scholars and leaders (and short responses by three other Anglican leaders), every one of them orthodox. The essays are expansions of short talks delivered at Beeson Divinity School's first annual Anglican Theology Conference, entitled "What Is Anglicanism?" The conference was held over September 25–26, 2018. Each essay addresses two questions: (1) What is the deep character of Anglicanism that distinguishes it from other Christian traditions? (2) Where should the Communion go in the future?

---

2. "Letter to the Churches, Gafcon Assembly 2018," GAFCON, June 22, 2018, https://www.gafcon.org/news/letter-to-the-churches-gafcon-assembly-2018.

3. Mary Frances Schjonberg, "Convention Lets Its 'Yes' Be 'Yes,'" *Episcopal News Service*, July 13, 2018, https://www.episcopalnewsservice.org/2018/07/13/convention-lets-its-yes-be-yes-agreeing-to-give-church-full-access-to-trial-use-marriage-rites/.

These essays give voice to a broad range of orthodox Anglicans. Some are from the Global North; others from the Global South. Some are within the Episcopal Church and the Anglican Church of Canada; most are in other Anglican churches. The fourteen writers come from low, broad, and high church perspectives. But all are committed to biblical orthodoxy, particularly on the presenting issues of our day—marriage and sexuality. They all agree that salvation comes from the triune God and none other, that human beings can be saved from sin, death, and the devil only through the life, death, and resurrection of Jesus Christ, the God-man. They all affirm the God-breathed character of Holy Scripture, that Jesus came to start a church (Matt. 16:18) whose constitution would be those inspired writings, and that the church ministers the life-giving power of God through its word and sacraments. They all profess the declarations of the three great ecumenical creeds without crossing their fingers behind their backs.

So why this book? Anglicanism is an important part of world Christianity today. Although recently fractured, its orthodox members are alive and well. They also constitute 80 percent of the worldwide Communion. This book is written by nine leaders from all over this worldwide church and two outside observers. Their essays provide a careful assessment of this vital movement, and therefore an important forecast of its future.

A Range of Answers

Archbishop Eliud Wabukala, from Kenya, writes that the Anglican Church is both catholic and Protestant in form, appeals to Africans because of its holistic approach to faith and life, and has developed a worldwide Communion because of its vision for world mission. He notes the growing success of Anglicanism in the Global South and thinks that Anglicanism is on the verge of a new global future. It has the historic opportunity to rediscover its distinctive reformed catholicity, which will give new life to the world. Wabukala suggests that it adopt a new conciliar leadership, and that the North learn from the vigor of the South.

Bishop Mouneer Anis, from Egypt, reminds us that we don't have to be English to be Anglican. In fact, he adds, the modern founders of Anglicanism, such as Thomas Cranmer and John Jewel, turned to North African theologians like Augustine and Cyprian, just as the early church was taught orthodoxy by the great theological minds of North Africa. Anis defines the Anglican Communion as a church that listens to the word of God in Scripture and also takes church tradition seriously—which places it between the Coptic Orthodox Church and various Protestant and reformed churches. Middle Eastern Anglicans help Anglicans in the North remember the suffering of the early church that is being repeated today. Anis has suggestions for future Anglicanism, such as a conciliar body of primates from which the new head of the Communion should be selected.

Ephraim Radner, from the Anglican Church in Canada, sees Anglicanism as a dying entity that is united not by theological agreement but by historical process. Genetic linkage provides continuity for the label "Anglican," but Anglicanism generally reflects the polarization, paralysis, and resentment of the larger social spheres in which Anglicans live. Radner thinks Anglicanism now has a post-Babel vocation in which it allows itself to be remade for some further divine purpose. Anglicans should be like the disciples after the crucifixion and resurrection, praying and listening for the emergence of new ecclesial communities.

Archbishop Foley Beach, of the Anglican Church in North America, argues that neo-paganism has infiltrated Anglicanism in the last half century. By this he means beliefs and practices that Christians once considered pagan. This counterfeit Anglicanism rejects classical Anglicanism's catholic, evangelical, and charismatic traditions. It often uses the same words but redefines Scripture, God, Jesus, Holy Spirit, evangelism, and moral and sexual ethics. Archbishop Beach calls for leaders of the Communion to protect orthodox doctrine and ethics by disciplining the Episcopal Church and any others who embrace neo-paganism. He says this crisis reveals the colonialism of the old wineskins. But he is hopeful that the new wine of Christ's continuing redemption will renew the churches among the nations.

Stephen Noll responds briefly to the first four chapters. Noll is the former dean of Trinity School of Ministry in Ambridge, Pennsylvania. He was also the chancellor of Uganda Christian University.

Pastor-theologian John Yates is concerned that in the movement of evangelicals to Anglicanism because of Anglican distinctives, the essentials of Anglican faith might be obscured. Those are living under the biblical word of God, proclaiming the gospel of justification through the body and blood of Jesus received by faith, revitalizing worship through the Book of Common Prayer, and serving the nation and common good. Anglicans must maintain their distinctives but realize that the essentials matter most.

Journalist and theologian Barbara Gauthier writes that Anglicanism is both reformed and catholic while being neither Roman nor (solely) Reformed. It appeals to the ancient fathers and the practices of the undivided church of the first five centuries. It joins the supreme authority of the Scriptures and the Patristic tradition, while emphasizing the ongoing sacramental life of the church. This reformed catholicism claims to be not the one true church but that part of the one, holy, catholic, and apostolic church that was brought to England and has been planted elsewhere. In the last century the Anglican Church has moved into all continents and among many races and nationalities so that Anglo-Saxons are now a minority of Anglicans. This new vibrant Anglicanism of its younger churches is growing, while the older Anglicanism of the older North is in decline.

Historian Gerald Bray identifies three defining characteristics of Anglicanism: its concentration on the fundamentals of Christianity while leaving disputed points aside, the centrality of the Bible, and its insistence on teaching Christianity to its own members and communities. But he also thinks it is still a concept in search of content. He claims that Anglicanism was never understood as a system of thought and theology until the nineteenth century, that it has been riven by conflict between its evangelicals and Anglo-Catholics, and that now its divide over marriage makes its future questionable. Because doctrinal unity is elusive, Bray suggests, in this ecumenical age, that Anglicans focus on what makes them Christians more than what makes them distinctively Anglican.

Bishop Chad Jones responds to Yates, Gauthier, and Bray. Bishop Jones is a coadjutor bishop in the Anglican Province of America.

Episcopal Cathedral dean Andrew Pearson proclaims that Anglicanism is the English witness to the biblical convictions of the Reformation. The latter was a rediscovery of the grace of God in Jesus Christ that had been largely lost because the authority of the Bible had been supplanted by man's wisdom. Pearson calls for Anglicans to use the Anglican formularies to renew their commitment to biblical orthodoxy, the gospel, the church, liturgical conviction, preaching, mission, and prayer. In sum, he says, this is a renewed commitment to the Lord Jesus Christ. Anglicans are to be comprehensive, but they must maintain a principled comprehensiveness. These are dark times, but we are a resurrection people.

I argue that Anglicanism was a distinctive way of living in the triune God for more than a millennium before the Reformation. Its distinctiveness can be seen in its spirituality, liturgy, sacraments, and theological method. It proposes a way forward in the twenty-first century when being evangelical is not enough, at least in those evangelical churches where experience is central and doctrine and church are minimized. Anglican sacraments and liturgy provide beauty and power that appeal to all five senses and to people of all capacities, which helps prevent an intellectualized gospel that attracts only the cognitively inclined. If Anglicans retrieve their ancient heritage of liturgy and sacrament, they will have something unique to offer this century when the "beauty of holiness" is resonant in ways it has not been for centuries.

Baptist theologian Timothy George is our first outside observer. He notes that the English Baptists emerged from the womb of Anglicanism by their opposition to the established Church of England. They opposed creedalism, infant baptism, prefabricated prayers, the episcopate, and enforcement of religion by civil magistrates. But, at the same time, they believed in an ecumenism of conviction that drills down to Christian essentials and is willing to see similarities. Younger Baptist theologians today talk about a Baptist catholicity that affirms catechetical use of the three ecumenical creeds and the doctrinal insights of the first seven ecumenical councils. They point to sacramental language in Baptist history and the same doctrine of justification that is found in the Thirty-Nine Articles. They have their own Baptist creed, and many Baptists find rich resources in the Book of Common Prayer. Both communions stress Christian mission, and in nineteenth-century England there was a Baptist-Anglican alliance led by the likes of Charles Simeon, Henry Martyn, and William Wilberforce.

Our Catholic observer is R. R. Reno, the editor of the influential journal *First Things* and a former Anglican. He sees Anglicanism as a *via media* (middle way) between Protestantism and Catholicism. That way of defining Anglicanism, he argues, captures the best of Anglicanism in its prejudice for what is old and its faith in outward forms through which God really does dwell on earth in sacred things and revitalized people. It also evokes the worst aspects of

Anglicanism: the spineless, muddling middle way that encourages a managerial mentality and inspires peace without principles. But Reno thinks Anglicanism might provide a template for the future of Christianity after Christendom: a differentiated vision of apostolic authority combined with tenacious loyalty to the objectivity of grace.

Bishop Ray Sutton responds to Pearson, McDermott, George, and Reno. Bishop Sutton is presiding bishop of the Reformed Episcopal Church.

In the conclusion, I talk about the present state of world Christianity and where Anglicanism fits in that picture. Then I discuss what contributions the new orthodox Anglicanism might make to the future of world Christianity. I also assess what we can learn from these eleven essays about the future of orthodox Christianity.

PART 1

REGIONAL PERSPECTIVES ON ANGLICANISM

1

AN EAST AFRICAN PERSPECTIVE

What Does the Lord Require of Anglicans?

Eliud Wabukala

What is Anglicanism? Its definition is rather elusive. Some say that Anglicanism is a product of incidental factors. It was never planned or strategically intended to be an expression of the Christian faith as we know it today. Instead, the rebellion by royalty in England against papal authority from Rome and the prevailing nationalist tendencies in England at the time combined to help produce what later became known as Anglicanism. These combined to bring about a separate church that from the onset retained strong elements of Catholicism while pushing toward Reformation ideals that were taking root in continental Europe.

This balancing of issues between Catholics and nationalist traditionalists in what became known as the "Elizabethan Settlement" gave rise to the form of Anglicanism that endures in its varied forms today. The form of Christian expression that emerged was broad and sometimes so vague as to be difficult to grasp, but usually felt and experienced as a thoroughly Christian way of life in its ethos, style, and outlook. Anglicans define themselves as those Christians whose worship originates from the Book of Common Prayer and whose intensive reading of Scripture is provided by the Anglican lectionary. The common use of the Prayer Book, which is thoroughly biblical, keeps Anglicans grounded in Scripture. But Anglicanism is also a sacramental way of following Jesus Christ. Because of this emphasis on both Scripture and sacrament, Anglicanism is both Catholic and Protestant in form.

When Anglicanism came to Africa, it took on a particular shape. In most parts of Africa—especially during its early life, as in Kenya—Anglicanism was characterized by a life of humility, faith in Christ and his cross, forgiveness of sin, and the expectation of a life of righteousness. But African Anglicans did not stick to themselves. They joined actively in fellowship with other Christians from other African churches. The East African Revival Movement reinforced this form of Christian expression—Anglicans and other Christians working together to serve their communities.

At first there was little intent to start a new Anglican church in Kenya. When Dr. Johann Krapf and John Rebmann were sent on mission from England to East Africa by the Church Missionary Society (CMS) around 1844, they did not intend to create an Anglican institution as we know it in Kenya today. Their aim was simply to convert people to the lordship of Christ as their Savior. They and others in the CMS encouraged literacy for the purpose of reading and understanding Scripture. They also taught elementary hygiene to combat disease that was prevalent because of a very harsh environment. The CMS strategy was to build schools and hospitals along with missions in order to teach the wholeness of the gospel. The result was a community of Christians whose approach to life was holistic. They downplayed the Anglican origin of the CMS so much that the older generation still refers to itself as CMS and not Anglican.[1]

Toward the Anglican Future

Some five hundred years after the Protestant Reformation, it is becoming clear that what some have called the "Anglican experiment" is not ending in failure but is on the verge of a new and truly global future in which the original vision of the Reformers can be realized as never before. We have had our problems, especially in the last sixty years. But rather than repudiating or belittling our history, we need to learn from it and set ourselves now to walk humbly with our God into the future that he has planned for us.

We should learn especially from the success of Anglicanism in the Global South, particularly in countries that were once British colonies. Here Anglicans have focused on the biblical tradition and have sought to interpret correctly the life and work of our Lord Jesus Christ. Members of these churches see themselves as recipients of the mission of Jesus Christ to share and teach the gospel as it was handed over by the apostles. Anglicans from these churches were leaders at the Lambeth Conference of 1998, where their unity was demonstrated by the passage of Resolution I.10, on human sexuality.[2]

Leaders from the Global North have led us down unhelpful paths. The so-called instruments of unity—the archbishop of Canterbury, the Anglican Consultative Council, and the Primates'

---

1. Much of what follows builds on my keynote address at the Global Anglican Future Conference in London, April 23, 2012.

2. Resolution I.10, "Human Sexuality," Anglican Communion (website), https://www.anglicancommunion.org/resources/document-library/lambeth-conference/1998/section-i-called-to-full-humanity/section-i10-human-sexuality?author=Lambeth+Conference&year=1998.

Meetings—have failed to provide unity and focus for effective mission. We all hoped that a solution to our recent crises (debate and division over sexuality) might come from a common Anglican Communion covenant. But this covenant was stillborn at its onset. Its nine-point promulgations were too general and noncommittal. They lacked the power to bring discipline in a fractured Communion. Their weakness lay in the fact that Scripture was overlooked as their source of authority. Yet only from Scripture can we know Jesus, the eternal Word and Lord of the church. To assert instead, as some of the proponents of the covenant did, that we need to recognize Jesus in each other's context was tantamount to a misinterpretation of the biblical text. For to be faithful to Scripture, our understanding of our context must submit to Scripture for renewal and transformation. Only by this submission will the church grow to become Christlike.

A Reformed Catholicity

But now we have a new and hopeful way forward. We need to realize that our time is not unique. Ours is not the first crisis in the history of Anglicanism or Christianity. Every crisis provides a new opportunity. By the mercy of God, he has given us this historic opportunity to rediscover the distinctive *reformed catholicity* of our Communion as shaped profoundly by the witness of the sixteenth-century Anglican Reformers. This is the answer to revisionist scriptural interpretations drawn by Anglican leaders in recent decades. We have a *catholic* heritage in our ancient sacraments and worship. And we are *reformed* because of our devotion to the word of God.

While we should uphold the hard work of biblical exposition, we can never disregard the plain teaching of the inspired text. It is that text that Archbishop Cranmer was so keen to have available in the English language in every parish church. The translation of the Scriptures into ethnic languages has been fundamental to the cultural transformation that the gospel has brought to Africa and the rest of the world. The division and confusion of past decades in Anglicanism are results of disregarding this plain teaching of the biblical text. Subsequent false teaching by leaders of Anglican Communion institutions has caused grievous divisions and endless debates since Lambeth 1998.

Communion in Mission

The way past those debates is to recognize that the Anglican Communion grew out of a vision for world mission. The first Lambeth Conference (1867) was organized in order to work with new Anglican churches outside of England. Similar outreach needs to be reenacted and reinterpreted in different ages and contexts. We need to remind ourselves that the church *exists* for mission to the world, so that without mission, the church loses its relevance.

The Anglican Communion in the past has seen itself as a family of churches who find their communion in mission. We need to realign our structures so that they can contribute toward our common goal for mission. In spite of our different contexts, the message of our mission should be the same: Jesus Christ revealed to us in Scripture, instructing us to follow him as our model, both in church as his body and in the community as a family of believers. He calls us to be friends with him and intends that we be brothers and sisters in this family created by his death on the cross and resurrection from the dead.

Mission is based on love. Jesus showed us that true love means we should be prepared to lay down our lives for each other. An Anglican Communion that can reach this level of mission will create structures that serve mission with effectiveness. Instead of taking different paths on essential issues of Scripture, members of the same Anglican family will humble themselves and repent in the face of biblical instructions.

Wisdom from Micah

My best advice is for us Anglicans to follow the exhortation of the prophet Micah. He too was writing at a time of crisis in the history of God's people. It was during the latter half of the eighth century BC, a time when the people of the northern kingdom of Israel had lost their identity, and the people of the South, Judah, nearly suffered the same fate.

In Micah 6:8, we read:

> He has told you, O man, what is good;
>   and what does the LORD require of you
> but to do justice, and to love kindness,
>   and to walk humbly with your God?

"What does the LORD require of you?" This is the greatest question facing the Communion in this era. The question demands that we have a clear understanding of the situation we are in and be willing to let go of comfortable illusions. It calls us back to what God has said and Micah affirms, that "he has told you, O man, what is good." It implies that discovering the will of God, what God requires, depends not on our ingenuity or imagination but on what God has already said. He spoke then in words that he speaks today—in the words of Scripture. The challenge is to all of us in the Anglican Communion. Will we allow the Holy Spirit to apply God's word to our hearts and obey it?

What *does* the Lord require? First, he requires that the Anglican Communion bring a *biblical mind* to the situation we face. None of us looked for our current crisis, and none of us can avoid it. We may be tempted to think we can get back to a time when the life of our Communion ran along more predictable and familiar lines. But that is an illusion. We should be bold and apply that biblical mind to our present crisis. We must face things as they are, in the confidence that God will act.

This will mean, second, examining our governance structures and correcting any hindrance to evangelism. As I have said above, the "instruments of unity" have failed us. But we Anglican Communion leaders must do more than simply distance ourselves from each other. We have to go back to the basic principles and develop new structures. We need to consider how we can *build on the model of a conciliar leadership*. Our Communion has come of age, and it is now time that its leadership should be focused not on one person or one church, however hallowed its history, but on the one historic faith we confess.

Third, to act justly and to love mercy means behaving toward one another with *honesty and fairness*. We must be careful not to be infected by cynicism and pragmatism that can creep in when issues of power and influence are at stake. Competing groups can act as prophetic movements, and God has given them some stern things to say; but the sternness should be all the more striking because of the kindness and generosity for which authentic prophets are known.

Fourth, all these things should be done with *humility and prayer*, not setting ourselves up above Scripture but recognizing that the word of God judges and searches us. We shall be alert to the fact that the word, which is God's truth for all cultures and all times, is not the privileged possession of any one culture or global gathering. Each of us has the potential to open up new perspectives on the unsearchable riches of Christ. But humility and prayer are required to get those new perspectives.

Fifth, to do what the Lord requires takes *courage*. We need leaders, lay and ordained, who are able to give a robust defense of apostolic faith in the global public square. Otherwise, secular ideologies that have so powerfully shaped liberal and revisionist Christianity in the Communion will tighten their grip on the church and prolong the trajectory of division.

We must also resist the temptation to be theologically lazy. Our aim for a renewed, reformed Anglican Communion will not be sustained if we are unwilling to support and encourage those who are gifted to do the training and the theological heavy lifting so essential to giving depth and penetration to our vision. We need to recover the vision of the Anglican Reformers, of ordinary believers knowing Scriptures and nourished by well-trained biblical teachers. In a hostile world this often requires fortitude. But it will be a bit easier if we build global partnerships to encourage evangelism and church planting.

So, sixth, *we need to recognize the different gifts in our Lord's body.* Our past efforts at these things have shown us that we need each other. The South can benefit from the experience of those in the North who have resisted and understood the dynamics of Western secularizing culture, for this culture is rapidly spreading around the globe. The North can benefit from the missionary enthusiasm and vigor that characterize the growing churches of the Global South. We all have learned that we must not be content with Anglicanism as a kind of chaplaincy to dwindling enclaves of those left behind by the receding tide of faith.

Tasks for Some Anglican Provinces in the Global South

All of this requires some special tasks for African Anglicans and others in the Global South:

1. Bishops should lead their churches to embrace and obey the Bible at parochial, diocesan, and provincial levels. In some areas in the past, the bishop was seen as an alien element in the life of rural congregations that came from the CMS. The resolutions of synods and the House of Bishops were not understood by the common Christians. They were imposed upon a bewildered following at the congregational

level. Bishops should resume their historic roles of pastoring pastors and ensuring that basic biblical preaching and teaching thrive across their dioceses.

2. Theological formation of the clergy should be stressed. Anglicans have always emphasized a well-trained clergy. It is particularly important that orthodox interpretation of Scripture and doctrine be maintained.

3. We Anglican leaders must teach our churches to beware of consumerism. Increased mobility and globalization have led people to choose churches based on what most satisfies their needs. We need to teach Anglicans that we are members of Christ's body, the church, and should think of what we can *give* to that body rather than what we can get.

4. We must lead in the responsible use of media. We should use it to advance mission that is biblical and life-giving, and beware of social media when it is counterproductive to the gospel.

5. We should advise Anglicans to consider tent-making ministry in villages and small towns as a way of reducing our financial burdens. This will prevent our overreliance on donors, both local and foreign.

In conclusion, a renewed appropriation of our reformed catholic tradition in Anglicanism will bring new life to the world. Using the gifts God has given Anglicans—the Prayer Book, sacraments, and plain-sense preaching from the Bible—we can trust that God will multiply the work we already see: refocused attention on God, deepened awareness of his holiness, his grace inspiring a deep sense of sin that causes repentance from sin, and a power that conveys profound forgiveness. This is new life and new hope in life. It all comes through our living Lord and Savior, Jesus Christ.

But this will not happen unless the Anglican Communion is bold enough to say no to the prevailing culture. We must realize that in Christ we have a message that offers salvation from the darkness and misery that have engulfed the entire cosmos. If we use the gifts God has given our Communion, there will be a recovery of orthodoxy, and new faith in the supernatural reality of the triune God. May he lead us and others to total conversion to our Lord and Savior Jesus Christ, to lives of holiness and outreach to the world around us.

2

A MIDDLE EASTERN PERSPECTIVE

Rooted in Egyptian Soil

Mouneer Hanna Anis

My Own Story

It is difficult for me to forget what the former archbishop of Canterbury Lord George Carey once said: "You don't have to be English to be Anglican." He said this during the Decade of Evangelism conference of 1990 in Kanuga, North Carolina. This conference was an eye-opener for me. Many laypeople, clergy, bishops, and archbishops gathered from around the Anglican Communion to share their stories of how the Lord was working in their churches. I will always remember the vibrant worship led by the Nigerian delegation. It encouraged all the conference participants to rejoice and dance as they were singing, "We are marching in the light of God."

This was the first time for me to see the rich diversity and global nature of the Anglican Communion. I also witnessed, during this conference, how happy and united this fellowship of Anglican churches could be. My understanding of Anglicanism was very narrow at that time, and I was not aware of the serious challenges that were waiting ahead to undermine the joy of this wonderful Communion.

I was then a lay minister at St Mark's Church, Menouf, Egypt, and the medical director of Harpur Memorial Hospital, the Anglican hospital in Menouf. Though I had been raised in a Coptic Orthodox family, my parents had been very open and had allowed me to go to other churches, such as Presbyterian and Catholic. This ecumenical context shaped my understanding and knowledge of the various local churches.

I first became aware of the presence of the Anglican Church in Egypt when I went to study medicine at Cairo University. It seemed to me to be a foreign church, not an indigenous one; I saw more expatriates in the church than Egyptians, and the worship style was more Western. Moreover, when I started to work for the Anglican Church hospital and became more involved in the church, I found that English was the common language used in the various church committees, as well as at the diocesan synod.

But as time passed, my appreciation for Anglicanism increased. It started to feel like my spiritual home. I decided to join the Anglican Church, and my wife and children became Anglicans as well. My bishop asked me, as a lay minister, to look after the daily church services in Menouf in addition to my work as a hospital director. Once a month a priest would come from Cairo to lead a Communion service for us. This arrangement continued for fifteen years until a permanent priest was appointed to St Mark's Church.

When I reflect on what drew me to Anglicanism, these eight things come to mind:

1. The word of God as revealed in the Holy Scriptures is given an important place in the church.

2. The gospel of our Lord Jesus Christ is preached in a very clear way.

3. The Holy Communion service is dignified and meaningful.

4. The church traditions that do not contradict the Scriptures place the Anglican Church in a middle position between the Coptic Orthodox Church and the various Protestant, reformed churches. In other words, it was not a big jump for me to join the Anglican Church after coming from an Orthodox family.

5. The family atmosphere that I experienced within the church was a great encouragement to me. The wonderful fellowship and the strong ties among members and workers inspired me. The whole diocese looked like one family, with the bishop as a uniting father of all.

6. There is an open-mindedness that accepts a variety of Christian thought and tradition while, at the same time, hewing to the ancient creeds. This leads to mutual respect between the traditional churches (Coptic and Catholic) and the Anglicans, which in turn has fostered excellent ecumenical relations.

7. There is a genuine desire to serve the community through Anglican hospitals, schools, and community development centers. These services are offered to all people regardless of their religion.

8. The good relations with the Muslim community and the engagement with them through interfaith dialogue has been inspiring.

The Birth of Christianity in the Middle East[1]

Some people forget that the story of Christianity began in the Middle East—the story of creation; the covenant with Abraham; the exodus; the presence of God in the midst of his people; the failures

---

1. Portions of this chapter draw from my earlier chapter "The Episcopal/Anglican Church in Jerusalem and the Middle East," in *The Wiley-Blackwell Companion to the Anglican*

and the victories of the people of God; the birth of Jesus Christ, our
Savior; his crucifixion, resurrection, and ascension; the first church;
and the first Christian mission to the world. It all began on the soil
of the Middle East.

So the church of Christ started in the Middle East two thousand years ago and continues to witness to the love of God today.
Jerusalem was the birthplace of the church. Antioch in Syria was
the place where people were first called "Christians." According to
Coptic Orthodox tradition and the writings of Saint Jerome, Saint
Mark himself established in Alexandria the first church in Egypt
and the first catechetical school in the world.[2] Carthage and Hippo
in North Africa shaped the Christian mind on many theological
issues.[3] Cyprus too played a significant role in the missionary jour-
neys of the apostles. Christians in Iran trace their history back to
the first century.

The Middle Eastern church fathers and mothers, the most famous being Saint Mark, were ready to shed their blood to keep
the faith once received from Jesus Christ through the saints. They
endured many hardships to combat heresies and to preserve the
apostolic faith. It is through their faithfulness that the Christian
faith spread to all the corners of the world. Without their witness,
Christianity would not be alive today in the Middle East.

Although the Anglican presence in the Middle East began
only at the beginning of the nineteenth century, Middle Eastern
Anglicans believe that they are rooted in the church of the first
century. Our ancestors were born there, and many of them were
martyred for the sake of our Lord in the Middle East. There is no

Communion, ed. Ian S. Markham, J. Barney Hawkins IV, Justyn Terry, and Leslie Nuñez Stef-
fensen (Chichester, UK: Wiley-Blackwell, 2011), 272–88.

2. Willem H. Oliver, "The Heads of the Catechetical School in Alexandria," *Verbum et
Ecclesia* 36, no. 1 (2015): 1–14.

3. See Thomas C. Oden, *How Africa Shaped the Christian Mind: Rediscovering the African Seedbed
of Western Christianity* (Downers Grove, IL: InterVarsity Press, 2007).

doubt that this early history has shaped our lives and thoughts ever since. More on this below.

Anglicanism in Egypt

The Anglican presence in the Middle East owes itself to the providence of God and gifted missionary evangelists. In 1819, the Church Missionary Society (CMS) of the Church of England sent its first missionaries to Egypt. After their arrival, they met the Coptic Orthodox patriarch and received from him letters of introduction to all monasteries in Egypt. They set out to visit the monks and distribute copies of the four Gospels in Arabic. They believed that the Coptic Church was to be encouraged to preach the gospel rather than simply focusing on the tradition and chanting the mass. In other words, they were hoping to help this great mother church to experience the same kind of reformation that the Anglicans experienced in the sixteenth century. This explains why Anglicans did not try to start Egyptian Anglican congregations for nearly a century beyond their arrival in Egypt. Another factor behind this strategy was a policy of the Anglican Church not to poach on the Orthodox Church's flock; instead, they would send new converts to the Coptic Orthodox Church to be nurtured in their faith.[4] Unfortunately, the Coptic Church often did not welcome these new converts. This unwelcoming attitude of the Copts disappointed CMS missionary Rev. Canon Temple Gairdner and prompted him to draft a new policy, which allowed for the establishment of the Egyptian Anglican Church in 1923.[5]

Two decades after the Anglicans' arrival, land in Alexandria was given to the Anglican Church by the Ottoman ruler Muhammad

---

4. Matthew Rhodes, "Anglican Mission: Egypt, a Case Study" (paper delivered at the Henry Martyn Centre, Westminster College, Cambridge University, May 2003), 3, htts://www.cccw.cam.ac.uk/wp-content/ . . . /Rhodes-Revd-Matthew-15-May-2003.pdf.

5. CMS Archives, G3/E/0/1925/15, University of Birmingham.

Ali Pasha (1839) to build its first church in Alexandria, which was then dedicated to Saint Mark. This marked the official presence of the Anglican Church in Egypt and its recognition by the government, but it was seen as a branch of the Church of England. As I will suggest below, it took a long time for this perception to change, and we are still in the midst of that change.

One reason for this is that the Anglicans who first came to the Middle East did not intend to start an indigenous Anglican Church. The objectives of the CMS missionaries were threefold: first, to preach the gospel to non-Christians; second, to provide pastoral care for English-speaking congregations; and third, to encourage and support the Coptic Orthodox Church and send new converts from Islam to join it. This third objective led to the establishment of a seminary for the Coptic Church in 1842, which continued until 1847. One of the monks who was trained in this seminary became a very famous pope of the Coptic Orthodox Church, Kyrillos IV, who was known later as Kyrillos the Reformer. He was the first pope to establish church schools in the main cities of Egypt. He also encouraged the education of girls.

Despite this focus on the Copts, the Anglican presence grew during the late nineteenth and early twentieth centuries. The CMS sent Rev. Llewellyn Gwynne, Dr. Frank Harpur, Rev. Douglas Thornton, Rev. Canon Temple Gairdner, Ms. Constance Padwick, and others to Egypt to plant churches and start Anglican institutions. They started the *Orient and Occident* magazine, built the Jesus Light of the World Church in Old Cairo, and established Harpur Memorial Hospital in Menouf. In 1920 the archbishop of Canterbury commissioned the Diocese of Egypt and the Sudan and appointed Llewelyn Gwynne as its first bishop. W. H. T. Gairdner and Douglas Thornton were the first leaders of what eventually became the Episcopal Church in Egypt.

Attempts to reach indigenous Egyptians took a big step forward when Gairdner arrived in 1899 and began a period of intensive Arabic study. By 1900 he was giving several addresses in Arabic each week, and by 1912 he was teaching Arabic to missionaries at the Cairo Study Centre. In 1917 he produced the book *Egyptian Colloquial Arabic*, followed in 1925 by *The Phonetics of Arabic*. Gairdner's linguistic abilities enabled him and his associate Douglas Thornton to dialogue with Muslims. Their discussions were marked by positive presentations of the Christian faith rather than negative point-scoring: "We need a song note in our message to the Muslims, not the dry cracked note of disputation, but the song note of joyous witness, tender invitation."[6] Gairdner used music, drama, poetry, and pictures—as well as articles and debate—to present the Christian faith. He brought the Episcopal Publishing House into existence and was the principal founder of *Orient and Occident*. This journal was circulated as far as Palestine, Syria, India, Sri Lanka, and Indonesia.

During these years, Gairdner came to reject the CMS policy of working principally with the Coptic Church. By 1921 he had concluded that the Coptic Church of his day was incapable of providing an effective mission to Muslims. It had too great a history of persecution by the Muslim majority to admit Muslim converts and so tended to pass them on to the Anglican Mission for baptism and nurture. "In the year 1921, I rose up in wrath and gathered my colleagues about me and declared that we should not go on like this any longer: in fact, that we must get on or get out."[7] Since the American (Presbyterian) Mission had already developed an indigenous evangelical church, Gairdner became convinced that an Egyptian Anglican church with its own pastors was a necessity in the short term. As his biographer, Padwick, put it, "Gairdner never dreamed

---

6. Constance Padwick, *Temple Gairdner of Cairo* (London: SPCK, 1929), 158.

7. Padwick, *Temple Gairdner of Cairo*, 263.

that this would be Egypt's final way of life and worship."[8] Small Anglican congregations with mostly Syrian and Palestinian Christians had already started to grow up in Cairo, but even Gairdner still thought their ultimate goal was to seed the Coptic churches with "evangelical militancy and Catholicity."[9]

In 1923 Gairdner drafted a policy statement that gained the approval of the archbishop of Canterbury:

> The primary aim of the Anglican Church in Egypt is the evangelization of the non-Christian population, and it does not desire to draw adherents from either the Coptic or the Evangelical Churches. Those who, in sincerity, find the Anglican Church their spiritual home are welcome to join it, but the Church does not set out to gain their allegiance. Instead, it seeks to extend the right hand of fellowship to the Coptic Church so as to render it every possible form of service, and at the same time it strives for closer co-operation and greater unity between all the churches in Egypt.[10]

While Gairdner worked hard to build up indigenous Egyptian congregations as interim means to someday reach Copts, he had a hard time persuading the bishop and his expatriate congregations to accept Egyptians as integral members of the Anglican Diocese of Egypt. The reason was Bishop Gwynne's low opinion of Egyptians. In one of his letters to the archbishop of Canterbury, the bishop wrote, "It is the policy of the British Foreign Office to say that the Egyptians are a most enlightened people with a strong sense of the good of their country and with high ideals of a righteous administration, but the real truth is that they are an uncivilized people."[11]

---

8. Padwick, *Temple Gairdner of Cairo*, 264.

9. Padwick, *Temple Gairdner of Cairo*, 264.

10. CMS Archives, G3/E/0/1925/15, University of Birmingham.

11. Bishop Gwynne to the archbishop of Canterbury, August 13, 1940, in "Archbishop's Correspondence 1921–1950," Box File 15, All Saints Cathedral Diocesan Archives, Cairo.

On April 25, 1938, the Feast of St. Mark (the patron saint of Egypt), Bishop Gwynne established All Saints' Cathedral in Cairo. William Temple, the archbishop of York, consecrated it. Unfortunately, the Anglican Church in Egypt was perceived by the Egyptian authorities, as well as by the people, as part of the colonial British government. That is why in 1955 all the properties of the church were confiscated and put under sequestration. In 1956 the Egyptian government forced all expatriates to repatriate, leaving only one Egyptian clergyman and one lay reader to look after all the parishes, schools, hospitals, and other institutions throughout Egypt. The future was unpredictable, which led to a growing spirit of fear that controlled many decisions made during this period.

Tragically, some Anglican churches and institutions in Egypt were destroyed, others were taken over by the government, and still others were given to other denominations. Several properties were sold at very low prices. Anglicans were relieved that in 1959 the Egyptian government returned the church properties to the diocese. But only a few years later, Harpur Hospital in Old Cairo and two schools in modern Cairo were confiscated. This was part of the government's vigorous reaction against Western colonial powers and the tension between the Egyptian and British governments. Many Western companies and organizations were nationalized. Consequently, many expatriates returned to their countries, and quite a few Egyptians migrated to North America and Australia. Many of those were Anglicans. It was a very difficult time for the church and its members.

These events made it clear that it was time for the bishop of Egypt to be an Egyptian. In 1974 the archbishop of Canterbury appointed Isaaq Musaad as the first Egyptian bishop of the Diocese of Egypt.

Jerusalem

The Anglican presence in Jerusalem started in 1841 as a joint venture between the Church of England (under Queen Victoria) and the

Lutheran Prussians (under King Frederick William IV). In 1841 the archbishop of Canterbury consecrated Michael Solomon Alexander, an ethnic Jew, as the first bishop of Jerusalem (1842–1845). Subsequent bishops were supposed to be nominated alternately by the English and Prussian sovereigns but consecrated as Anglican bishops.

On December 30, 1846, the second bishop arrived in Jerusalem. Bishop Samuel Gobat served there from 1846 to 1879. It is said that Gobat, a Swiss Calvinist, believed that the way to evangelize the people of the Ottoman Empire was through the members of the Middle Eastern churches. Since, however, he considered those churches to be "wayward and in deep spiritual sleep, they had to be awakened and restored to the true and pure faith, namely, to the evangelical faith that is founded on the Bible alone, the sole authority for faith."[12]

It was not until the mid-twentieth century that a Middle Eastern diocese was led by an indigenous bishop. In 1956 the "majma" (synod) in Jordan unanimously passed a resolution advising the archbishop of Canterbury to appoint an Arab priest from the diocese as the next Anglican bishop in Jerusalem. To set up a new framework in which this could happen, Archbishop Geoffrey Fisher of Canterbury decided to elevate the Diocese of Jerusalem into an archbishopric in 1957. He then appointed Archbishop Angus Campbell MacInnes to oversee the entire region. The new archbishopric became an extraprovincial jurisdiction of the archbishop of Canterbury. A new Diocese of Jordan, Lebanon, and Syria was formed, and the archbishop of Jerusalem had oversight over it. In 1957, Najib Cubain, the first Arab bishop, was consecrated as the bishop of Jordan, Lebanon, the West Bank, and Syria. He served as an assistant to the archbishop in Jerusalem.

---

12. Rafiq Frarah, "Evangelical Missions and Churches in the Middle East II: Palestine and Jordan," in *Christianity: A History in the Middle East*, ed. Habib Badr (Lebanon: Middle East Council of Churches, 2005), 729.

The Formation of the Province of Jerusalem and the Middle East

After several decades of leadership under MacInnes and George Appleton, "The Episcopal/Anglican Province of Jerusalem and the Middle East" was inaugurated in 1976. Metropolitical authority was transferred from the archbishop of Canterbury to the Provincial (Central) Synod. The following bishops have since served as president bishops or primates of the province: Hassan Dehqani-Tafti (1976–1986), Samir Kafity (1986–1996), Ghais Abdel Malik (1996–2000), Iraj Mottahedeh (2000–2002), Clive Handford (2002–2007), Mouneer Hanna Anis (2007–2017), and Suheil Salman Ibrahim Dawani (2017–present).

Iran

It was only after Henry Martyn (1781–1812) came to Iran as a chaplain of the East India Company and translated the entire New Testament into Persian that the Bible became accessible to Persian speakers around the world.[13] Martyn, a protégé of Charles Simeon, wrote in his journal on January 1, 1812, in Shiraz: "If I live to complete the Persian New Testament, my life after that will be of less importance. But whether life or death be mine, may Christ be magnified in me."

Missionary work in Iran began in the 1820s. The third bishop of Iran was William James Thompson (served 1935–1961), and one of his Iranian pupils, Hassan Dehqani-Tafti, became the next bishop on April 25, 1961. Dehqani-Tafti wrote in 1976:

The present day Church in Iran grew out of the C.M.S. Mission . . . with [its] medical service and later, schools. The first church building was put up in Isfahan in 1909, the first

---

13. Padwick, *Temple Gairdner of Cairo*, 291–97.

[indigenous] Persian pastor ordained in 1935, and Bishop Hassan Barnabas Dehqani-Tafti, consecrated in 1961. . . . He [was] the first Persian bishop for over a thousand years, for in pre-Islamic days Iran was a country with a strong church with over eighty "bishops" and sent missionaries to India, China and the Far East.[14]

The Iranian Revolution of 1979 brought new oppression to the Anglican Church in Iran. There was an attempted assassination of Bishop Hassan; when this failed, government agents assassinated his only son. Several members of the Iranian Anglican Church, alongside some British missionaries, were imprisoned. All institutions of the Anglican Church were confiscated. After Bishop Hassan's retirement, Iraj Mottahedeh (a convert from Judaism) served as bishop from 1986 to 2007. His successor, Azad Marshall, proclaimed at his installation in 2007, "My Christ did not come for only Christians; my Christ is for the whole world. With your help and cooperation, I will seek to serve both Muslims and Christians because Christ came to serve all." The church in Iran still seeks to faithfully serve all people.

Cyprus and the Gulf

Reporting on unique opportunities to interface with Muslims, Bishop Michael Lewis of Cyprus has written:

> In 1976, when the new Province of the Episcopal Church in Jerusalem and the Middle East was inaugurated, Cyprus, Iraq, Kuwait, Qatar, Bahrain, Abu Dhabi, the United Arab Emirates, Oman, Yemen, Aden and the Canterbury Group formed the Diocese of Cyprus and the Gulf, providing support for

---

14. Hassan Dehqani-Tafti, in "Partners in Mission," quoted by Mouneer Hanna Anis, "The Episcopal/Anglican Church in Jerusalem and the Middle East," in Markham et al., *Wiley-Blackwell Companion to the Anglican Communion*, 280.

the Chaplaincies in the expatriate communities which exist throughout the region.[15]

The origins of the Anglican presence in the Gulf can be traced back to an Act of Parliament in 1877 that established the Diocese of Lahore and included Delhi, East Punjab, Kashmir, Pakistan, and the southern states of the Arabian Gulf. Its first bishop was Thomas Valpy French (1825–1891). However, the Anglican Church was not formally established in the Arabian Gulf until the 1930s. Congregations continue to be composed mostly of expatriates, except in Cyprus and Iraq, where there are large numbers of indigenous Christians from other denominations.

Lessons from Our History

We can learn many lessons from our history in the Middle East. As I discuss these lessons, I will focus mainly on the Egyptian experience, which may be similar in many ways to the experience of other dioceses of the Middle East and beyond.

1. *Expanding God's kingdom should be at the core of our mission* and the reason for our presence in any region. Spreading the good news (the gospel) requires that we, as an Anglican community, should be good news for the society in which we live, as well as for the other churches around us. In order to be good news, we need to be humble in our attitude. We should listen to others with respect, share with love, and serve with compassion and without a hidden agenda.

The world around us not only wants to hear the teaching of Jesus but also wants to see Jesus himself, who went around doing good to all people and preaching the kingdom of God with love and compassion. As we seek to plant a church in an area, we need

---

15. Michael Lewis, "Diocese of Cyprus and the Gulf," Jerusalem and Middle East Church Association (website), accessed August 6, 2019, https://jmeca.org.uk/christianity -middle-east/anglicanepiscopal-diocese/cyprus.

to think of the physical and material needs of the people there. However, it is important to be alert, taking care that we not preach a social gospel only. Jesus brought both healing and teaching to the crowds on whom he had compassion, recognizing that they needed both (Matt. 9:35–38).

2. *Our presence in Egypt and North Africa reminds us constantly of the pains and suffering of our early church fathers and mothers.* They were ready to shed their blood for the sake of Jesus Christ. This history, which I dare say became part of our DNA, helps remind us that hardships are *inseparable* from the life of the church.

Many of our Muslim neighbors were amazed by the tolerance and forgiveness of Christians who lost their loved ones in recent terrorist attacks against the churches.

Pope Tawedros II said that suffering is not a new thing for the church in Egypt. Personally, I can even say that a bit of hardship keeps the church strong and faithful: "Indeed, all who desire to live a godly life in Christ Jesus will be persecuted" (2 Tim. 3:12).

3. *We need to build up local leaders* from the first day of our presence in any area. Jesus called his disciples to join him as soon as he came out of the wilderness. When the local leaders become well equipped, they become more capable of serving, witnessing, facing challenges, and engaging with their societies. They need to catch the vision, if they do not share it already, and to be trained theologically. We know that some of them will fail, but this is an inevitable risk that must be taken when we invest in training leaders. Bishop William James Thompson of Iran took this risk when he discipled Hassan Dehqani-Tafti, who (as I have mentioned) was consecrated in 1961 as the first indigenous bishop of Iran.

It is important to trust God as we equip local leaders, and to trust them as well. Lack of confidence in the locals leads to a church that is confident in neither her Lord nor herself.

4. It is important to make efforts to enculturate Anglican liturgy and worship so that people may worship from their hearts. Failure in this process of enculturation made the Anglican Church in Egypt a church only for the educated and the intellectuals. This hindered its spread in villages and poor areas where illiterate people live.

I believe that the structure of Anglican worship is very biblical. However, we need to be creative and flexible while keeping this structure. For example, it would be easier for an illiterate person to sing a confessional song than to struggle with reading the general confession.

5. We need to be more aware, if we are reaching out to a new country or area, that we are at risk of developing a colonial attitude. Such an attitude can creep into our minds and hearts without our intention, leading us to impose our ways of doing things on the local people.

There are ways to avoid such a colonial attitude. For example, we should use a participatory approach while developing a strategy or policy. Locals must have their say in this. We should also listen carefully to locals and encourage them to own their church. Finally, we should avoid using financial pressures to promote our own ways of doing things.

6. One of the great lessons we can learn from Temple Gairdner and Douglas Thornton is how to interact with Muslim friends. Gairdner's words are worth repeating: "We need a song note in our message to the Muslims, not the dry cracked note of disputation, but the song note of joyous witness, tender invitation."[16] Unlike some other missionaries, Gairdner chose a friendlier interfaith dialogue with Muslims. He also encouraged the church to get involved in community development and services. The Diocese of Egypt is still building on this foundation; many of its churches now have a community development center attached to them.

---

16. Padwick, Temple Gairdner of Cairo, 158.

Our Challenging Context in the Middle East

Our context as Anglicans in the Middle East is both a blessing and a challenge. This region is the cradle of many diverse civilizations that influenced each other, having a huge impact on all people in the region. This multiculturalism is, in part, what has shaped the unique and beautiful Middle Eastern culture that exists today.

For example, our presence among the first-century churches like the Oriental Orthodox, Greek Orthodox, Chaldean Catholic, Assyrian, and Armenian Churches is a real gift to us as Anglicans. We have much to learn from these churches, which received their teaching directly from the apostles. Their faithfulness and experience of martyrdom give us excellent examples of how to resist heresies and stand firm for the orthodox faith.

We can also learn from their weaknesses and mistakes, which led to many divisions. We need to do this with great humility, however, recognizing our own weaknesses and not gloating over theirs.

We need to develop cordial ecumenical relations with these traditional churches. But how can we build trust and fill the gaps between us without compromising our convictions? One way is to have a serious theological dialogue with these churches before we make very important decisions, such as whether or not to ordain women. If we believe in "one, holy, catholic, and apostolic church," we should avoid making unilateral decisions that widen the gap between us. This would violate the oneness of the church. Ecumenical dialogue strengthens our relations even if we do not agree on some issues. We need always to keep in mind the manner of walk Saint Paul describes: "Eager to maintain the unity of the Spirit in the bond of peace" (Eph. 4:3).

Another challenge for Anglicans in the Middle East comes from living at the heart of the Islamic world. Islam and Christianity are two missionary religions. Evangelism and disciple-making are at the core of the Christian faith. Daawa (calling people to Islam) is also an integral part of the Islamic faith. How then can followers of these two missionary faiths coexist in one society? What makes this tricky is that most Muslims believe that Christians have omitted passages from the Bible that tell about the prophet Muhammad. In addition, the divinity of Christ and the doctrine of the Trinity are difficult for Muslims to accept. Because of these differences Muslim fundamentalists consider Christians as *mushrikin* (infidels or idolaters or polytheists). These factors might seem to make coexistence impossible. But we cannot deny the reality of fourteen centuries of coexistence. This shows that, throughout these centuries, many Muslims have been tolerant.

On the other hand, we Christians cannot say that Islam is a heavenly religion. We have serious differences, and such differences contribute to misconceptions, tension, and sometimes sectarian clashes.

Recently there has been a strong wave of Islamic fundamentalism, extremism, and terrorism. Partly as a result, Christians over the last sixty years (Anglicans included) have tended to isolate themselves from wider society. This withdrawal has created more misconceptions. But after the revolutions of January 2011 and June 2013, in which the people of Egypt rose up and expressed their deep frustration with how they were governed,[17] the attitudes of Christians changed and they started to speak up. Muslim reformers, too, started to appear in the media, questioning Islamic traditions that call for hatred and violence.

In the midst of all this, the Anglican Church in Egypt has committed itself to building bridges and promoting harmony. We have established two cultural centers in Cairo and Alexandria to bring Christian and Muslim youth together through art, music, and community services.

---

17. In 2011, they rose up against the dictatorial and oppressive government under Mubarak; in 2013, they rose up again, this time against the way the Muslim Brotherhood was running the country, excluding moderate Muslims and Christians.

The Future of the Anglican Church in the Middle East

In the four decades since the Province of Jerusalem and the Middle East was launched in 1976, many changes occurred in each of the four constituent dioceses and in the political map of the wider Middle East. Let me sketch the most important of them.

First, the diocese of Egypt with North Africa and the Horn of Africa has grown considerably. Two Episcopal areas have grown so much that they may become their own dioceses. The Gambela area of Ethiopia in the Horn of Africa is one of them, and North Africa the other. Table 1 shows how the diocese of Egypt and these two areas have grown.

Table 1

Category	1976	2018
Number of Anglicans (approx.)	2,000	15,000
Number of congregations	18	172
Number of institutions	5	30
Number of ordained clergy	6	61

Because of this growth we are asking to become an independent province. All eight countries in which we live (Egypt, Libya, Tunisia, Algeria, Ethiopia, Eritrea, Djibouti, and Somalia) lie in the north and east of Africa, so it would make good sense to be part of the Council of the Anglican Provinces in Africa (CAPA). This would make us more coherent and would provide an opportunity for expansion, reaching out to other African countries like Chad and Mauritania.

Second, the Diocese of Jerusalem should become the seat of an archbishop once more. It has always been, and still remains, a significant and historic diocese within the whole of the Anglican Communion. Although many Anglicans migrated because of the long-standing conflict in the Holy Land, the ministry of the diocese through its institutions is growing. For both theological and political reasons, it is crucially important to keep a strong Anglican presence in Jerusalem. To achieve this, we may need to restore the status of Jerusalem as an archbishopric before our region is recognized as a province. We will have far more growth if the situation in Syria and Lebanon improves and peace prevails.

Third, we also need to review the structure of the Diocese of Cyprus and the Gulf. Cyprus is now a part of the European Union. It has a good number of churches and can function as a diocese on its own. If Europe itself were to become a province, the three countries of Cyprus, Malta, and Greece could form one of its dioceses.

Iraq and the Gulf constitute another area of great potential. The number of congregations is huge. However, these congregations are less than coherent because they are formed of congregants who are intimately linked with dioceses in India, Pakistan, Bangladesh, Nigeria, and the Philippines. Moreover, these churches do not have Arabic-speaking congregations. Anglicans need to plant churches for the many Arabs who live and work in the Gulf. This region could be a province with overlapping dioceses designed on the basis of nationalities. For example, an Indian bishop could oversee all Indian congregations across the Gulf, and the same arrangement could be made for the Pakistani congregations. Such bishops could select their own president bishop or primate for a term.

A well-structured Anglican presence in the Gulf would provide needed oversight for the Christians there who frequently complain of being ignored. At the time of writing (2018), the various Asian congregations in the Gulf are not represented in the synod of the Diocese of Cyprus and the Gulf. They deserve representation.

The situation in the Diocese of Iran is sad. Many churches and properties were seized at the time of the Islamic Revolution. Most of the Iranian Anglicans have migrated to Western countries. It is not possible to sustain a diocese there because there are only three churches and very few members. But they represent a faithful remnant. It might be worthwhile to add Turkey with its three Anglican churches to the diocese of Iran. Yet this would require the restructuring of Europe as a diocese or province as well.

Of course, I am fully aware that as an individual I do not have the authority to mandate all these changes. But I do have the freedom to dream of what could be done to create a better-functioning and more powerful Anglican presence in the Middle East. I dream because I am convinced that Anglicanism has beauty and the ability to contribute to this important region.

A Future Model for Planting New Churches in the Middle East

We have found in Egypt what we think is a successful model for a holistic ministry that involves the physical, social, and spiritual dimensions of mission. It involves establishing a community development center as well as a multipurpose hall that can be used as a church. This model has gained praise from our non-Christian neighbors. They appreciate the loving community services that we offer to the whole community regardless of religious background. Muslim neighbors do not mind that we hold spiritual meetings. In fact, they encourage us in many ways.

This is the way new Anglican congregations engage their communities, sharing with them God's love through both words and deeds. Our community development programs convey a welcoming and helping spirit by providing literacy classes, empowering women to establish small businesses, bringing health awareness, and offering nurseries for working women. In all these ways, our neighbors see that we Anglicans care not only about their souls but also about their material conditions.

Our View of the Current Crisis of the Anglican Communion

The following paragraphs represent my own views, though I think they are shared by our people in the Diocese of Egypt and by most of my colleagues in the Global South Anglicans movement. I am aware that some of my colleagues in the province may have different opinions.

In our view, the principal cause of the current crisis of the Anglican Communion is what the Windsor Continuation Group described as an "ecclesial deficit."[18] The word "deficit" is used by accountants to describe what happens when expenditure exceeds income. This is what has happened within the Anglican Communion. Ideally we should have a good balance between diversity and interdependence. But, in reality, diversity of theological judgment has exceeded (by far) interdependence among the churches of the Communion.

Any church must limit theological diversity in order to maintain theological coherence. But what we Anglicans call our "Instruments of Communion"[19] have not had the authority—or have not exercised their authority—to maintain theological coherence and protect the essentials of the Christian faith. Therefore, there has not been a healthy balance between diversity and interdependence.

We believe the following are needed to restore a proper balance.

1. The essentials of Christian orthodoxy must be defined, and member churches of the Communion must uphold them and guard them.

2. To achieve and guard these essentials, we must form a conciliar body of the primates in the Communion (archbishops of each

---

18. Windsor Continuation Group Report, 11, https://www.anglicancommunion.org/media/100354/The-Windsor-Continuation-Group.pdf.

19. The archbishop of Canterbury, Lambeth Conference of Bishops, the Primates' Meeting, and the Anglican Consultative Council.

province), plus other elected bishops, and this council should have the authority to make binding decisions and guard the faith.

Toward this end, the Windsor Report[20] made an excellent suggestion of "An Anglican Covenant" as a framework for our diversity to insure mutual accountability and interdependence. We believe that such a covenant will not only heal the current crisis but also enable the Communion to be a well-functioning member of the body of Christ. Rowan Williams, the former archbishop of Canterbury, put it well at his last meeting of the Anglican Consultative Council:[21]

> I still hope and pray, speaking personally, the Covenant has a future, because I believe we do have a message to give the Christian world about how we can be both catholic and orthodox and consensual, working in freedom, mutual respect and mutual restraint. Without jeopardizing the important local autonomy of our Churches, I think we still need work on that convergence of our schemes and systems, and I say that because I believe we all need to wake up to the challenges here if we are not to become less than we aspire to be as a Communion.[22]

The Windsor Continuation Group also recommended that authority be given to the primates as the body responsible for guarding the faith, and pointed out that this was suggested by Lambeth resolutions of 1988 and 1998.[23] Furthermore, the group observed

---

20. *The Lambeth Commission on Communion, the Windsor Report 2004* (London: Anglican Communion Office, 2004), 65–71, https://www.anglicancommunion.org/media/68225/windsor2004full.pdf.

21. The Anglican Consultative Council (ACC) is made up of representatives from the different provinces of the Anglican Communion, as well as representatives from the Primates' Meeting. The ACC seeks to develop common policies with respect to the world mission of the church, including ecumenical matters.

22. Rowan Williams, in his final address to the Anglican Consultative Council, November, 2012, St Mary's Cathedral, Auckland, New Zealand.

23. A Lambeth resolution (1988, 18.2a) "urges that encouragement be given to a developing collegial role for the Primates' Meeting under the presidency of the Archbishop of

that the Anglican Consultative Council was meant to be consultative but has wrongly assumed authority, and that, instead, the authority of the archbishop of Canterbury and the Lambeth Conference both should be augmented.

Unfortunately, these recommendations, made in successive Lambeth Conferences by the Windsor Group, were not followed. Our ecclesial deficit has led to many unilateral decisions by Anglicans of all persuasions, which has kept the crisis unresolved and fueled fragmentation and division.

3. We also need to deal with the challenge of poverty within the Anglican Communion. We should exert every effort to help member churches become self-supporting. That will help guard against the unhealthy use of financial resources by wealthier provinces to manipulate poorer provinces and dioceses.

4. Another important, related issue is theological education. The provision of quality orthodox theological education is critical for preventing younger generations from being carried away by heretical doctrine.

A Communion Owned by All

Anglicans all over the world appreciate the Church of England as the mother church that gave birth to our other Anglican churches outside England. The martyrs who gave their lives both before and after the Reformation are a great source of inspiration to us all. We Anglicans in the Middle East are indebted to the Church of England missionaries who came to us, driven by God's love, to encourage us and open our ears to hear afresh the gospel message.

Canterbury, so that the Primates' Meeting is able to exercise an enhanced responsibility in offering guidance on doctrinal, moral and pastoral matters"; "The Lambeth Conference Resolutions Archive from 1988," https://www.anglicancommunion.org/media/127749 /1988.pdf., Lambeth Resolution III.6a (1998), "reaffirms Resolution 18.2(a) of Lambeth 1988." "The Lambeth Conference Resolutions Archive from 1998," https://www.anglican communion.org/media/76650/1998.pdf.

Most of them knew they might not return to their families in Britain. In fact, many of them died and are buried in Egypt and the other Middle Eastern countries. We will continue to look at Canterbury Cathedral as our mother church, and Saint Augustine of Canterbury as a great inspiration to us.

We also know that the Anglican Communion began as an initiative of Archbishop Charles Longley in 1867 when he called for the first "Pan-Anglican conference of British, colonial and foreign bishops."[24] Archbishop Longley had a vision of Anglican identity as something that was no longer confined to the British Isles or North America. Meeting under the umbrella of the archbishop of Canterbury was appropriate to the structure of the British Empire at that time. Almost all the bishops and metropolitans then were citizens of the British Empire.

But now, after 150 years, the nature of the Communion has changed a great deal. Anglicans in the Global South represent more than 80 percent of the members of the Anglican Communion. Courage is now needed to review and revise the current structure and representation within the Communion. I would recommend the following:

1. The head of the Anglican Communion should be elected from among the primates for a term to be decided. This person needs to work in a collegial way with the other primates of the Communion.

2. Regional meetings of provinces should play a more active role in the life and witness of the church. Such meetings need to become more conciliar in nature. Networks should be developed for the different ministries within

---

24. "In 1867 76 Anglican bishops attended the first Lambeth Conference following an invitation from Archbishop of Canterbury Charles Longley." Quoted in "What Is the Anglican Communion?," Anglican Communion (website), https://www.anglican communion.org/structures/what-is-the-anglican-communion.aspx.

each region to promote the mission of Christ in the region. For example, provinces in the Middle East need to have a strategy for engaging with the Islamic world; provinces in Africa need to develop a strategy for sustainable development of the continent; provinces in North America and Europe may need to develop an approach toward the progressive and innovative secular society in which they live; and so forth.

3. Nongeographical renewal movements should be encouraged and welcomed by the provinces as partners rather than threats—for example, the Evangelical Fellowship in the Anglican Communion and the Global South Anglicans Fellowship.

Whatever new structure is developed, our main aim should be to help the Anglican Communion become and remain a faithful member of the body of Christ. We need to trust God's promise that the gates of hell will not overcome the building of his church (Matt. 16:18). He will protect his church. Our role is to remain faithful until Jesus comes again. We need to remember that there will always be weeds growing alongside the wheat. God allows both to grow together for now, but at the end they will be separated by him and him alone. It was out of this conviction that Saint Athanasius remained within the church of Alexandria even when the Arians had power in the church and continually repudiated him. He was convinced that God's truth would prevail in the end.

An African Note

Archbishop George Carey's words are worth repeating: "You don't have to be English to be Anglican." Similar words probably could have been said at the time of the sixteenth-century Reformation of the church in England: "You don't have to be Roman Catholic to be an English Christian." When he made his statement, Carey was not promoting a split between Anglican churches in various parts of the world and the Church of England. Rather, he was encouraging the leaders of Anglican churches around the Communion to healthily enculturate the worship and mission of their churches within their own contexts.

But there is good historical reason for Carey's statement. If we were to ask what is the actual origin of Anglicanism, we could do no better than to turn to Thomas Oden's book *How Africa Shaped the Christian Mind.*[25] Oden argues that Western Christianity (and we would include Anglicanism) has its theological origins in Africa. The greatest theologians of the first centuries were Africans: Augustine of Hippo; Tertullian and Cyprian of Carthage; Clement, Origen, Cyril, and Athanasius of Alexandria. They fought heresy and developed the great doctrines of the Trinity and Christology. They corrected and taught the heretical semi-Arians and full Arians of Europe. Orthodox theology moved from South to North to develop doctrine, shape the church, and establish the great monasteries. During the Reformation period, the magisterial Reformers returned to the theologians of Alexandria and North Africa for inspiration and guidance. So did the English Reformers, such as Thomas Cranmer and John Jewel, as they sought to interpret the Bible properly and be a faithful church. We may well conclude, then, that Anglicanism is actually rooted in the soil and theological riches of Egypt and North Africa. In other words, we in Africa own Anglicanism as much as our British brothers and sisters do. This is something to be immensely proud of, in our Lord.

It is my hope that my Anglican brothers and sisters in the Middle East may realize that it was God's plan and purpose for us to be there. The fact that the Anglican Church has flourished despite

---

25. See footnote 3.

its many challenges means that the Lord is with us. He wants us to continue the mission he started two thousand years ago right in our backyard. We need to renew our confidence that he can use us for his glory, right where we are, as he builds his kingdom among us.

3

A CANADIAN PERSPECTIVE

Process, Providence, and Anglican Identity

Ephraim Radner

Any definition can be either ideal or empirical, prescriptive or descriptive. Thus, we can define democracies in a certain way that can either prescribe how they function ideally (all the people of a society or state have an equal role in making corporate decisions) or describe how they in fact function in this or that place (modern Western democracies are influenced by blocs of interest groups and often swayed by financial manipulation). When it comes to the Christian church, definitions tend to combine the ideal and the empirical, and for good theological reasons: what the church is "ideally" (e.g., the pure bride of Christ), takes part of its meaning from how the church empirically acts (e.g., as a collection of sinners) even as this empirical subject is in fact redeemed and transformed by God in Christ. Both the ideal and the empirical must be held together with respect to the church so that the actual work of God that forms and disposes of the church can be discerned.

Defining Anglicanism, then, is an exercise that demands that we think both of what Anglicanism is (or might be) ideally, even as we take seriously what Anglicanism is empirically, so that we can begin to discern what God is actually up to with this reality we call "Anglicanism."

In this light, the following essay argues that Anglicanism, as an integral reality that might help shape the healthy future of the world's ecclesial life, may be a fading entity. It is not dead yet, however. Dying and death itself are, in any case, necessary elements in God's offering of new life. That is, dying and death are gifts of God themselves, which he has refashioned for overcoming the crushing elements of morbidity that sin has brought upon us. This giftedness of death is true for human persons; but it is equally true, as the Scriptures point out, for our communities of faith—Israel and the church both.[1] The ideal for the church is always new life in God; but the empirical may well be a dead body.[2] Yet, taken together, we can begin to see the grace of God as the latter becomes the means to the former. Even though Anglicanism may be dying as an ecclesially constructive entity, in historical terms, Anglicanism in this very condition may therefore also be a place of God's action and, potentially, of a divine action we can identify as gracious.

In what follows I will do three things:

---

1. See Ezek. 37 for a paradigmatic example. This theme has been worked out at length in Ephraim Radner, *The End of the Church: A Pneumatology of Christian Division in the West* (Grand Rapids, MI: Eerdmans, 1998).

2. 2 Cor. 4:10.

1. Define Anglicanism as a providential historical process of Christian life together worked out in the face of social challenge. This is my most detailed section.
2. Outline the development of these challenges in our day and explain the ways that Anglicanism has proved unable to meet them and still survive as truly Anglican.
3. Suggest that this failure is an opening to something new and good ecclesially—not so much a new Anglicanism, but a path of Christian witness and healing that represents the future promise of the church, not its past.

Anglicanism as a Historical Process

Anglicanism is not a church or a confession or a set of attitudes. Each of these points is discussed below. But taken together, none of them amounts to a particularly controversial claim, even if it is unconsciously resisted. Strictly speaking, "Anglicanism" only refers to a set of churches and their life, located now around the world, as these developed out of the Church of England. The semantic issue here is different, for instance, from that involved in the use of the term "catholic" for a church. "Catholic" is a qualification whose meaning is determined by a range of theological definitions that can be tested and applied to various church bodies, teachings, and attitudes *wherever* they may be found. The "Anglican" of Anglicanism, however, is a kind of sociological designator rather than a fundamentally theological descriptor. This is because of what Anglicanism actually constitutes in its own self-understanding, at least as confirmed retrospectively by contemporary ecclesial debate: we can trace what is Anglican by purely historical means.

First, Anglicanism is not a church. This is a formal theological and ecclesial truism: there are various Anglican churches, each of which is governed by individual constitutions and canons, none of which is jurisdictionally subordinate to another, and few of which have, even in their constitutions and canons, normative self-definitions that are given in concrete terms of other churches.[3]

One could, of course, claim theologically that there is some sort of sacramental reality that binds together Anglican churches on the level of ecclesial identity. Anglican bishops (and priests) recognize each other's orders, as well as, more fundamentally, the baptisms and Eucharists of each other's churches. These mutual recognitions might indicate some kind of common Anglican ecclesial reality. In fact, though, such common recognition among Anglican churches did not emerge until the mid-nineteenth century; it is now shared with many non-Anglican churches (e.g., Lutheran, Methodist, etc.); such mutual recognition is, in any case, no longer consistent and uniform even among Anglican churches (e.g., within the currently divided Anglican Communion, where divisions over women's ordination, sexual practice, and other matters have limited some mutual recognitions).[4]

To be sure, one might well want to appeal to such an underlying ecclesial identity among Anglicans, as it may inform all distinct and mostly divided Christian churches in the world, saying, for instance, that "we are all baptized into the body of Christ, and hence we are all joined somehow to one church." But when we do this, we are talking not about Anglicanism in any specific way but only about Christian churches in general. While appealing to such a Christian identity for Anglican churches is surely correct, this general Christian identity does not illuminate Anglicanism in particular.

---

3. See Norman Doe, *Canon Law in the Anglican Communion: A Worldwide Perspective* (Oxford: Oxford University Press, 1998); Doe, *The Principles of Canon Law Common to the Churches of the Anglican Communion* (London: Anglican Communion Office, 2008).

4. On just the recent matter of the permission and affirmation of gay partnerships and gay marriage, an estimated twenty-two of the thirty-eight Anglican Communion provinces are in some sort of "impaired communion" with the American Episcopal Church. See Kerry O'Halloran, *The Church of England: Charity Law and Human Rights* (New York: Springer, 2014), 135.

Second, Anglicanism is not a shared confession. The various Anglican churches are no longer bound by any clear confessional identity. They may once have been, although that is arguable; and even within the Church of England, such a clear identity, if it can be established, began to unravel by the first half of the seventeenth century. The single Church of England was a caldron of disagreement, conflict, antagonism, and outright violence around confessional matters in the sixteenth and early to mid-seventeenth centuries.[5] Puritan émigrés to America and their persecutors (e.g., Archbishop William Laud) were all "Anglicans" together.[6] The confessional differences were fundamental but nonetheless part of the same church.

One could easily overstate these differences of confessional commitment, given the more quotidian realities of parochial life and pastoral witness, in worship and catechism. Britain, it turns out, became one of the most widely catechized nations of Europe.[7] Yet this very success, using a theologically diverse set of materials, set the stage for confessional indifference. By the early eighteenth century, and after a good bit of religious conflict, theologians of many stripes were arguing for a national Christian religion—"Anglican"—that would be defined by a set of such broad theological and practical fundamentals that it might include within it a range of other and quite distinct churches.[8]

---

5. The conflictual interpretation is well established but has been solidified by recent works of, e.g., Eamon Duffy (*The Stripping of the Altars: Traditional Religion in England c. 1400–1580*, 2nd ed. [New Haven, CT: Yale University Press, 2005]), and Diarmaid MacCulloch (e.g.,, *Tudor Church Militant: Edward VI and the Protestant Reformation* [London: Allen Lane, 1999]).

6. For a good overview of the current discussion of the relationship of Puritanism to Anglicanism leading into the seventeenth century, see Peter Lake, "The Elizabethan Puritan Movement (1967)," *History* 100, no. 342 (October 2015): 517–34. On Winthrop, see Francis J. Bremer, *John Winthrop: America's Forgotten Founding Father* (New York: Oxford University Press, 2003).

7. Ian Green, *The Christian's ABC: Catechism and Catechizing in England c. 1530–1740* (Oxford: Oxford University Press, 1996).

8. Stephen W. Sykes, "The Fundamentals of Christianity," in *The Study of Anglicanism*, ed. Stephen W. Sykes and John Booty (London: SPCK, 1988), 231–45. On one prominent ex-

As it turned out, this press for "comprehension" gave way to a more modest acceptance of "toleration," where an increasing number of distinct churches were permitted to flourish alongside the established church, but not within it. This still opened the door to a quite nonconfessional dynamic within England as a whole; where everything is permitted, it is difficult to stake out what is truly important. In this increasingly nonconfessional context, church people in the eighteenth century debated the value of clergy subscribing to the Thirty-Nine Articles, and later, of confessing the creeds.[9] This did not preclude *local* confessions, as it were; these were evident in the missionary societies, for instance, and finally led to fragmentation within them.[10] But these dynamics of local commitment underscore the difficulty of linking Anglicanism itself with an integral confessional substance.

Certainly, a variety of doctrinal outlooks (even if not legislated by local canons) now exists throughout the Anglican world, given the demise of the 1662 BCP as a common standard, a trend that began already in the eighteenth century.[11] Despite significant pleas and arguments for the Prayer Book as undergirding a coherent Anglican theology, the hope for this—regretfully, perhaps—has been subverted by actual changes across the world among Anglican

ponent—Isaac Watts—of a broad established church based on common "fundamentals," see J. F. Maclear, "Isaac Watts and the Idea of Public Religion," *Journal of the History of Ideas* 53, no. 1 (January 1992): 25–45.

9. The debate over whether clergy should be made to subscribe to the Articles of Religion was formal and vociferous in the latter eighteenth century already. By the next century, even the creeds—especially the Athanasian Creed—had come into question. See Richard B. Barlow, "Anti-Subscription and the Clerical Petition Movement in the Church of England, 1766–1772," *Historical Magazine of the Protestant Episcopal Church* 30, no. 1 (March 1961): 35–49. On nineteenth-century debates over the Athanasian Creed, see D. Henderson, "The Devil's Law Cases," *Ecclesiastical Law Journal* 15, no. 1 (January 2013): 28–58.

10. Steven S. Maughan, *Mighty England Do Good: Culture, Faith, Empire, and World in the Foreign Mission of the Church of England, 1850–1915* (Grand Rapids, MI: Eerdmans, 2014).

11. This was already pointed out at the 1948 Lambeth Conference, in the Carrington Report, report 4: "The Anglican Communion," in *The Lambeth Conferences (1867–1948)* (London: SPCK, 1948), 81–94.

churches, including those often committed to regaining some kind of confessional or at least theologically articulate commonality of identity. African as much as Western Anglican churches now have a range of worship options available to them that stand outside any strict BCP lineage (at least as defined by a 1662 norm).

There are certainly those who would wish for a single confessional standard to identify Anglicanism, as in other traditions. But this can only be a wish. It simply would not apply to the wide variety of Anglican life over the last three hundred years. While many Anglican theological instructors (the present writer included) teach a certain kind of *sola Scriptura*, BCP Anglicanism and commend it to students, we are not so naive as to think it is anything more than a personal ideal, sustained by happy historical exemplars.

Finally, Anglicanism is not a set of attitudes. The notion that there is some set of "attitudes" that is particularly Anglican—comprehension, moderation, *via media*, learned study, Reformed catholic—cannot be demonstrated empirically. The attitudes exist; but they are inconsistent, subjectively identified, and transient throughout the history and geography of Anglicanism.[12] The only way proponents of this or that claim to a coherent Anglican "spirit" could argue their views would be to ignore or exclude vast numbers of other Anglicans from the start, or to erase the conflict, division, civil wars, and schisms that the pretense to comprehension obscured. This is mostly recognized by historians of Anglicanism, even if some

---

12. Newman's Tracts 38 and 41 on Anglicanism as a "via media" between Rome and Geneva ("Romanists and Reformers") have become classic statements; he begins to change his views, even while an Anglican, of course, leading to his final conversion to Rome. On Maurice, see Jeremy Morris, F. D. *Maurice and the Crisis of Christian Authority* (Oxford: Oxford University Press, 2005). Cf. Martin Thornton, *English Spirituality: An Outline of Ascetical Theology according to the English Pastoral Tradition* (London: SPCK, 1963); H. R. McAdoo, *Anglican Heritage: Theology and Spirituality* (Norwich, UK: Canterbury Press, 1991). Aidan Nichols, *The Panther and the Hind: A Theological History of Anglicanism* (Edinburgh: T&T Clark, 1993), is tendentious, but useful in exposing intrinsic theological contradictions within Anglicanism, if Anglicanism is read in a purely confessional fashion.

theologians prefer to avoid the topic. Theologians, instead, have tended to gather like-minded scholars to promote their brand of Anglicanism—whether featuring "incarnation," "mission," or "reason"—but the variety of these efforts points to their inadequacy as consistent rules.[13] In any case, if Anglicanism has a "spirit," it is difficult to know how one might measure it according to contemporary experience. Analyzing the larger Communion's numerical trajectories—at present, this would mean a set of evangelical attitudes would come to the fore—does not seem historically fair. Using as one's standard the ecclesial dynamics internal to local churches appears to be likewise constrained.

What, then, is Anglicanism? The brief discussion above points to a more positive category in which one should locate the adjective "Anglican": Anglicanism is a particular historical process. Specifically, it is a historical process (or set of processes) that provides genetic linkage between specific groups of Christians and orders subsequent interaction among these groups. Speaking broadly, this process moves from the reformed Church of England of the sixteenth century (a complex story in itself) and continues through episodes of struggle, conflict, expansion, mission, and local change. The fact that one can, and indeed must, write "histories" of the Reformation, or of early modern Anglicanism, and then of Anglicanism itself, indicates that temporal and social complexity is built in to the identity of Anglicanism in an essential way. The fact, furthermore, that such histories are contested analyses and subject to debate and revision means that this identity, even in its historicality, is opaque.[14]

---

13. *Essays and Reviews*, ed. John W. Parker (London: Parker, 1860); *Lux Mundi: A Series of Studies in the Religion of the Incarnation*, ed. Charles Gore (London: John Murray, 1889); *Essays Catholic and Critical*, ed. Edward Gordon Selwyn (London: SPCK, 1926).

14. One need only read, among contemporary historians, the varying evaluations of early Anglicanism by Patrick Collinson, Eamon Duffey, and Alex Ryrie to recognize this.

Any church is part of a historical process, of course. But the point here is to discern the particular parameters of such a process for Anglicanism. These are strict and few: the only two criteria for the use of the term "Anglican" in this case are that it be a self-designation and that causal genetic linkages for such designations can be demonstrated. That is, one must call oneself an Anglican, and the name must derive from some relationship one has with other Anglicans, either through self-conscious borrowing or through self-conscious receipt, or (usually) both. The element of mutual "recognition" enters in just here. Thus, Lutheranism is not Anglicanism, because Lutherans don't call themselves Anglicans. Similarly, someone who writes "Anglican" on the census form, despite having never entered an Anglican church and having neither parents nor schooling or literature that is Anglican, is either mistaken or fraudulent.

But self-designation and genetic linkage together would still not be a sufficient definition for Anglicanism. We must, therefore, add a third criterion to this category of historical process, one that involves a certain deliberate religious purpose. This third criterion is that those who meet the first two criteria are in fact engaged in trying to understand these connections and in sorting out the divine meaning that brought them to be. This criterion is about self-consciousness, cognitively and religiously. After all, Anglicans self-designate or connect within a specific frame of intentionality that is subjectively assumed and ordered to a Christian purpose, however that may be understood. This implies a relational practice of some kind, embedded in the historical process itself. Any Anglicans who are not engaging other Anglicans—for better or worse, in friendship or in struggle—have removed themselves from the historical process that is Anglicanism's identity in the first place, one that involves answering the questions Who am I? Where did

---

Earlier histories, e.g., Thomas Fuller's, Peter H. Heylyn's, and Gilbert B. Burnet's, are no different in this respect.

I come from? and Why am I here? Nonrelational Anglicans are, as it were, Anglican dead ends in definitional terms. That is not yet a *theological* judgment, though it has theological implications; it is, rather, a historical evaluation, simply pointing out that such Anglicans disappear, leaving little behind that might further order the genetic dynamic of their identity.

One should note that the mere fact that one might appeal to a "Communion" as a context for defining Anglican churches points to the interesting reality that over time, a formal ordering of relationality emerged for Anglicans that expressed, practically and then structurally, the inner dynamic of the three criteria outlined above. Even though it is true that the Communion itself is and has been contested—there have been split-offs over time and into the present—the Communion did not simply appear out of nothing.[15] It was itself the evolving result of a process, one that was driven by assumptions and hopes held variously by Anglicans about the character of God at work in the world and, as a result, given social form. This is a nontheological version of Desmond Tutu's purported quip that the chief characteristic of Anglicans is that "we meet."[16]

Anglicanism, then, is a historical process in which certain individuals and groups call themselves Anglicans because they have received the meanings of that self-designation from other Anglicans,

---

15. After the late eighteenth-century Non-Juror schism, which eventually disappeared, there have been "evangelical" pressures on division, as in nineteenth-century South Africa. See Anthony Ive, *The Church of England in South Africa: A Study of Its History, Principles, and Status* (Cape Town: Church of England Information Office, 1966); on one major nineteenth-century split in the United States, see Allen Guelzo, *For the Union of Evangelical Christendom: The Irony of the Reformed Episcopalians* (University Park: Pennsylvania State University Press, 1994); on the various "continuing churches" within Anglicanism, see Douglas Bess, *Divided We Stand: A History of the Continuing Anglican Movement* (Berkeley, CA: Apocryphile, 2006).

16. The phrase is only attributed to Tutu by the Canadian primate Michael Peers and has been much quoted. Cf. *Living Communion: The Official Report of the 13th Meeting of the Anglican Consultative Council, Nottingham, 2005*, comp. James M. Rosenthal and Susan T. Erdey (New York: Church Publishing, 2006), 67.

and they continue to wrestle with what God is up to in this process. Put this way, it is clear that there are indeed theological implications to this broad definition, one that moves from the empirical to the ideal. One might explore these implications in a number of directions, but a good case could be made for the following outline, focusing on the nature of historical experience in Christian theology and on the shape of Anglican experience in particular.

One might begin with the presupposition that a historical process is interesting or even compelling theologically because one believes that this process itself is tied to God. Traditionally, this presupposition is explained in terms of divine providence.[17] If history, then, belongs to God, any theological reflection on Anglicanism is bound up with a conviction of God's providence at work within Anglicanism's development. God is "up to something here," we might say, and the question is What? At this point, the theologian collates the data—the various events that have distinguished Anglicanism as a historical phenomenon. That historical process is one marked by theological, social, and cultural diversity; by mission; by international multiplication of diverse Anglican national churches; by conflict, cooperation, and struggle; and finally by uncertainty in the midst of these and other elements. From this we can surmise that just this kind of complex set of engagements is central to God's providential work with Anglicans over time, and it is in this set that we are to discern divine purpose.

This kind of analytic move is not, theologically, a novel one for Anglicanism. It was already given form by early eighteenth-century Anglicans—for example, Gilbert Burnet, who liked to talk about the Church of England's divine vocation in terms of a noncoercive, patient, and charitable evangelism, distinct from other European

---

17. Cf. Francesca Aran Murphy and Philip G. Ziegler, *The Providence of God: Deus Habit Consilium* (London: T&T Clark, 2009).

churches.[18] By the early twenty-first century, in the nuanced work of the Anglican ecclesiologist Paul Avis, this kind of providential reading of Anglicanism's historical process involves a difficult form of decision-making now within a Communion of churches that can dynamically work though the balancing of an array of inbuilt ecclesial tensions.[19] Not unrelated to Gilbert's vision of three hundred years earlier, Avis links Anglicanism's vocation to the "practice" of "the grace of walking together without coercive constraints."[20]

Theological interpretations, like Avis's, of Anglican decision-making in council—what is called "synodality"—are not easily articulated.[21] Providential readings of ecclesial history entail "vocation," to be sure, but vocation given in Christological terms. The traditional way that history, church, and Christ have been coordinated in such providential readings is through a scriptural figure. This approach is itself scriptural: Paul, for instance, compares the church to Israel in the desert and actually identifies Christ with aspects of Israel's journey; the book of Revelation (see chap. 12) is filled with figural imagery to explain the history of the church and Israel. This kind of figural reading is consistent with early Anglican understandings of providential history itself.[22] For example, Foxe's Book of Martyrs casts Edward VI as the new Josiah. Figural reading of history, as the primary form of providential theological analysis, makes use of typology, certainly, but also of a broader range of

---

18. See Tony Claydon, "Latitudinarianism and Apocalyptic History in the Worldview of Gilbert Burnet, 1643–1715," in The Historical Journal 51, no. 3 (September 2008): 577–99.

19. For Avis, these balanced elements include "catholic and reformed, episcopal and synodical, universal and local, biblical and reasonable, traditional and open to fresh insight"; see Paul Avis, The Vocation of Anglicanism (London: Bloomsbury T&T Clark, 2016), 182.

20. Avis, Vocation of Anglicanism, 186.

21. A "synod" is a gathering, or literally, "walking together," of decision-makers. Almost all traditions have some form of synodality—meetings, conferences, conventions. How these are organized, however, differs enormously.

22. John Foxe's monumental Actes and Monuments (first English edition in 1563)—popularly known as Foxe's Book of Martyrs—was filled with figural-providential readings of church history. It was a popular approach, including for Puritans.

coordinative elements, from allegory to moral exemplarism.[23] The point of a figural reading of the Bible and hence of history, both ecclesial and human—which is, in part, what a faith in providence entails—is the broad conviction that God shapes history "in accordance with" Scripture.

There is perhaps a range of ways one might work out a figural reading of Anglican history.[24] Such a reading will inevitably shift as more historical data becomes available, both in looking at the past and in terms of accumulated experience as history continues to unfold. Tyndale's early ruminations on the English Church, driven by their focus on persecution for the gospel as the key thread, must inevitably look very different from a perspective that takes in the British seventeenth century, the North American experience, or the missionary expansion in Southeast Asia. Figural readings of the church are necessarily provisional and find their fittingness usually within a small temporal compass.

From such an evolving and provisional vantage, nonetheless, it is possible to argue for more or less appropriate interpretations of the church. And from the perspective precisely of a now challenged worldwide Communion, a good argument can be made that God has, until the present, been using Anglicans as a figural outworking of Christian reconciliation in a fragmented, post-Babel world.[25] God is, of course, using other churches in this larger work, but Anglicans seem to have played a specific role within this divine economy,

23. This last element—moral exemplarism—proved a central Anglican approach for all parties and was established early on in Tyndale's figural-providential readings of church history. On the background, see Ryan McDermott, *Tropologies: Ethics and Invention in England, c. 1350–1600* (Notre Dame, IN: University of Notre Dame Press, 2016).

24. One influential element in my own thinking here is Sykes's discussion of fundamental contestation itself as a part of Christian life. See Stephen Sykes, *The Identity of Christianity* (Philadelphia: Fortress, 1984), 250ff.

25. On the figure of Babel, so powerful in the Christian tradition, especially in the Middle Ages, see the four-volume German work on the interpretation of Babel by Arno Borst, *Der Turmbau von Babel: Geschichte der Meinungen über Ursprung und Vielfalt der Sprachen und Völker* (Stuttgart: Hiersemann, 1957–1963).

informed by the very particular context of civil and international diversity and conflict that has marked their ecclesial life and the environment of their missionary expansion and structural relations. It is as if God posed the question to Christian responsibility Can such post-Babel reconciliation happen, and if so, how within the common life of a civilly engaged Christian body?

In this light, Anglicanism's theological meaning might therefore trace a providential story that moves from a certain kind of local pacific reformation to one of an extended resolution of evangelical missionary diversity within a global reach. The figural import of the church establishment in England, with its initial press for a scriptural and reformed common life shaped by the Book of Common Prayer, founds this story in a peculiar way. It first orders national and religious difference according to a set of clear, if contested, ecclesial practices of Scripture reading and worship, as well as of church order, all in a way that is unique to divided Europe at the time. The story moves from this beginning, then, along a trajectory of intra-Christian conflict in the seventeenth century, and then follows the rise of that unparalleled British character of uneasy religious toleration within the liberal state in the eighteenth century. This increasingly variegated religious scene is reshaped and refocused (rather than simply exploded), through local forms of social renewal, that lead to the astonishing missionary expansion of Anglicans out of these peculiar British outlooks. Anglican mission itself—to the Americas, India, Australasia, Africa, and finally Asia itself—has moved along lines that involve a certain combination of scriptural, moral, and civil truths and goods, and then evolved in unexpected ways.[26]

---

26. Brent Sirota, *The Christian Monitors: The Church of England and the Age of Benevolence, 1680–1730* (New Haven, CT: Yale University Press, 2014). While focusing on mission to and among British colonials, Hilary Carey offers good discussion of the Anglican missionary societies in *God's Empire: Religion and Colonialism in the British World, c. 1801–1908* (Cambridge: Cambridge University Press, 2011).

One can track this evolution, in the form of the Anglican Communion's particular structures and relationships, with the twentieth century's secular evolutions of internationalism and disputed democracies. This has involved, for both church and society, a cultural and moral struggle with political liberalism.[27] This broad movement of Anglican-global twinning has now taken form in a decades-long struggle not only over gendered leadership and sexual morals but also in the steady challenge to (and often the uneasy dismantling of) broader forms of social order and authority, which involve episcopal and synodical, provincial, diocesan, and congregational decision-making.[28]

It is important in this outline to see the continuity between late twentieth-century Anglicanism and sixteenth-century English ecclesial life with respect specifically to the challenge of social reconciliation. For the figural aspect of Anglicanism's providential shape lies in the identification of a consistent grappling with what one might call the "civil Pentecost" of modern human life. What makes Anglicanism peculiar is the modern form of its social challenges—immediately pressing diversity within a given nation and then within a concentrated international scene—which are engaged within an ecclesial microcosm. What makes this peculiar story figural in a Christian sense, however, is its rooting in the scriptural reality of pneumatic mission set out in Acts 2—the bringing together of diverse peoples and languages into a common understanding of God—which itself builds on the fragmenting human history that follows Babel, in Genesis 11.

---

27. See Ephraim Radner, "The Anglican Communion and Anglicanism," *Oxford History of the Anglican Communion*, ed. Jeremy Morris, vol. 4 (Oxford: Oxford University Press, 2017), 303–28.

28. The often-bitter debate over the Anglican Covenant in the years after 2007 is symptomatic of these struggles. Good references to the debate and strong argument in favor of the covenant can be found in Paul Avis, "Anglican Ecclesiology and the Anglican Covenant," *Journal of Anglican Studies* 12, no. 1 (May 2014): 112–32.

Anglicans not only have uniquely participated in but also have self-consciously sought to embody these developments ecclesially and ecumenically. Many of the elements misleadingly associated with an "Anglican ethos"—mission, understanding, Christian faithfulness, reconciliation, social concern, even scriptural commitment—are the markers of a figural history as it has been worked out in this manner. Whether in England, Scotland, and Ireland, or in the United States, or in Burundi, China, and New Zealand, these historical markers of ecclesial life are more deeply the providential hooks by which Anglicans have been caught up in the larger challenges to human communal flourishing in the face of divisive sin. The identity of Anglicanism is simply, and richly in this case, what God has done with Anglicans "in accordance with the Scriptures."

Present Developments

The identity of Anglicanism is given in just this historical process. But one must say more about such an identity in light of recent history. Providence takes in the present. Indeed, the convergence of larger contemporary political realities with Anglicanism's own political limitations may indicate that Anglicanism has reached the limit of its usefulness in this post-Babel vocation. Levels of post-Babel social chaos seem to have reached a pitch that Anglicanism's forms of engagement simply can no longer sustain constructively.

From a sociopolitical perspective, I would point to two elements among many that have informed Anglicanism's fading providential role: complexity and social incapacity.

Social decision-making in the twenty-first century now involves so many people (and peoples), and so many layers of concern, that actual engagement of cultural, social, and ideological diversity within polities, whether civil or ecclesial, has become stymied. Nations like the United States, with its population of 325 million, dwarf the size of all of Europe in 1600 (less than 80 million). The whole of England in 1600 was a fifth the population size of the single city of Lagos today.[29] Decision-making and resultant conflict in Reformation England was difficult enough.[30] Today, it has become almost impossible in the face of complex challenges like climate change, corruption, and poverty. No one person or group knows enough, there are no clear mechanisms for fair and useful knowledge exchange and learning on these matters, and the means of decision-making simply cannot cope, as it were, with the numbers involved—of people and of truths.[31] Polarization and paralysis are the rules of the day, underneath which boil the fat and gristle of human resentment.

Anglicanism is but a microcosm of this challenge of numbers and complexity. Local and international decision-making bodies, whether diocesan conventions or Lambeth Conferences, grind to a halt and fragment into unreconcilable bodies of antipathy. This trajectory of increasing disagreement and incapacitated decision-making contrasts with Anglicanism's remarkable work and witness over the last century, in particular, within expanding and complexifying social contexts. A simple glimpse at the Lambeth Conference reports from the late nineteenth century on, including the astonishing 1920 gathering after World War I, demonstrates this.[32] Other ecclesial traditions have had their own callings; but few were driven into these matters with such open and desirous

29. For overviews of European demographics more broadly, see Massimo Livi-Bacci, *The Population of Europe: A History*, trans. Cynthia De Nardi Ipsen and Carl Ipsen (Malden, MA: Blackwell, 2000).

30. See the overview in John Coffey, *Persecution and Toleration in Protestant England, 1558–1689* (Harlow, UK: Longman, 2000).

31. Cf. Dag Ankar, "Small Is Democratic, but Who Is Small?," *Arts and Social Sciences Journal*, vol. 2010: ASSJ-2; Adrian Little, *Democratic Piety: Complexity, Conflict and Violence* (Edinburgh: Edinburgh University Press, 2008); Robert Geyer and Samir Rihani, *Complexity and Public Policy: A New Approach to Twenty-First Century Politics, Policy and Society* (London: Routledge, 2010).

32. See the various chapters in Paul Avis and Benjamin M. Guyer, eds., *The Lambeth Conference: Theology, History, Polity and Purpose* (London: Bloomsbury, 2017).

energies as Anglicanism. These energies, in turn, proved effectively influential in broader political discourse and reform throughout the world.[33]

But in the face of now clearly overwhelming global complexity, as it were, these energies—which were always under strain—have cracked. When the 2008 Lambeth Conference eschewed deliberated resolutions, it did so in the wake of a threatened (and partially realized) boycott by numerous African bishops and with the recognition that acceptable definitive decision-making had now exceeded the conference's grasp.[34] Subsequent efforts to mend this breach, including the proposed Anglican Covenant, have foundered.[35] As it stands, neither Communion churches nor alternative Anglican groups that have formed outside of Communion structures have developed alternative means to consulting, deliberating, and deciding across lines of difference that actually bring vying groups together rather than divide them from the start.

Anglicans are thus no longer at the forefront of post-Babel Christian witness, but are increasingly examples of the seeming intractability of this condition. They mimic the polarization, paralysis, and resentment of the larger social spheres in which they live. Proposals have been made to get beyond this impasse, involving new forms of intra-Anglican or interparty synodalism, but these remain hopes

---

33. On a key moment in this development, full of tension and debate, see the provocative study by William J. Bulman, *Anglican Enlightenment: Orientalism, Religion and Politics in England and Its Empire, 1648–1715* (Cambridge: Cambridge University Press, 2015).

34. "Anglican Communion: More Than One in Four Bishops to Boycott Lambeth Conference," *Daily Telegraph*, July 11, 2008, https://www.telegraph.co.uk/news/religion/2286131/Anglican-Communion-More-than-one-in-four-bishops-to-boycott-Lambeth-Conference.html.

35. Official responses to the formally submitted section 4 of the covenant—and there were many unofficial debates, on the Internet especially—can be found at http://www.anglicancommunion.org/media/100895/collated_ridley_cambridge_reponses.pdf. The contentious 2009 ACC meeting in Jamaica gave rise to a revision of this section that itself remains contested. The final text can be found, via a link, at http://www.anglicancommunion.org/identity/doctrine/covenant.aspx.

that have not yet been taken up.[36] Most importantly, their scope remains so limited and their enactment, were it to happen at this point, so delayed that the character of Anglican witness, no longer promises wider ecclesial influence. This limitation does not mean that these proposals are not worth pursuing or that, once pursued, they cannot bear converting fruit. God's providential ordering of such efforts is, by definition, outside of human manipulation, and thus faithfulness demands that efforts be expended for the good, whatever their predicted outcomes. Nonetheless, providential discernment also seeks to order such efforts according to the shape of God's gifts and judgment both, and on this score Anglicans need to join sober-mindedness with hope.

Future Promises

The contemporary ecclesial and political challenges of Anglicanism are both real and reflectively provocative. Nonetheless, they portend not ecclesial disappearance or irrelevance but rather change. Anglican churches are not vanishing any time soon. Some will, no doubt.[37] But there are vital Christian communities all over the world that call themselves Anglican. Their vitality and strength, however, have little to do with this self-designation and much to do with their Christian core. For my third criterion for Anglicanism—engagement in understanding the connections involved in and sorting out the divine meaning of the historical process itself that Anglicanism represents—is fading for almost all Anglican churches who meet the first two criteria (self-designation and genetic link-

---

36. See "The Way of Anglican Communion: Walking Together before God," Communion Partner, http://communionpartners.org/the-way-of-anglican-communion-walking-together-before-god/; Philip Ashey, *Anglican Conciliarism: The Church Meeting to Decide Together* (Newport Beach, CA: Anglican House Media, 2017).

37. See statistics in David Goodhew, *Growth and Decline in the Anglican Communion: 1980 to the Present* (New York: Routledge, 2017), and recent articles like Goodhew, "Facing More Episcopal Church Decline," *The Living Church*, August 30, 2018, https://livingchurch.org/covenant/2018/08/30/facing-more-episcopal-church-decline/.

age), however vital these churches are according to numerical measures. The uncertain state and only vaguely gestured outcomes of the Lambeth Conference point to this. Instead, it seems that Anglicans are in a time of discernment: what would God do with this fading identity? Discernment is a pneumatic and sacrificial task. That is, discernment requires that we give ourselves up and follow Jesus to his cross, where the Spirit reveals to us God's life. Discernment about Anglicanism's future in this context, then, may mean letting go of Anglicanism itself as a discrete ecclesial vocation and allowing its historic and contemporary forms to be remade for some further divine purpose.[38] Certainly, this does not mean leaving this or that Anglican community for some other—we commend ourselves over to death in Christ; we do not run away from it.[39] To be remade by God is not to watch ourselves from afar but to be subjected to change in the very place we find ourselves.

Rather, as in all deaths, Anglicans are being disrobed, denuded, so that—as with Job's nakedness in birth and death both—we can see, and become visible as, the basic Christian children we are.[40] Some of today's most vital Christian witness by Anglicans—from Nigeria to Pakistan—comes in this posture. Bit by bit, Anglicans are giving up buildings, trust funds, gloriously attired bishops, seminaries, synods, and structures; many people, after all, have lost trust in them, and they increasingly do not fulfill their purpose.[41]

---

38. Arthur Michael Ramsey, *The Gospel and the Catholic Church*, 2nd ed. (London: Longmans, Green, 1956) is still the best ecclesiological statement of Anglicanism in this vein, whatever its limitations. Drawing on Ramsey's vision, Stephen Bayne famously said that "the vocation of Anglicanism is to disappear because Anglicanism does not believe in itself but believes only in the Catholic Church of Christ; therefore it is forever restless until it finds its place in that one Body." See S. F. Bayne, "Anglicanism—the Contemporary Situation: This Nettle, Anglicanism," in *Pan-Anglican: A Review of the World-wide Episcopal Church* 5, no. 1 (Epiphany 1954): 43–44.

39. See Eph. 5:2.

40. See Ephraim Radner, "The Naked Christian: Baptism and the Broken Body of Christ," *Pro Ecclesia* 26, no. 1 (Winter 2017): 25–42.

41. The difficult, painful, and still unfinished consequences of the drawn-out property litigation among Anglicans in the United States especially is but one instance of this

However, Anglicans are not simply replacing them with repristinated versions, that is, with better bishops or better structures. Perhaps—in providential terms once again—the history that is Anglicanism has reached its current end for just this purpose: to expose the nature of grace within divided human communities in an ever-more-critical fashion.

Perhaps we are being driven deeper into the days after crucifixion and resurrection, as in Acts 2—days of simple gathering, days of prayer, days of listening, days of sharing all. We cannot be sure of what this will look like. Perhaps we are looking into the emergence of new ecumenical communities—something that the Saint Anselm group at Lambeth may well be a glimmer of; or the Catholic Chemin Neuf Community, which works with them, combining ecclesiality, mission, and stark mutual obedience and sharing with unexpected ecumenical openness; or something else.[42] To change in this way, of course, requires certain desires, habits, and skills involving profound trust in divine guidance and sustenance, self-expenditure, and forgiveness. These are aspects of a Christian spirit and practice that have waned in recent decades within the larger church (and not just within Anglicanism), and their growth and flourishing are matters for prayer. This is not my generation's promise; it is another's, a younger generation's, still attuned to the radical gift of their being, nakedly wonderful; and to their being in Christ, nakedly exposed in love. I will continue to be an Anglican and to follow along, as best I can, the historical process that it embodies. I meet, I listen, I teach. But I am looking, in hope, beyond.

---

process. The Church of England has a much larger set of material challenges to grapple with in the face of numerical decline and the changing economics of state support.

42. On the Community of St. Anselm, see http://stanselm.org.uk/; on Chemin Neuf, see https://www.chemin-neuf.org/en/home. See also communities like Alleluia, in the United States, http://www.yeslord.com/.

4

A NORTH AMERICAN PERSPECTIVE

Neo-pagan Anglicanism

Foley Beach

In January 2016 I attended the Primates' Meeting of the Anglican Communion called by the archbishop of Canterbury in Canterbury, England. The meeting began with the cathedral being closed to the public. The primates were invited to a private, three-hour prayer time in the cathedral. On my way through the cathedral I came upon a tablet honoring all the archbishops of Canterbury, beginning with Augustine. I was struck that Thomas Cranmer (served 1533–1555), often treated as the father of Anglicanism, was over halfway down the list. It was a stark reminder that Anglicanism did not begin in the sixteenth century with the English Reformation but had it roots in the very earliest days of Christianity.

Anglicanism goes back at least to Augustine, the first archbishop of Canterbury appointed by the Holy Roman Church in 597. The

English form of Christianity can be traced back even earlier, since the gospel came to England in the first century. But under the influence of the continental Reformation, the English Church broke with Rome during the bloody and fiery church battles of the mid-sixteenth century. Later in that century, under Queen Elizabeth (1558–1603), the Anglican Church began to find its identity with the Elizabethan Settlement. This new establishment finalized the English Church's separation from the Roman Church, made the English monarch the "Supreme Governor of the Church of England," required the Bible to be read in English in all churches, reaffirmed the Book of Common Prayer's worship for the Church of England, and made the Thirty-Nine Articles of Religion the doctrinal basis of the Church of England.

Through the years, Anglicanism has grown in evangelical zeal and witness into its own expression of the church catholic with its Book of Common Prayer, biblical scholarship, missionary endeavors, majestic and diverse worship services, magnificent architecture, and breadth of robust Christian theology. By the late nineteenth century, Anglican bishops were confident enough to start ecumenical dialogue. The 1888 Lambeth Conference approved what has been called the Lambeth Quadrilateral, which sets forth a minimum set of doctrines of the Anglican Church:

- the Holy Scriptures of the Old and New Testaments as "containing all things necessary to salvation," and as being the rule and ultimate standard of faith;
- the Apostles' Creed and the Nicene Creed as sufficient statements of the Christian faith;
- the two sacraments of baptism and the Lord's Supper, which were ordained by Christ himself, ministered with the use of Christ's words of institution, and the elements ordained by him;

- the historic episcopate, locally adapted in the methods of its administration to varying needs of the nations and peoples God called into the unity of his Church.[1]

The Lambeth Quadrilateral not only helped develop the ethos of a broad and comprehensive attitude toward other denominations of the Christian faith, but also impacted the formation of new provinces of the Anglican Communion as their nations gained their independence from the British Empire. These foundational principles served as a guide as these provinces developed in their various cultures.

Anglicanism has brought into Christianity the Authorized Version (King James) of the Bible, the Book of Common Prayer, the Thirty-Nine Articles of Religion, evangelical catholicism with the Oxford Movement, and the rigorous intellectualism of C. S. Lewis; the Bible scholarship and preaching of Charles Simeon, John Stott, J. I. Packer, Leon Morris, Derek Kidner, J. Alec Motyer, C. F. D. Moule, Joyce Baldwin, and N. T. Wright; the poetic and moving music of so many great hymns, such as "Holy, Holy, Holy," by Bishop Reginald Heber, "Amazing Grace," by John Newton, "When I Survey the Wondrous Cross," by Isaac Watts, "Rock of Ages Cleft for Me," by Augustus Toplady, and "O Little Town of Bethlehem," by Bishop Phillips Brooks; and numerous missionary agencies such as the Church Missionary Society (CMS), the Society for the Propagation of the Gospel (SPG), the Society for the Promotion of Christian Knowledge (SPCK), the Church's Ministry Among the Jews (CMJ), and the Society of Missionaries and Senders (SAMS), which have taken the gospel of Jesus Christ all around the world.

The Rise of Neo-pagan Anglicanism

Any discussion of Anglicanism in our present context must include the rise of neo-pagan Anglicanism in many Anglican churches

---

1. Lambeth Resolution 11. See "The Lambeth Conference Resolutions Archive from 1888," https://www.anglicancommunion.org/media/127722/1888.pdf.

around the world, especially in the West. This movement has created a battle raging worldwide for the soul of the Anglican expression of Christian faith. Like other times in the history of the one, holy, catholic, and apostolic church, many leaders in the present-day Anglican Church have drifted away from their biblical roots, catholic heritage, and evangelical zeal. They have been enticed by the philosophies and moralities of modern culture. Affronted by what they see as the rigidity of biblical morality, many Anglican leaders have accepted uncritically certain social-scientific assumptions at odds with the biblical vision. As a result, they have undermined the authority of the Old and New Testaments, and called into question the historic underpinnings of the Christian faith. This has created unprecedented conflict and dissension in their churches. Anglican leaders themselves have lamented this "tearing [apart of] the fabric of the Communion at the deepest level" (Primates' Meeting, 2003).[2]

This departure from the "faith that was once for all delivered to the saints" (Jude 3) has created an ecclesiastical war within the Anglican Communion. Revisionists have battled those who adhere to the historic and catholic teachings and practices of the Christian faith. The consequences of this conflict have been manifold: the loss of the anointing of the Holy Spirit for many congregations; a distorted gospel message presented to an unbelieving world; the loss of millions of dollars of historic church assets and buildings; millions and millions of dollars of sacred monies redirected to pay legal and court fees; public division and scandal in churches (local, national, and international); and an increase in the persecution of Christians throughout the world.

Anglicanism—with its rich heritage of biblical scholarship, liturgical formation, profound music, uplifting architecture,

---

2. "This Will Tear the Fabric of Our Communion," *The Guardian*, October 16, 2003, https://www.theguardian.com/uk/2003/oct/17/gayrights.religion.

missionary success, and deep spirituality—is on the brink of succumbing to a cultural correctness which academic elites and the political left have tried to impose. Brandishing economic rewards (which create economic dependency and therefore slavery) and threats of institutional disloyalty, Anglican progressives have introduced an ever-expanding neo-paganism into the worldwide Anglican Communion.

What do I mean by neo-paganism in Anglicanism? I am referring to a modern form of Anglicanism that performs the historic forms of worship within historic Anglican structures while embracing beliefs and practices that Christians once considered pagan. Theological beliefs once deemed unbiblical and even heretical are taught as Christian doctrine, and moral practices once seen as sinful and offensive to God are now taught and embraced in the name of love and compassion. No one is excluded from the kingdom of God, as God's love conquers all, which is a new form of the old heresy of universalism. Theologies and moralities from which one was once required to repent are now welcomed as Christian.

These Anglican progressives believe (mistakenly) that science has shown us that biblical theology and morality are simply vestiges of ancient patriarchy and therefore need to be removed from the life of the church. They have embraced the new pluralism's demands for personal rights, radical inclusiveness, and nondiscrimination in a way that erases emphatic biblical distinctions, granting to these modern concepts more authority than the historic teachings of the Bible and four thousand years of Judeo-Christian tradition. This is a counterfeit Anglicanism. It rejects the breadth of classical Anglicanism's catholic, evangelical, and charismatic traditions. It repudiates orthodox belief and practice that come from the plain teachings of the Bible, the historical catholic faith, the English Reformation, the Oxford Movement, and the Book of Common Prayer. Oddly, it even denies the Anglican tradition's history of offering a contextualized countercultural witness. Neo-pagan Anglicanism seeks to draw people into the church by accommodating non-Christian beliefs and practices prevalent in the culture. Progressive Anglicans think this will grow their congregations, but in almost every case, they have been proved wrong.

Neo-pagan Anglican theology and morality are now being taught as normal Christianity in certain provinces of the Anglican Communion. I am not suggesting this is being done overtly. Pagan deities are not being explicitly commended in churches and cathedrals. Or, if they are, this is very rare. Rather, what I am suggesting is that the real danger has come in through the back door. Liberal innovations in theology and sexual ethics are pushing Anglicans toward an understanding of God, gender, and sexuality that has more in common with pagan theology and ethics than with historic Christianity. But progressives have been clever in all of this: they have changed the theological content of belief while maintaining the facade of orthodoxy. They still speak of Jesus, the gospel, and the Spirit, but the meanings of all these words have changed drastically. As the apostle Paul wrote two thousand years ago, they preach "another Jesus . . . a different spirit . . . [and] a different gospel" (2 Cor. 11:4).

The Bible

The Bible, for the neo-pagan Anglican, is simply a moral guide to our historical roots; it shows how our distant fathers thought. It is a way to get in touch with our spiritual forebears. Neo-pagans leapfrog over two thousand years of theological tradition and history, and filter the Bible according to the most recent declarations of sociologists and psychologists. They no longer believe that the Bible is the word of God; at best, for them it *contains* the word of God. Their thinking is that since the church created the Bible, the church can recreate the Bible according to the latest fashions of academics. As a recent Episcopal bishop of Pennsylvania preached: "We wrote the Bible. We can rewrite the Bible."[3] In another sermon, this bishop preached: "The Scriptures are internally contradictory on the surface. Their interpretation varies according to the needs of the hearer."[4]

Neo-pagan Anglicans still read the Bible in worship, but they often add poems and scripture texts from other world religions. Worse, they sometimes treat these other scriptures as having authority equal to that of the Bible. In recent years many Episcopal churches have included readings from the Qur'an among the lectionary readings from the Bible. These churches often say that the central meaning of the Bible's teachings is that we should love our neighbors and come together in unity. The rich variety of doctrines and disciplines taught in the Gospels and the Epistles (not to mention the Old Testament) is overlooked or deliberately ignored.

God

The historic Christian understanding of God as Father is considered by neo-pagan Anglicans to be patriarchal and masochistic. Calling on or praying to God as Father is too limiting for God and unrealistic for contemporary personal experience. It lacks the breadth of all the other religions, the argument goes. God is beyond gender and the title Father, so other forms and names may be used: Mother, Creator, Sustainer, Redeemer, and so on. But calling God "Father" or "he" is judged to be too narrow and offensive.

These teachings and practices have become commonplace in many Anglican churches. In September 2018, England's most senior female bishop said the church should stop calling God "he" because it is a turnoff to young people. Bishop Rachel Treweek is quoted in

---

3. Sermon at the Church of the Good Samaritan in Paoli, Pennsylvania, *Virtue OnLine*, November 29, 2005.

4. Sermon at St. Luke's Church, Newtown, Pennsylvania, July 8, 2004.

the *Daily Mail* as saying, "I don't want young girls and boys to hear us constantly refer to God as 'he.'" She goes on to say that non-Christians feel alienated from the church if the image of God is painted as only masculine.[5] In my experience the opposite is often the case. Informed Christians know that calling God "she" is a return to ancient paganism, and that using terms such as "Godself" denies the profound personhood of God that is so attractive to young people seeking love and spiritual reality in God. After all, to deny masculine pronouns for God is to reject Jesus's own language for God.

In February 2018 the Episcopal Diocese of Washington, DC, voted to limit the use of masculine pronouns in referring to God in order to be more inclusive.[6] Linda Calkins of St. Bartholomew's Episcopal Church in Laytonsville, Maryland, said:

> I am still waiting for the Episcopal Church to come to the place where all people feel that they can speak God's name. Many, many women that I have spoken with over my past almost 20 years in ordained ministry have felt that they could not be a part of any church because of the male image of God that is systemic and that is sustained throughout our liturgies. Many of us are waiting and need to hear God in our language, in our words and in our pronouns.[7]

But many others yearn to hear the language Jesus and the early church used for God. Some of them have suffered from their fathers' abuse and need not only reminders that their heavenly Father is not like that, but also the healing that only God the Father can

---

5. Leigh McManus, "Britain's Most Senior Female Bishop Says Church Should Stop Calling God 'He,'" *Daily Mail*, September 16, 2018, https://www.dailymail.co.uk/news/article-6173387/Bishop-says-Church-stop-calling-God-young-people-religion.html.

6. Dave Bohon, "D.C. Episcopal Diocese Embraces Genderless God, Transgender Inclusiveness," *New American*, February 6, 2018, https://www.thenewamerican.com/culture/faith-and-morals/item/28221-dc-episcopal-diocese-embraces-genderless-god-transgender-inclusiveness.

7. Bohon, "D.C. Episcopal Diocese Embraces Genderless God."

provide. Two years ago, a dear friend decided she could no longer attend her Episcopal church in Clayton, Georgia, when the priest changed the Lord's Prayer to "Our Mother in Heaven." Another friend left his Fredericksburg, Virginia, Episcopal church when the priest changed words in the Lord's Prayer to reflect Mother Earth as the creative being of the universe. This is pagan theology; it's not Christian and it's not Anglican.

God is obviously beyond gender. And yet, traditional Anglicans would argue that God has revealed to us his preferred pronouns. As I have suggested above, we haven't been left wondering. The Bible isn't silent on the matter. Over 160 times in the Gospels, God has been revealed to us as Father. Jesus called God *his* Father, *the* Father, *my* Father. Jesus taught his followers to pray, "*Our* Father." Jesus said that he and the Father were one (John 10:30). Jesus said that when you saw him, you saw the Father (John 14:9). C. S. Lewis explains it this way:

> Suppose the reformer stops saying that a good woman may be like God and begins saying that God is like a good woman. Suppose he says that we might just as well pray to "Our Mother which art in heaven" as to "Our Father". Suppose he suggests that the Incarnation might just as well have taken a female as a male form, and the Second Person of the Trinity be as well called the Daughter as the Son. Suppose, finally, that the mystical marriage were reversed, that the Church were the Bridegroom and Christ the Bride. . . . Now it is surely the case that if all these supposals were ever carried into effect we should be embarked on a different religion. Goddesses have, of course, been worshipped: many religions have had priestesses. But they are religions quite different in character from Christianity.[8]

8. C. S. Lewis, "Notes on the Way," in *Time and Tide* 29 (August 14, 1948), reprinted as "Priestesses in the Church?," in *God in the Dock: Essays on Theology and Ethics* (Grand Rapids,

Lewis is correct. Even with the best of motives, one cannot make a seemingly small change regarding pronouns without necessarily effecting a much larger change—a change that ultimately results in a religion quite different in character from Christianity. However, this change has been widely accepted in many Anglican provinces.

Jesus

For neo-pagans, Jesus the Christ is merely the *Christian* way to God. He should not be promoted or required of other religionists, such as Muslims, Hindus, or Jews. Progressive Anglicans teach that all three faiths of the Abrahamic tradition are actually worshiping the same God. Others teach that *all* religions are expressions of worship to the same God and are therefore equally valid ways to God. They believe Christians should not impose their imperialistic religious perspective on others. A recent bishop of the Episcopal Diocese of Los Angeles issued an apology to Hindus worldwide for what he called "centuries-old acts of religious discrimination by Christians, including attempts to convert them." The apology was read by Bishop Jon Bruno in a statement to over one hundred Hindu leaders at an Episcopal Eucharist. The ceremony started with a Hindu priestess blowing a conch shell three times and included sacred Hindu chants. Episcopal priest Karen MacQueen, who was deeply influenced by Hindu Vedanta philosophy and opposes cultivating conversions to Christianity, added, "There are enough Christians in the world."[9]

For this sort of Anglican, Jesus is teacher, lover, joy-giver, and Redeemer. He is not uniquely the Son of God, but the son of God as each of us is a son or daughter of God. He is not considered *the* way

---

MI: Eerdmans, 1970); see http://www.episcopalnet.org/TRACTS/priestesses.html. Emphasis added.

9. Arthur J. Pais, "Episcopal Christians Apologise to Hindus for Discrimination, Proselytisation," *India Abroad*, February 25, 2008, https://www.rediff.com/news/2008/feb/25 apology.htm.

to the Father (or God) for all people (as in John 14:6) but is only a way for Christians to relate to God. Others may or may not believe that Jesus's death on the cross atones for their sins, and may or may not believe that Jesus physically rose from the dead after he was cruci-fied. Jesus is not taught as the coming Judge who will separate the sheep from the goats and who will judge each person's sin. Yet each Sunday the Nicene Creed is recited and the Eucharist is celebrated. As one archbishop, whom I would classify as embracing neo-pagan Anglicanism, said in a recent Primates' Meeting I attended, "We still say the Creed each week," as if this justifies his unbiblical teaching about Jesus and marriage.

A recent presiding bishop of the Episcopal Church said: "Chris-tians understand that Jesus is the route to God. Umm—that is not to say that Muslims, or Sikhs, or Jains, come to God in a radically different way. They come to God through . . . human experience . . . through human experience of the divine. Christians talk about that in terms of Jesus."[10] These neo-pagans go further, insisting that Jesus had the "Christ-spirit" (that is, that the messianic anointing came on him for his time on earth, which actually reduces him to less than fully God) and that he just happened to be male because this was culturally acceptable at the time. Some change Jesus's maleness into femaleness, calling him/her "the Christa." This transgender Jesus can be found in New York's (Episcopal) Saint John's Cathedral, where a female Jesus hangs on the cross in one of the chapels.

The Holy Spirit

The Holy Spirit, according to neo-pagan Anglicanism, is what feels right for the moment, not actually a distinct person of the Godhead who calls the believer to repentance from sin and transforms the

---

10. Presiding bishop Katharine Jefforts Schori, interview on NPR's "Here and Now," October 18, 2006, http://www.standfirminfaith.com/index.php/site/article/1384/.

believer into biblical holiness and righteousness. I say "what feels right" because there seem to be no revealed boundaries for the Holy Spirit in neo-paganism. For example, while the catechism in the 1979 BCP of the Episcopal Church clearly says that one recognizes truths taught by the Holy Spirit "when they are in accord with the Scriptures," the Episcopal Church continues to embrace teachings and practices opposed to Scripture. I remember hearing the Episcopal bishop of Atlanta explaining to his diocese why he voted to affirm the consecration of a bishop who had divorced his wife and was partnered with another man: "I followed the guidance of the Holy Spirit."[11] Apparently he had rejected the Anglican tradition's insistence that the Holy Spirit does not contradict Scripture. In contrast to that tradition, the neo-pagan Anglican believes that the purpose of the Holy Spirit is to motivate the people of God to love, accept, and welcome everybody to the gospel without insisting, as the gospel does, on repentance from their sins.

Evangelism

For this heretical Anglicanism, evangelism is simply getting people into church, not calling people to repentance of their sins and to faith in Christ. Caring for people's needs is what all good Christians do, but for neo-pagans, introducing someone to Jesus as Lord and Savior is too evangelistic and smacks of fundamentalism. They may be concerned about their congregations getting grayer and older, but their remedy is to think of creative ways of filling the pews other than conversion to the historic Christian faith. Their emphasis is on growing the church roll instead of growing people into deeper relationships with Jesus Christ. The current presiding bishop of the Episcopal Church, Michael Curry, calls people to

---

11. Bishop Neil Alexander to the Diocese of Atlanta conservative clergy gathering, September 2003.

Jesus and speaks of the Jesus Movement. However, the Jesus he calls people to is one who speaks love and acceptance without addressing sin. Yet the Jesus of the Gospels called people out of their sins into the ways of God: "Repent and believe the good news." He welcomed sinners with love and acceptance but then insisted that they could not remain in unrepented sin. Otherwise they would never experience his love. They would remain enslaved to attitudes and actions which alienate them from that very love.

Moral and Sexual Ethics

Jesus's new commandment was to love one another (John 15:12). Neo-pagans have said this means to love everyone and accept everyone as they are. Of course this is not a bad thing! But their "gospel" message stops there. There is no call to repentance for personal sins other than repenting of the systems and structures that have oppressed people because of Western civilization. They have set aside the moral ethics of the Bible regarding marriage and sexuality, and traded them for the sexual enlightenment of the 1960s. Premarital sex, homosexuality, bisexuality, transgenderism, and a host of other nonbiblical sexual practices are embraced and promoted. These expressions of sexual behavior and lifestyle were once considered practices of pagan religions but are now embraced and celebrated in Anglican churches.

The Scottish Episcopal Church, the Anglican Church in Canada, the Episcopal Church (USA), the Episcopal Church in Brazil, the Province of Anglican Church of Aotearoa, New Zealand, and Polynesia, and many dioceses in the Church of England now openly allow these pagan practices. The Diocese of New Westminster (Canada) authorized the blessing of same-sex unions in 2003. The Episcopal Church (USA) consecrated a noncelibate homosexual in a partnered relationship in 2004. Since then, marriage has been redefined away from biblical norms to pagan models in Anglican provinces in Canada, the United States, Scotland, Brazil, Wales, and New Zealand.

Most of the provinces in these countries promote pagan lifestyles and practices by supporting and participating in gay-pride parades in their cities; yet they look with horror on those who teach that one can change his or her sexual preferences by obeying Jesus Christ in the power of the Holy Spirit. The biblical teachings on these issues are considered obsolete and irrelevant because they conflict with the claims of some contemporary social scientists. Those who struggle with same-sex attraction and are trying to live in biblical fidelity and purity are often chastised. They are urged to live out their same-sex desires and assured that there is no other possibility for them. Neo-pagans dismiss as misguided any concerns about the genuine temptations their teachings create for these followers of Jesus.

Neo-pagan Anglicanism is embedded in establishment Anglicanism centered at Lambeth Palace, the Anglican Consultative Council, and the Anglican Communion Office. Calls to the archbishop of Canterbury to discipline, rebuke, and hold accountable those bishops, archbishops, and provinces that have abandoned historic and biblical Anglicanism have fallen on deaf ears. Power, finances, influence, and perception are powerful gods, and not easily contested. Rather than resist neo-pagan Anglicanism, the current archbishop of Canterbury has embraced these unbiblical teachings and moralities as valid options among Anglicans by saying we can disagree about marriage, sex, and gender and still walk together. He calls this "good disagreement" and avoids giving a biblical response to these questions. When asked in an interview for GQ magazine if gay sex is sinful, he responded, "You know very well that is a question I can't give a straight answer to." The reporter pressed further by asking, "Why can't you?" The archbishop answered:

Because I don't do blanket condemnation and I haven't got a good answer to the question. I'll be really honest about that. I know I haven't got a good answer to the question. Inherently, within myself, the things that seem to me to be absolutely central are around faithfulness, stability of relationships and loving relationships.[12]

Neo-pagan Anglicans often use the same words as evangelicals and Anglo-Catholics, but they have embraced new and unbiblical meanings for these words: "Jesus," "evangelism," "Bible study," "blessings," and "marriage." Unless one listens carefully to the ways these words are used, neo-pagan sermons and teachings can sound orthodox and biblical. But deeper examination proves that progressive Anglicans have redefined all these words.

This redefinition is occurring mostly in the West but is now making its way into parts of Africa and South America. Spreading like a highly contagious virus, it is well funded from sources within the Episcopal Church, the Anglican Church of Canada, and their various parishes, dioceses, and foundations, such as the Compass Rose Society and Trinity Church Wall Street. With their resources and the blessing of the establishment within the Anglican Communion, these neo-pagan Anglicans are infecting significant sectors of Anglicanism with this unbiblical virus. Unsuspecting and (financially) needy provinces and dioceses around the Communion are taken in by monetary generosity, airplane tickets, lavish meetings, and friendship—but without realizing what is in the Trojan Horse being brought into their churches.

Neo-pagan Anglicanism is beautifully packaged in some of the most elegant liturgy, music, and tradition in Christianity. But it has become liturgy for the sake of liturgy, music for the sake of

---

12. George Conger, "What Does Justin Welby Think about Same-Sex Marriage?," *Anglican Ink*, May 25, 2018, http://www.anglican.ink/article/what-does-justin-welby-think-about-same-sex-marriage.

music, and tradition for the sake of tradition. As the apostle Paul wrote, they are "having the appearance of godliness, but denying its power" (2 Tim. 3:5). And as Athanasius argued against Arius's heresy, the Jesus whom they promote is not the Jesus of which the Bible speaks.

Movement to Reform the Anglican Communion

At the end of the twentieth century, neo-paganism's presenting issue became the main topic of the 1998 Lambeth Conference, a once-in-a-decade gathering of all the Anglican bishops from around the Anglican Communion. The neo-pagan West, with its insistence on the acceptance of homosexual lifestyles and marriages, was confronted by the theologically and biblically conservative bishops of the Global South. The Lambeth Conference of Bishops voted overwhelmingly (526–70), in Resolution I.10, against the neo-pagan agenda. This resolution affirmed that faithful and godly sexual relationships were appropriate only in the context of the lifelong marriage between a man and woman, and that the unmarried are called by Scripture and tradition to abstinence. The resolution also called for special pastoral care for same-sex-attracted persons. But it clearly named same-sex practice as "incompatible with Scripture." It rejected both the authorization of same-sex marriage rites by the church and the ordination of anyone in a same-sex union.[13]

Just a few years later, the Episcopal Church (USA) and the Anglican Church of Canada defied the resolution by pushing ahead with their nonbiblical agenda (as mentioned above), claiming that the Anglican Communion had no authority to impose resolutions on their particular provinces. Acting on their own and in defiance of

---

13. "1998 Lambeth Resolution I.10," GAFCON, https://www.gafcon.org/jerusalem-2018/key-documents/resolution-110.

the above Lambeth resolution, the Episcopal Church (USA) conse-crated a noncelibate homosexual man who was in a partnered rela-tionship. Many of the provinces in other parts of the Communion responded by breaking communion with these two provinces or stating that they were in a state of "impaired" communion.

When the archbishops of all the Anglican provinces (the "pri-mates") met after these events, they called on these two provinces to repent and return to the teaching of the Bible. In 2007, the Pri-mates' Meeting in Dar es Salaam instructed the archbishop of Can-terbury to carry out their desired discipline and hold the provinces accountable. The primates thought he agreed not to include these provinces in future meetings until they showed evidence of repen-tance. But when Archbishop Rowan Williams failed to uphold his part of the agreement and instead invited these provinces to the 2008 Lambeth Meeting, the trust and leadership of the office of the archbishop of Canterbury was severely damaged.

Frustrated by the archbishop's lack of leadership, by the accep-tance of sinful practices in the life of the Communion, and by being insulted by arrogant Western bishops, primates of the Global South called forth the Anglican Future Conference (GAFCON) in Jerusa-lem in 2008. Stephen Noll summarizes the result of the historic conference in Jerusalem:

> In the Jerusalem Statement and the Jerusalem Declaration, the 2008 Global Anglican Future Conference took up the challenge of restoring Biblical authority (and the teaching on human sexuality in particular) by affirming the primacy of the Bible as God's Word written and going back to the other sources of Anglican identity—the Creeds and Councils of the ancient church, the 39 Articles, the 1662 Book of Common Prayer, and the Ordinal. The Conference also constituted a Primates Coun-cil and authorized it to recognize Anglican churches in areas

where orthodox Anglicans have been deprived of their church property and been deposed from Holy Orders.[14]

After 2008, things continued in the same direction with neo-pagan Anglicanism being not just tolerated but embraced by the Anglican establishment. The bodies known as "Instruments of Communion" (the archbishop of Canterbury, the Lambeth Conference of Bishops, the Primates' Meeting, and the Anglican Consultative Council) ignored the concerns precipitated by the rise of neo-paganism in the Anglican Communion. Rather than disciplining and correcting those who were teaching and promoting doctrines contrary to the Bible and the Anglican Communion, they began to incorporate these practices and beliefs into the life of the Anglican Communion structures.

The current archbishop of Canterbury called for a gathering of the primates in 2016 for the purpose of "disciplining" the Episcopal Church over its approval of same-sex marriage in its province. (He used those exact words in a phone call inviting me to the "gathering"). But when the meeting was finished, there was no public word about discipline. Instead it was announced that "consequences" were imposed on the Episcopal Church for a three-year period, until its General Convention would meet in 2018 and could show the church's repentance by restoring traditional marriage as the norm. The consequences imposed on Episcopal Church leaders were that (1) they were not to serve in leadership capacities in the Anglican Communion, (2) they were not to represent the Anglican Communion in ecumenical gatherings, and (3) they were not to be a part of any decisions regarding doctrine and polity.

As I write in December 2018, the three years have passed, and the consequences have not been enforced. The 2018 General Conven-

---

14. Stephen Noll, *Letter to the Churches: The Text with Commentary* (Newport Beach, CA: Anglican House, 2018), 6.

tion of the Episcopal Church went even further down the road of renouncing biblical marriage as the norm by forcing all dioceses to allow same-sex marriages. The archbishop of Canterbury has promoted the Episcopal Church's presiding bishop by giving him unprecedented opportunities, such as preaching at the royal wedding of Prince Harry and Meghan Markle, and using the bishop in a video highlighting the Church of England's nation-wide prayer campaign.

The archbishop of Canterbury has insisted that we can "walk together" in the midst of our disagreements, and that our disagreement over marriage, homosexual practice, and ordination should not divide us. He has thereby compromised Resolution I.10 from Lambeth 1998. In effect he has said that these neo-pagan practices are acceptable in parts of the Anglican Communion and we should just agree to disagree.

With GAFCON's release of the Jerusalem Statement[15] and the Jerusalem Declaration in 2008[16] and its "Letter to the Churches" in 2018,[17] the archbishops and bishops who represent the majority of the Anglican Communion have drawn an orthodox line in the sand. In these documents they are saying that we need to do the following in order to proclaim Jesus Christ faithfully to the nations in our generation: (1) restore the Bible as the authoritative, clear, and sufficient word of God; (2) remind the church that sexual ethics are a salvation issue (see 1 Cor. 6); and (3) understand that walking together with false teachers is unbiblical. To walk together with false teachers is a tacit admission that false teaching on salvific matters falls within the acceptable boundaries of pastoral

---

15. "Jerusalem Statement—June 2008," GAFCON, June 29, 2008, https://www.gafcon.org/jerusalem-2018/key-documents/jerusalem-statement.

16. "The Jerusalem Declaration," GAFCON, June 29, 2008, https://www.gafcon.org/resources/the-jerusalem-declaration.

17. "Letter to the Churches—Gafcon Assembly 2018," GAFCON, June 22, 2018, https://www.gafcon.org/news/letter-to-the-churches-gafcon-assembly-2018.

and theological diversity. This cannot be so. It violates the word of God (1 Cor. 5:9–12).

GAFCON is a reform and renewal movement. It calls on Anglicans throughout the world to do as Jude 3 says: "to contend for the faith that was once for all delivered to all the saints." This movement calls on all Anglicans to repent of our sins, return to the Lord, return to the historic teaching of the Bible and church tradition, and resist the economic and political pressures to compromise biblical faith.

Together with leaders from Global South Anglicans, these godly leaders are attempting to address what has been described as the "ecclesial deficit" in the Anglican Communion. The lack of leadership by the Instruments of the Communion, and specifically the archbishop of Canterbury, to address the neo-pagan takeover of certain provinces in the Communion is tearing the Communion apart. The 2016 Global South Anglicans Communique speaks to this very clearly:

> This deficit is evident in the inability of existing Communion instruments to discern truth and error and take binding ecclesiastical action. The instruments have been found wanting in their ability to discipline those leaders who have abandoned the biblical and historic faith. To make matters worse, the instruments have failed to check the marginalisation of Anglicans in heterodox Provinces who are faithful, and in some cases have even sanctioned or deposed them.[18]

The communique goes on to suggest that changes need to come to Anglican structures of authority:

> The instruments are therefore unable to sustain the common life and unity of the Anglican Churches worldwide, especially in an increasingly connected and globalising world, where dif-

---

18. "The Sixth Trumpet: Communiqué from the 6th Global South Conference, Cairo 2016," Global South Anglican Online, October 8, 2016, http://www.globalsouthanglican .org/index.php/blog/comments/communique_sixthGSC.

ferent ideas and lifestyles are quickly disseminated through social media. This undermines the mission of the Church in today's world.[19]

The colonial wineskins are no longer working. We are in a post-colonial era, and the Anglican Communion's establishment has failed to change in this crucial respect. It still seeks to control, manipulate, patronize, and order its life on a dependency paradigm. It is failing in its servant leadership to the Communion, and because of this, many people are suffering. The normalization and promotion of sin and the lack of leadership from the Communion establishment threatens to tear the Communion asunder. The words of Jude 18–19 should pierce our hearts: "'In the last time there will be scoffers, following their own ungodly passions.' It is these who cause divisions, worldly people, devoid of the Spirit."

Because of this, the godly leaders of GAFCON and the Global South have stood tall. They have refused to compromise the Scriptures. They have put an end to "business as usual" with provinces that have adopted theologies more in line with ancient paganism than with historic Christianity. Many, at great sacrifice and personal cost, have turned down large financial gifts from such provinces, dioceses, and churches. They have sacrificed their salaries, office staffs, funding for schools, childcare, church buildings, food banks, and medical clinics. They have done so in order to stand up for the historic faith of the church. It has been tough, but God has honored their faithfulness with vibrancy of faith, miraculous provision, and freedom from economic slavery to the West.

Moving Forward

We live in a world in need of the gospel of Jesus. Heresy is a decadence that cannot be tolerated within the church. It steals our time

---

19. "The Sixth Trumpet."

and resources. It robs us of energy that ought to be used to share the gospel of Jesus and make disciples. Millions are going to their graves without hearing about Jesus and his saving work. Millions need to be snatched from the fire. Millions need to be shown mercy and loved out of their sin. Millions are going to bed hungry and with severe needs. Millions are being persecuted because of their faith in Jesus.

As Anglican Christians, we are called to be in the world—taking the gospel to these millions, calling people to repent of their sins, feeding the hungry, healing the sick, clothing the naked, and helping all in need.

We must love people enough to tell them the truth—the truth about their sin and our sin—and to call them to join us in repentance. Yet neo-pagan Anglicanism threatens to put an end to all of this by diluting the gospel and dividing the church.

Will that happen? Will the gospel be diluted and the church divided? We must remember that this is God's church, and the gates of hell will not overtake it (Matt. 16:18). The church catholic—the real church, which is made up of true believers and followers of Jesus—this church will continue. Its shape may change, but its mission will continue until the end of the age. As colonial and aging wineskins continue to promote neo-pagan beliefs and practices, the new wine of Christ's continuing redemptive work will burst out to transform lives and renew our churches among the nations.

Response to the Regional Perspectives

Stephen F. Noll

It is difficult, it seems to me, to read the four presentations on Anglican identity in this section without experiencing a kind of whiplash. The essays by Archbishop Eliud Wabukala and Bishop Mouneer Anis portray a noble history of Anglican missionaries who brought the gospel to East Africa and the Middle East, ushering in a spirit of cooperation among the older churches and other missionary bodies, along with a zeal to reach peoples who did not know salvation in Christ. These past successes continue into the present where Global South Anglicans have managed to expand their evangelistic work even as the colonial sponsors have withdrawn.

Looking to the Anglican future, these two writers are more hopeful than confident. Archbishop Wabukala asks, "What does the Lord require?" and lists desiderata for the Communion, yet he warns that reform "will not happen unless the Anglican Communion is bold enough to say no to the prevailing culture." Bishop Anis also cites recent futile attempts to reform the Communion while commending the example of Athanasius, who remained in the church despite the Arian dominance.

Ephraim Radner notes the inexorable decay of Anglicanism in the "post-Babel" culture but thinks this process may birth "something new and good ecclesially," something to be discerned in terms of a "scriptural figure." Whatever that figure might be, he does not conceive that "something" as a movement that has abjured Anglican institutionalism in the name of biblical and historic Anglican teaching.[1] It seems to me his "figure" combines something of the pessimism of Ecclesiastes with the wistfulness of the Chronicler, who projected a postexilic restoration of the temple establishment. In any case, his view does not entail a call to action in response to today's cultural crisis within the Communion.

One might conclude from the three presentations that travelers on the Anglican way today merely face some lane diversions. But what if head-on collision is imminent? This is the question that causes whiplash when one turns to the chapter by Archbishop Foley Beach on "neo-pagan Anglicanism."

First of all, who is Foley Beach to speak on Anglicanism? His title is archbishop and primate of the Anglican Church in North America. He has a seat on the "Primates Council" of the Global South Anglican Network (chaired by Bishop Anis), and he is chairman of the GAFCON Primates Council (Archbishop Wabukala is a former chairman). So he is recognized as an Anglican primate by the vast majority of Anglicans worldwide. But in the eyes of the archbishop of Canterbury and the other "Instruments of Unity," Archbishop Beach, whatever his titles, is *not an Anglican at all*—nor are any of the members of his church.[2]

---

1. In this essay and other writings, Radner has virtually nothing to say about the GAFCON movement, which is an odd oversight, considering events of the past twenty years. On the other hand, he commends the "nuanced work" of Paul Avis, who is a prime apologist for the Canterbury Establishment. See my comment on Avis in *Global Anglican Communion: Contending for Anglicanism 1993–2018* (Newport Beach, CA: Anglican House, 2018), 353–54.

2. See the "Communique from the Primates' Meeting, Canterbury Cathedral, England, 2–6 October 2017," 2, https://www.anglicancommunion.org/media/311326/communiqu%C3%A9-primates-meeting-2017.pdf: "It was confirmed that the Anglican Church of

Second, is Archbishop Beach simply scaring the sheep with his talk about "neo-pagan Anglicanism"? I leave that for the reader to judge, but I shall add two items from late 2018 that might justify the title of his chapter.

The first item comes from Canada: "The [Anglican] Diocese of Toronto congratulates Bishop Kevin Robertson and Mr. Mohan Sharma, who were married today at St. James Cathedral in the presence of their two children, their families and many friends, including Archbishop Colin Johnson and Bishop Andrew Asbil."[3] Bishop Robertson is an Anglican in the eyes of Canterbury, and no doubt he and his spouse will be welcomed to the 2020 Lambeth Conference.

The second item comes from the Mother Church itself, whose bishops have issued "Pastoral Guidance" concerning baptism (or its renewal) for "trans people."[4] The bishops instruct clergy "to identify the preference of the transgender in respect of their name and gendered (or other) pronouns." So if Adam Jones awakes one day convinced that he is Eve, "she" can go to the vicar and ask for a new baptismal identity.

These outrageous violations of God's creative will and of Scripture, tradition, and sacrament are hardly bumps in the road. They are more like the abomination of desolation set up in the temple. I do not think Athanasius would choose to attend a council where these false shepherds were seated. They justify the severity of Archbishop Beach's title.

The emerging movement that Foley Beach represents is an alternative figural reading of Anglican history, one drawn from the

North America is not a Province of the Anglican Communion. We recognised that those in ACNA should be treated with love as fellow Christians."

3. "Bishop Robertson Married at Cathedral," Diocese of Toronto, Anglican Church of Canada (website), December 28, 2018, www.toronto.anglican.ca/2018/12/28/bishop -robertson-married-at-cathedral/.

4. "Pastoral Guidance for Use . . . in the Context of Gender Transition," https://www .churchofengland.org/sites/default/files/2018-12/Pastoral%20Guidance-Affirmation -Baptismal-Faith.pdf.

Old Testament prophets, who spoke repeatedly of judgment, exile, repentance, and reform. The shape of this prophetic vocation, I believe, can be discerned in three major events and statements framing the past two decades.

Lambeth 1998. In 1998, the churches of North America presented the Lambeth Conference with "facts on the ground" emerging from the sexual revolution, including homosexual ordinations and same-sex blessings. The conference rejected these innovations overwhelmingly and articulated its view in Resolution I.10, which reaffirmed the norm of heterosexual marriage or abstinence and stated that homosexual practice was "incompatible with Scripture."

In effect, the Lambeth Conference echoed the word of the Lord spoken through Jeremiah,

> Stand by the roads, and look,
>   and ask for the ancient paths,
> where the good way is; and walk in it.

And the North American bishops went home and said, "We will not walk in it" (Jer. 6:16). The official "Instruments of Communion" dithered for a decade, which led directly to the "Global Anglican Future Conference" (GAFCON) in Jerusalem.

GAFCON 2008. In its conference statement, the nearly twelve hundred participants and three hundred bishops indicted the North American churches for promoting a false gospel, and the official Instruments for failing to discipline these churches. The statement went on to reaffirm the classic definition of Anglican identity from Canon A5[5] of the Church of England and supplemented it with a

---

5. Canon A5 states: "The doctrine of the Church of England is grounded in the Holy Scriptures, and in such teachings of the ancient Fathers and Councils of the Church as are agreeable to the said Scriptures. In particular such doctrine is to be found in the Thirty-

fourteen-point Jerusalem Declaration.[6] Finally, the conference established an extraordinary Primates Council with authority to recognize alternate jurisdictions in provinces that had promoted practices contrary to the teaching of Scripture and the norm of Lambeth I.10.

GAFCON 2018. Over the past decade, GAFCON leadership has sought a hearing from the archbishop of Canterbury and Communion Office, who have steadfastly ignored the movement and insinuated that it is schismatic. The 2018 conference, attended by nearly two thousand delegates, predominantly from the Global South, adopted the theme "Proclaiming Christ Faithfully to the Nations." Its "Letter to the Churches" states:

> Over the past twenty years, we have seen the hand of God leading us toward a reordering of the Anglican Communion. Gafcon has claimed from the beginning: "We are not leaving the Anglican Communion; we are the majority of the Anglican Communion seeking to remain faithful to our Anglican heritage."[7]

This statement reiterates GAFCON's prophetic critique of recent Anglican history, which includes themes of judgment and hope, seeing God's hand at work in the crisis of the past twenty years and claiming an inheritance and vocation to reform, restore, and reorder the Anglican Communion.

GAFCON is a prophetic and ecclesial "movement of the Spirit." I do not think one can answer the question What is Anglicanism? without taking this prophetic paradigm into consideration.

nine Articles of Religion, *The Book of Common Prayer*, and the Ordinal." See "Of the Doctrine of the Church of England," The Church of England (website), https://www.churchof england.org/more/policy-and-thinking/canons-church-england/section-a#b5.

6. "The Jerusalem Declaration," GAFCON, June 29, 2008, https://www.gafcon.org /resources/the-jerusalem-declaration/.

7. See my *Letter to the Churches: The Text with Commentary* (Newport Beach, CA: Anglican House, 2018); also Stephen Noll, "Commentary on the 'Letter to the Churches,'" GAFCON, October 11, 2018, https://www.gafcon.org/news/rev-dr-stephen-nolls-commentary-on -the-letter-to-the-churches.

PART 2

VOCATIONAL PERSPECTIVES ON ANGLICANISM

5

A RECTOR AND SCHOLAR

Our Anglican Essentials

John W. Yates III

The question What is Anglicanism? emerges from an ongoing existential crisis in our global Communion. To ask it is to probe much deeper questions about the identity and mission of the church: Who has authority? What is the role of Scripture in our common life? How are we to be held accountable?

We are by no means the first to ask these questions. These and many other questions were posed by the Reformers of the Church of England in the sixteenth century. They did not set out to build a global Communion. They set out amid the constraints and dangerously mixed motives of their era to reform the church of Christ in a particular nation at a particular time by addressing fundamental issues about the identity and mission of the church. In many ways our task is the same, though the stage is noticeably bigger.

The identity and mission of the global Anglican Communion are at stake.

In this context I wonder if one way to address the question of Anglican identity is to ask a related question rooted in our shared history: What did the Reformers think they were doing? No era exerts a greater shaping influence on who and what we are as Anglicans than does the Reformation. We still look back to the formularies—the Thirty-Nine Articles, the Homilies, and the Ordinal and the Book of Common Prayer—as constitutive of our Communion.[1] It therefore makes sense to return to these as resources in our present season of uncertainty.

Of course, this approach has its limitations. Anglicanism is not merely a Reformation reality. Our shared history stretches back many centuries prior to the Reformation of the sixteenth century, and post-Reformation developments continue to shape Anglicanism in fundamental ways. I do not imagine that all the answers are somehow simplistically found in the sixteenth century. However, there is no better age to which we can turn, and no more complete and coherent set of answers provided to our questions than those given by the Reformers. If the Reformation has no answer to the question What is Anglicanism? perhaps there is no coherence to our tradition after all.

So what did the Reformers think they were doing? I want to argue that among the varied agendas of the age of Reformation, four essential tasks were paramount. The Reformers thought that they were living under the word of God, proclaiming the gospel, revitalizing worship, and serving the nation. I would like to reflect briefly on each of these, considering why they remain important

---

1. Anglicans generally recognize the 1662 BCP as the authoritative version of the Prayer Book, to which our worship must conform. Cranmer's versions of 1549 and 1552, however, fundamentally shaped the 1662 edition and provided the theological impetus for the English Prayer Book tradition. Typically, I will refer to these earlier prayer books in this chapter.

today and concluding with a few thoughts on the difference between Anglican "essentials" and Anglican "distinctives."

Let me add, here, that I speak as a pastor-theologian who has, in the traditional language of the church, "cure of souls." At the end of the day, it is the lived reality of pastoral ministry that drives my argument as much as the history of our Anglican Communion. This is not a theoretical conversation. We must not lose sight of the fact that our understanding of Anglican identity will shape the ministries of our churches and the lives of our friends, neighbors, and loved ones. My hope is that this chapter will be a help and encouragement particularly to clergy, those training for ordination, and lay men and women engaged in the leadership of the church, for these men and women are on the front lines of the church's ministry.

Living under the Word of God

Thomas Cranmer's "Homily on Scripture," which stands at the head of the collection of Homilies of 1547, begins with an unambiguous declaration: "Unto a Christian man there can be nothing either more necessary or profitable than the knowledge of Holy Scripture: forasmuch as in it is contained God's true Word, setting forth his glory and also man's duty."[2] It is hard to overemphasize the importance of Scripture to the Reformers.[3] For it is in the Scriptures that God is to be found and known; and it is in the Scriptures that God's people are to find and know themselves. For this reason, chief among the priorities of the Reformers was the desire to see the church in England brought under the guiding influence of the life-giving word of God.

---

2. Ronald B. Bond, *Certain Sermons or Homilies (1547) and A Homily against Disobedience and Wilful Rebellion (1570): A Critical Edition* (Toronto: University of London Press, 1987), 61; the English in all quotations from this text has been modernized.

3. See John W. Yates III, *"Sola Scriptura,"* in *Reformation Anglicanism: A Vision for Today's Global Communion*, ed. Ashley Null and John W. Yates III (Wheaton, IL: Crossway, 2017), 77–104.

One of the first great battles to be fought and won by Cranmer was for royal consent that the Bible be published in English and made publicly available in every parish church across the country. Consent was given in 1537, and in April 1539 the "Great Bible" was published. Cranmer was convinced of what he wrote in his preface to the first edition: "If anything be necessary to be learned, of the holy scripture we may learn it."

The Reformers believed that all people, even the illiterate and uneducated, can be transformed by the reading or hearing of Scripture. This is because the Bible speaks the very word of God. It feeds the soul, convicts of sin, imparts saving knowledge, and leads to the justification of sinners. Simply making Scripture available to the people was not enough, however. The Reformers knew that it must be read in a thorough and disciplined manner, and that this must be built into the worshiping life of the church through a cycle of daily readings. This led to Cranmer's insistence on the inclusion of a lectionary in the Book of Common Prayer.

In his preface to the 1552 BCP, Cranmer explains the purpose and use of a daily lectionary by describing its origin among the fathers of the church:

> For they so ordered the matter, that all the whole Bible (or the greatest part thereof) should be read over once in the year intending thereby, that the clergy and specially such as were ministers of the congregation, should (by often reading and meditation of God's word) be stirred up to godliness themselves, and be more able also to exhort others by wholesome doctrine, and to confute them that were adversaries to the truth.[4]

Clergy who have been sated by Scripture will live in accordance with God's will, encourage others to do the same, and defend the

---

4. *The First and Second Prayer Books of Edward VI*, Everyman's Library (London: Dent, 1964), 321, spelling modernized.

truth of the gospel. This practice of daily Bible reading in the local parish was meant to spill over into private homes. As Cranmer wrote in his preface to the Great Bible, citing John Chrysostom, "I exhort you . . . and ever have and will exhort you, that ye (not only here in the church) give ear to that that is said by the preacher, but that also when ye be at home in your houses, ye apply yourselves from time to time to the reading of holy scriptures."[5]

The daily reading of Scripture was central to the program of reformation because the Reformers believed that God's word had the power not just to bring salvation but also to improve the lives of people amid the challenges of everyday life. Cranmer explained this with *pathos* in his preface:

> Thy wife provoketh thee to anger; thy child giveth thee occasion to take sorrow and pensiveness; thine enemies lie in wait for thee; thy friend (as thou takest him) sometime envieth thee; thy neighbor misreporteth thee or picketh quarrels against thee; thy mate or partner undermineth thee; thy lord, judge, or justice, threateneth thee; poverty is painful unto thee; the loss of thy dear and wellbeloved causeth thee to mourn; prosperity exalteth thee, adversity bringeth thee low. Briefly, so divers and so manifold occasions of cares, tribulations, and temptations, beset thee and besiege thee round about. Where canst thou have armor or fortress against thine assaults? Where canst thou have salves for thy sores but of holy scripture?

At the heart of Anglicanism is the desire that God's people should live under the word of God and be transformed by it. This is not merely for the sake of uniformity of doctrine but also for the good and godliness of all.

---

5. Gerald Bray, ed., *Documents of the English Reformation 1526–1701* (Cambridge: James Clarke, 2004), 236.

The Reformers had great confidence in the power of Scripture. They were not, however, naive when it came to human nature and our ability to misconstrue the meaning of God's word. It was clear to them that Scripture must be carefully taught and explained. It is no mere coincidence that the first of the formularies produced under the reign of Edward VI was the Homilies.[6] This collection of short addresses was distributed to all clergy, and they were to be preached in every parish across England. Edward's preface to the Homilies clearly states their purpose, which was "the true setting forth and pure declaring of God's word, which is the principal guide and leader unto all godliness and virtue."[7]

Cranmer and his fellow Reformers knew that the only way to ensure the deep reformation of Christ's church was by enlivening the preaching of the church with a clear proclamation of gospel truth that rested in the explanation and exposition of Scripture. This came through in the Ordinal, where the bishop asks those being ordained to the priesthood:

> Be you persuaded that the holy Scriptures contain sufficiently all doctrine required of necessity for eternal salvation, through faith in Jesus Christ? And are you determined with the said scriptures, to instruct the people committed to your charge, and to teach nothing, as required of necessity, to eternal salvation, but that you shall be persuaded may be concluded, and proved by the scripture?[8]

Scripture is the living, breathing, life-giving word of God. Because of this, the Reformers were committed to the surprisingly difficult task of bringing this word before God's people so that they

---

6. The formularies include the Articles of Religion, the Ordinal, the Book of Common Prayer, and the Homilies.

7. Bond, *Certain Sermons or Homilies*, 55.

8. From the Ordinal, 1549, in *First and Second Prayer Books of Edward VI*, 309, spelling modernized.

might live under it. They did so by making Scripture widely avail-able in the language of the people, by guiding them in the daily reading of Scripture, and by prioritizing the ministry of preaching. Our task today is the same. Anglicans are still people of the word. We must not only make Scripture available where it is not already available; we must also teach people how to read and reflect on it. And we must support their daily reading with preaching that takes Scripture seriously and explains it with care. Sadly, much of the confusion and consternation over Anglican identity lies in the fact that we have removed ourselves, step-by-step, from daily engage-ment with Scripture. If we are to recover our identity, we must first recover the importance of living under God's word.

Proclaiming the Gospel

The Reformers' enthusiasm for the Bible lay in the fact that in Scrip-ture they had discovered the joy of the gospel long hidden by the complexities and superstitions of medieval doctrine and worship. Central to the program of reformation, therefore, was their desire to see this gospel clearly proclaimed. This is evident in Cranmer's "Homily on Salvation," which begins with a summary explanation of the gospel emphasizing the need for all people everywhere to hear and receive it.

> BECAUSE all men be sinners and offenders against God, and breakers of his law and commandments, therefore can no man by his own acts, works, and deeds—seem they never so good— be justified and made righteous before God; but every man of necessity is constrained to seek for another righteousness, or justification, to be received at God's own hands, that is to say, the remission, pardon and forgiveness of his sins and trespasses in such things as he hath offended. And this justification or righteousness, which we so receive of God's mercy and Christ's

merits, embraced by faith, is taken, accepted, and allowed of God for our perfect and full justification.[9]

The universal message of the gospel is the justification of sinners through the body and blood of Jesus Christ received by faith. What Cranmer articulates thoroughly in the Homilies is affirmed concisely in the Thirty-Nine Articles. Article 11 states: "We are accounted righteous before God, only for the merit of our Lord and Savior Jesus Christ by faith, and not for our own works or deservings. Wherefore that we are justified by faith only is a most wholesome doctrine, and very full of comfort."

This brief, doctrinal statement concludes with a pastoral note of personal comfort. The Reformers believed that justification by faith alone through Christ alone was not just good theology; it was good for the soul because it offered assurance of salvation. According to the Homilies and Articles, salvation depends not on works or personal merit, or the mediation of the church, but on the righteous love of Jesus demonstrated on the cross. Part of what makes this good news *good* is that those who trust in the saving love of Christ do so without fear of losing it. The pastoral note of Article 11 matches the overall tone of Cranmer's preface to the "Great Bible" and the logic of his "Homily on Salvation." Throughout the Anglican formularies there is an emphasis on the blessings and benefits of the gospel.

The centrality of the gospel message of justification by faith is emphasized by J. C. Ryle, the great bishop of Liverpool, in his collection of essays *Knots Untied*. Ryle notes that the only anathema pronounced in the Thirty-Nine Articles relates to this doctrine and appears in Article 18, which reads:

They also are to be had accursed, that presume to say, that every man shall be saved by the law or sect which he professeth, so

9. Bond, *Certain Sermons or Homilies*, 79.

that he be diligent to frame his life according to that law, and the light of nature. For Holy Scripture doth set out unto us only the name of Jesus Christ, whereby men must be saved.

As Ryle points out, the Council of Trent "anathematizes continually," but we do so only once, on this most crucial of doctrines.[10]

It is commonly said that Anglican theology walks a "middle way" or *via media* between Catholic and Protestant traditions. This *via media* is reflected in Anglican ecclesial culture as well, which has a reputation for broad-mindedness and moderation. It is true that many contemporary Anglicans attempt to walk a "middle way" between Rome and Canterbury, often mixing beliefs and practices that are fundamentally incompatible. But this is decidedly *not* true of the Reformers. In his brief but brilliant book on the Thirty-Nine Articles, Oliver O'Donovan writes:

> There was nothing particularly "middle" about most of the English Reformers' theological positions—even if one could decide between what poles the middle way was supposed to lie. Their moderation consisted rather in a determined policy of separating the essentials of faith and order from adiaphora. . . . Anglican moderation is the policy of reserving strong statement and conviction for the few things which really deserve them.[11]

The Reformer's understanding of the gospel as the message of justification by faith alone through grace alone is one of those essentials warranting strong statement.

Inherent within this understanding of the gospel is a robust doctrine of sin. Justification is meaningless where there is no sin

---

10. J. C. Ryle, *Knots Untied: Being Plain Statements on Disputed Points in Religion from the Standpoint of an Evangelical Churchman* (Moscow, ID: Nolan, 2000), 28.

11. Oliver O'Donovan, *On the Thirty-Nine Articles: A Conversation with Tudor Christianity*, 2nd ed. (London: SCM, 2011), 8.

to atone for. And the cross is emptied of its power if Christ is merely a martyr. Much of the identity crisis we have experienced within the Anglican Communion can be traced to a gradual weakening of the doctrine of sin. The Reformers understood just how important a clear doctrine of sin is to the proclamation of the gospel. This is most clear in the ordering of the Homilies. Cranmer begins with the "Homily on Scripture," but before proceeding to the "Homily on Salvation" he introduces our great need for salvation in the homily traditionally titled "Of the misery of all mankind, and of his condemnation to death everlasting by his own sin." The homily begins, "The Holy Ghost in writing the Holy Scripture is in nothing more diligent than to pull down man's vainglory and pride, which, of all vices, is most universally grafted in all mankind, even from the first infection of our first father Adam."[12]

In my experience as a pastor it is honest teaching on sin that opens the door both to conversion and to a more profound grasp of the good news of the gospel for those who already believe. This, of course, is also the doctrine that elicits the most violent denunciations against our cause. Contrary to the teaching of many—particularly in the West—the gospel we proclaim is not a universal message of affirmation but a message of salvation for those who believe and trust in Jesus for the forgiveness of sin.

If we are to reclaim the Anglican identity of our global Communion, it must be built on an unapologetic return to the strong and simple proclamation of the gospel found among the Reformers rooted in a robust understanding of human sin. Bishop Ryle puts it well: "We cannot be too careful to add nothing to, and take nothing away from, the simplicity of the gospel."[13]

---

12. Bond, *Certain Sermons or Homilies*, 70.
13. Ryle, *Knots Untied*, 21.

Revitalizing Worship

Worship is both expressive and instructive. It expresses what we believe and, at the same time, instructs us as to what we ought to believe and how we ought to behave. The Reformers, particularly Cranmer, understood this. They sought, therefore, to revitalize the worship of God's people in such a way that reflected the true nature of the gospel and formed the convictions and affections of God's people accordingly. Cranmer's chief tool in this work of revitalization was Scripture.

Oliver O'Donovan writes, "If the first cause of the Anglican Reformation was the English Bible, its decisive form was the English Prayer Book."[14] Cranmer would have agreed and likely added that the movement from one to the next was natural. As Scripture brought clarity to the message of salvation, so the worship of God's people necessarily changed. In his preface to the 1549 BCP, Cranmer explains his purpose in setting out the English liturgy:

> Here you have an order for prayer much agreeable to the mind and purpose of the old fathers, and a great deal more profitable and commodious than that which of late was used. It is more profitable, because here are left out many things, whereof some be untrue, some uncertain, some vain and superstitious, and is ordained nothing to be read but the very pure word of God, the holy scriptures, or that which is evidently grounded upon the same; and that in such a language and order, as is most easy and plain for the understanding, both of the readers and hearers.[15]

Cranmer recognized that the revival of true religion in the Church of England would take place only as the church's worship was revitalized through simplification, presentation in the common language of the people, and grounding in Scripture. Scriptural

---

14. O'Donovan, On the Thirty-Nine Articles, viii.
15. First and Second Prayer Books of Edward VI, 322.

quotations and allusions are found in nearly every line of his liturgy, reflecting not just Cranmer's prioritization of the biblical text but also the complete saturation of his imagination with the language and imagery of the Bible.

This scriptural grounding of the liturgy led to a form of Eucharistic worship that presented the doctrine of justification by faith alone. This is most powerfully expressed in the revised prayer of consecration of 1552:

> Almighty God, our heavenly father, which of thy tender mercy didst give thine only son Jesus Christ, to suffer death upon the cross for our redemption, who made there (by his one oblation of himself once offered) a full, perfect and sufficient sacrifice, oblation, and satisfaction, for the sins of the whole world, and did institute, and in his holy Gospel command us to continue, a perpetual memory of that his precious death, until his coming again: Hear us O merciful father we beseech thee; and grant that we, receiving these thy creatures of bread and wine, according to thy son our Savior Jesus Christ's holy institution, in remembrance of his death and passion, may be partakers of his most blessed body and blood.

Dom Gregory Dix describes Cranmer's 1552 Book of Common Prayer as "the only effective attempt ever made to give liturgical expression to the doctrine of 'justification by faith alone.'"[16]

Cranmer had set out not to create something novel or new, however, but to root this revitalized worship in the work of the fathers of the early church. His private notebooks are filled with carefully selected quotations from the fathers, demonstrating his respect for them and dependence on them as he set about this work.[17] Cran-

---

16. Dom Gregory Dix, *The Shape of the Liturgy* (London: Dacre, 1945), 672.

17. See Ashley Null, *Thomas Cranmer's Doctrine of Repentance* (Oxford: Oxford University Press, 2000), 254.

mer did not cast aside the traditions of the church but revised and rewrote as he pressed them through the sieve of Scripture and justification by faith alone. The result was nothing less than one of the most significant works in the history of the English language.[18]

The Book of Common Prayer is one of the great strengths of our tradition and essential to our identity as Anglicans. It roots us in the rich tradition of the church back to the Patristic age and in the language and imagery of Scripture. We are not, however, shackled to this tradition. Part of its strength is its dynamism. In his additional note on ceremonies at the beginning of the 1552 Book of Common Prayer, Cranmer writes:

> Every country should use such ceremonies as they shall think best to the setting forth of God's honor or glory, and to the reducing of the people to a most perfect and godly living, without error or superstition. And that they should put away other things which from time to time they perceive to be most abused.

Cranmer was wise enough to know that in other times and places theological error would arise in different forms. These errors would need to be taken into account in the revising of ceremonies for use in worship. His understanding of the Book of Common Prayer thus took into account the necessity of *semper reformandum*— the need for constant reform within the church. At the same time, however, his Prayer Book was shaped by a constant return to and engagement with the doctrine and practice of the early church. In this sense, Cranmer kept to the Reformation principle of *ad fontes* (to the sources).

---

18. For a very helpful, though occasionally flawed, history of the Prayer Book, see Alan Jacobs, *The Book of Common Prayer: A Biography* (Princeton: Princeton University Press, 2013). For further discussion, see my review in the *Bulletin of Ecclesial Theology* 3, no. 1 (2016): 179–84.

In an era of uncertainty within our Communion, we must hold on to the Prayer Book tradition. At its best it is richly biblical and theologically profound. We must embrace the rootedness of this tradition, while also appreciating the need for dynamism in revision. In this work of revising our liturgies, however, we must keep Cranmer's priorities in mind. Our liturgies must use language that is understandable to God's people. They must be filled with Scripture not just by means of direct quotation but also by employing the imagery and language of the Bible. Our liturgies must present the gospel of justification by faith alone clearly and without equivocation. Furthermore, in this work we must always be sensitive to the tendency to reflect our culture's idolatries rather than to challenge them.

Revitalizing worship in the Prayer Book tradition remains central to the ongoing reformation of the church and to our identity as Anglicans. We need to take corporate worship seriously. We must ensure that every word and movement matters, and that the logic of our worship leads us to the gospel. At the same time, we must refuse to uncritically privilege the fixed forms of previous eras or to canonize particular aspects of ceremony. We will need updated liturgies. But as we revise, we must keep to the principles and priorities of Cranmer in the crafting of the Book of Common Prayer.

Serving the Nation

There is one final aspect of the English Reformation for us to consider. This is that the Reformers believed wholeheartedly that by reforming the church, they were serving the nation and seeking the common good.

Today most Anglicans are uncomfortable with the fact that Cranmer and other Reformers affirmed the divine right of the king as supreme governor of the church. In our multicultural and international Communion this is difficult to swallow, and few still share this conviction. It would be a mistake, however, for our concerns about the relationship between church and state to distract from the simple fact that in the minds of the Reformers, fundamental to the life of the church was the call to serve the nation and seek the common good. This vocation began with the king himself and extended down to every member of society.

Cranmer may not have uttered the words below, but they capture this mission well. They purportedly come from his charge to the boy king Edward VI at his coronation:

> Your majesty is God's vicegerent, and Christ's vicar within your own dominions, and to see, with your predecessor Josiah, God truly worshipped, and idolatry destroyed; the tyranny of the bishops of Rome banished from your subjects, and images removed. These acts be signs of a second Josiah, who reformed the church of God in his days. You are to reward virtue, to revenge sin, to justify the innocent, to relieve the poor, to procure peace, to repress violence, and to execute justice throughout your realms.[19]

The king, as sovereign over the church, was to be shepherd to the nation. He was to seek the good of his people by conforming the laws of the nation to the law of God in Scripture. This work extended to those in leadership under him. In the 1662 rite of Holy Communion, just after the prayer for the king, the church prays for all rulers, that they "may truly and indifferently minister justice, to the punishment of wickedness and vice, and to the maintenance of God's true religion and virtue." In the homily on "Good Order and Obedience," we are urged to pray for kings and those in power.

> Let us pray for them, that they may have God's favor and God's protection. Let us pray that they may ever in all things

---

19. John E. Cox, ed., *Miscellaneous Writings and Letters of Thomas Cranmer* (Cambridge: Parker Society, 1846), 127.

have God before their eyes. Let us pray, that they may have wisdom, strength, justice, clemency, and zeal to God's glory, to God's verity, to Christian souls, and to the commonwealth. Let us pray that they may rightly use their sword and authority for the maintenance and defense of the catholic faith, contained in Holy Scripture, and of their good and honest subjects, and for the fear and punishment of the evil and vicious people.[20]

As these prayers suggest, the king and his counselors were called upon to seek the good of the nation by bringing it into conformity with the truth of God revealed in Scripture. The measure of a king and his counselors was the extent to which they fulfilled this element of their vocation. The logic of these prayers need not lead to an attempt by the church to take over the levers of power present in the state. At a much more fundamental level they lead us to a commitment to justice and a hunger for the common good.

It is often lost on modern readers that the Book of Common Prayer was "common" in the sense that its uniform cycle of prayer and praise was intended for the entire populace of England. It was meant to catechize a nation and, through that instructional work, to bring about societal renewal. Part of the Anglican impetus is to seek and shape the common good through the church's faithful worship. As Cranmer explained in the note on ceremonies in his preface to the 1552 Prayer Book, "Every country should use such ceremonies as they shall think best to the setting forth of God's honor or glory, *and to the reducing of the people to a most perfect and godly living*" (my emphasis). This can take place where the king is head over the church or where a latter-day Cyrus rules instead. The church must seek justice, the welfare of the poor, the establish-

20. Bond, *Certain Sermons or Homilies*, 169–70.

ment of civil peace, and the end of violence in whatever commonwealth it finds itself.

We who are in the United States inhabit a cultural moment where some within the broader evangelical community are calling for a calculated withdrawal from the public square. This is not an option for Anglicans. The force of our mission will always be *into* the earthly city, not out of it. It is well worth remembering that while Latimer, Ridley, and Cranmer all went to their deaths as victims of the state, they went first and foremost as servants of the commonwealth.

Concluding Reflections

Among the complex and varied motives of the Reformers, several central aspirations rise to the top. Cranmer and others believed that they were living under Scripture, proclaiming the gospel, revitalizing worship, and serving the nation. By turning our attention to the question What did the Reformers think they were doing? I have sought to focus on what might be called these "Anglican essentials" rather than "Anglican distinctives," those things that distinguish us from other branches of Christ's church. It would be fair to say that these essentials of Anglicanism could be used to describe other branches of the Protestant church around the world. I do not wish to downplay our distinctives or neglect their affirmation. There is, however, a theological and pastoral intent behind my approach.

One of the hallmarks of our situation in North America is the movement of large numbers of evangelical Christians out of various denominations, and nondenominational congregations, into Anglican churches. These men and women are drawn to our rich traditions, polity, sacramental theology, and liturgical worship. It is pleasing to me to see so many friends and peers joining us in this movement. However, a word of caution is appropriate. Much of what draws these friends into the Anglican fold are the distinctives of Anglicanism—those things that set us apart from other reformed or Protestant traditions. They enter into our fellowship because they find Anglicanism to be a fresh and vibrant context in which their evangelical beliefs can flourish.

In the transition, however, the "essentials" of Anglicanism are merely assumed. This, I believe, is a dangerous trend. While we must maintain our distinctives, we must always be aware that the essentials matter most. I have seen far too many evangelical friends enter the Anglican fold only to become increasingly precious about certain traditions and formalities. The things that first drew them in become the things they cherish most.[21] In this process, secondary matters become primary, and the church community becomes inwardly focused on what makes them different from other churches in a competitive ecclesial marketplace. Far too many new member courses at Anglican churches focus primarily on the intricacies of Anglican worship and polity rather than on the essentials of the gospel of Jesus Christ.

We must not lose sight of the Reformers' basic aims: to live under the word of God, to proclaim the gospel of salvation by grace alone through faith alone, to continuously revitalize the worship of the church for the good of God's people, and to serve the nations where we live by seeking the common good. So we ought to ask: Is our teaching and preaching reflexively scriptural? Is our pastoral care rooted in the good news of salvation by grace alone through

---

21. A further observation is warranted at this point. Many of my evangelical peers are drawn to Anglicanism through a particular local expression of our tradition. They come to believe that the local expression they have encountered is a complete representation of "true Anglicanism." They are unaware of the diversity of our tradition and, as a result, become wedded to a particular expression—often tied to local ceremonial. All too often I discover in conversation that fundamental convictions about "what is Anglican" are derived from a peculiar local expression with little understanding of broader, theological convictions and the essentials of the faith articulated in the formularies.

faith alone? Does our worship bring people to the cross of Christ? Do we enter into the life of the world seeking the common good and the communication of the gospel? If we allow these essentials of our faith to become secondary, our distinguishing marks will matter very little in the end.

6

A JOURNALIST AND THEOLOGIAN

Reformed Catholicism

Barbara Gauthier

What is the distinctive character of Anglicanism? What distinguishes it from Rome on the right and Geneva on the left? In good Anglican fashion, I will respond to these two questions by posing a third: Whence came the space between Rome and Geneva where Anglicanism now stands?

Why the Gap between Rome and Geneva?

At the beginning of the sixteenth century that gap did not yet exist, and all those looking toward the future were in basic agreement that the Western church was seriously in need of reform. All agreed that ungodly elements had crept in and were at work in the church to the detriment of the faithful. The church needed to be cleansed, and these aberrations of faith undone and cast aside. But there was little agreement on the best way to accomplish the reform. Where had things begun to go astray? What should be removed, and to what extent? How could the church once again be set on the right path?

As C. S. Lewis put it, "A sum can be put right: but only by going back till you find the error and working it afresh from that point, never by simply going on."[1] The answer would be to go back to the point where the error began and fix it. But correcting a church is far more complicated than correcting a sum. There first has to be agreement on exactly what the error is. Next there has to be agreement on the nature of the error and where it began. There also has to be agreement on how far back prior to the error the reform should go to ensure that the roots of that error are removed as well. It is only then that the church may be worked "afresh from that point."

Some of the Reformers thought that the church need only correct the abuses that had developed. Others were more concerned about correcting the error that had given rise to the abuses. Still others were determined to identify and correct the doctrinal root of the error that had led to the abuses.

Whenever an essential truth of the apostolic deposit of faith is being ignored or forgotten, a doctrinal root of error can find its way into the church. Joseph Cardinal Ratzinger, in a 1988 address, explained that schisms occur in the church when an essential truth is being neglected:

> One of the basic discoveries of the theology of ecumenism is that schisms can take place only when certain truths and certain values of the Christian faith are no longer lived and loved within the Church. The truth which is marginalized becomes autonomous, remains detached from the whole of the

---

1. C. S. Lewis, *The Great Divorce* (New York: Harper Collins, 2001), viii.

ecclesiastical structure, and a new movement then forms itself around it. . . . We should allow ourselves to ask fundamental questions, about the defects in the pastoral life of the Church, which are exposed by these events. . . . We can make such schism pointless by renewing the interior realities of the Church.[2]

Ratzinger's point is that when the church refuses to receive necessary correction, it cannot restore the fullness of the apostolic faith, and the error remains. Moreover, those who break with the church take with them the essential truth they had championed, but in their turn neglect other truths by leaving them behind.

William Reed Huntington describes the anatomy of a schism from the vantage point of those who leave:

The founder of a "denomination" is generally a man who has a singularly clear and strong perception of some one truth of religion. Thus, the planetary centre around which all his own thoughts revolve, becomes, as a matter of course, the pivot of the system he imposes on his followers. . . . Whatever [this cardinal truth] is, the sectarian mind dwells on it to the exclusion of all else, so that gradually the articles of the faith which, at the start, no one would have thought of disavowing, fall into the background and are lost.[3]

In short, the church is left impoverished; those who have left become impoverished; and the fullness of faith is divided.

Martin Luther and later Reformers were convinced that the Roman Church had laid aside the authority of the apostolic Scriptures and, with it, the doctrine of salvation by grace through faith

---

2. Joseph Cardinal Ratzinger, "Cardinal Ratzinger's Remarks on the Lefebvre Schism," *Wanderer*, June 22, 2000, https://www.catholicculture.org/culture/library/view.cfm?id=3032&repos=1&subrepos=&searchid=292734.

3. William Reed Huntington, *The Church Idea* (New York: Dutton 1870; Nashotah, WI: Nashotah House, 2012), 92. Citations refer to the Nashotah House edition.

as a gift of God through the death and resurrection of Jesus Christ, having replaced it with the authority of tradition and works of human striving. While the Protestant Reformers insisted on the importance of Scripture in establishing Christian doctrine, they developed different emphases within that cardinal truth. For Luther, it was justification by faith alone. Calvin focused on the sovereignty of God. The Anabaptists embraced believer's baptism and emphasized individual salvation.

These Reformers also differed in how far back they should go in the tradition of the church to make sure that the doctrinal root of Roman error had been removed. Luther chose to keep the office of bishop but not the tradition of apostolic succession or the magisterium as a source of authority. Calvin rejected Catholic orders and embraced instead the early apostolic understanding of the church as related congregations overseen by elders, retaining an emphasis on Christian community and keeping infant baptism as a rite of initiation into the company of the elect. Anabaptists such as Zwingli and Menno Simons decided to wipe the slate clean and start over with only what could be supported by their idiosyncratic reading of the New Testament itself: independent congregations, adult baptism, no creeds, no bishops, and no tradition apart from Holy Scripture itself.

Where Does Anglicanism Fit within the Gap?

The Anglican Reformers were different. The Reformation in England had no one single theological figure to stamp his system and name on those who followed him. There are no Cranmerians, no Ridleyans, no Jewelists or Hookerites to stand alongside the Lutherans, the Calvinists, the Zwinglians and Mennonites of the continental Reformation. For the most part, the Anglican Reformers shared a common vision, and like the biblical householder "who brings out of his treasure what is new and what is old" (Matt. 13:52), they welcomed the new emphasis on Scripture as the ultimate authoritative basis of Christian faith and doctrine. But valuing the old as well, they continued to embrace that which had been part of the church's understanding of Scripture and practice from the very earliest times.

In keeping with this broader vision, the Anglican Reformers of the sixteenth century differed significantly from their continental counterparts. They were determined to maintain the entire deposit of apostolic faith as received by the apostolic church: to keep the apostolic truths that had been preserved in Catholic faith and practice (sacraments, liturgy, holy orders) and to restore those apostolic truths that had been neglected (Scripture, personal faith, and holy living). By examining the faith and practice of the early church more closely, one might be able to discern the proper balance of scriptural faith and apostolic practice for the renewal of the church in England.

This approach is clearly in evidence in the development of the Book of Common Prayer. In his preface to the 1549 BCP, Archbishop Thomas Cranmer (1489–1556) harkened back to the ancient fathers of the church and their use of Scripture as a model for church worship and prayer.[4] Cranmer's changing theological views led to some

---

4. Cranmer wrote:

There was never any thing by the wit of man so well devised, or so sure established, which in continuance of time hath not been corrupted: As, among other things, it may plainly appear by the Common Prayers in the Church, commonly called *Divine Service*. The first original and ground whereof if a man would search out by the ancient Fathers, he shall find, that the same was not ordained but of a good purpose, and for a great advancement of godliness. For they so ordered the matter, that all the whole Bible (or the greatest part thereof) should be read over every year; intending thereby, that the Clergy, and especially such as were Ministers in the congregation, should (by often reading, and meditation in God's word) be stirred up to godliness themselves and be more able to exhort others by wholesome Doctrine, and to confute them that were adversaries to the Truth. . . .

So that here you have an Order for Prayer, and for the reading of the holy Scripture, much agreeable to the mind and purpose of the old Fathers, and a great deal more profitable and commodious, than that which of late was used. (Thomas Cranmer, preface to *The booke of the common prayer and administracion of the Sacramentes, and other rites and ceremonies of the Churche: after the rite of the Church of England* [London: Edward Whitchurch, 1549])

departures from this approach in his later work; however, it is the approach set forth in the preface to the 1549 BCP, rather than Cranmer's later views, that has molded Anglicanism over the centuries.[5]

Four hundred years later, the legacy of Cranmer's preface to the 1549 BCP could still be seen. At the 1958 Lambeth Conference, the bishops gathered there established certain guidelines for revisions of the Book of Common Prayer to be used in the various provinces of the Anglican Communion. In addition to requiring what is "essential to the safeguarding of our unity, i.e., the use of canonical Scriptures and Creeds, Holy Baptism, Confirmation, Holy Communion, and the Ordinal," Lambeth Resolution 74 also urged "that a chief aim of Prayer Book revision should be to further that recovery of the worship of the primitive Church which was the aim of the compilers of the first Prayer Books of the Church of England."[6]

One of Cranmer's contemporaries, Nicholas Ridley (1500–1555), held the witness of antiquity to be more authoritative than did Cranmer, especially when it came to discerning more accurately between apostolic truth and heresy in the church. Ridley was drawn in particular to guidelines set down by a fifth-century Gallic monk, Vincent of Lérins, who distilled his reflections on the essence of authentic apostolic Christian belief into this simple dictum: "That faith which has been believed everywhere, always, by all."[7] This rule became for some the touchstone of the ancient church and a useful

---

5. In the 1549 BCP, Cranmer reintroduced the epiclesis (prayer for the Holy Spirit to sanctify the elements) into the Eucharistic prayer, consistent with Patristic models. While the epiclesis was the norm in the ancient church, its form had substantially diminished in the liturgy of the Western church over the centuries. However, in the 1552 BCP, he removed the epiclesis from the Communion service, consistent with his changing theological views.

6. Lambeth Conference, "The Lambeth Conference Resolutions Archive from 1958," 20, http://www.anglicancommunion.org/media/127740/1958.pdf.

7. Vincent of Lérins, "Commonitory," in *Nicene and Post-Nicene Fathers*, Series 2, ed. Philip Schaff and Henry Wace, trans. Charles A. Heurtley, vol. 11 (Buffalo: Christian Literature, 1894), 2.6.

plumb line for helping to discern the true doctrine of the primitive apostolic church.

The Vincentian canon, as it has been called, also proved useful to Reformers seeking to distinguish what was authentic to the primitive church from heretical additions that had developed in later centuries. One of Vincent's corollaries proved helpful to Ridley and his allies in their efforts to restore the ancient faith:

> [Vincent of Lérins] was often quoted by the Reformers and Anglican divines in their controversy with Rome. In his disputation at Oxford, Ridley said, when doubts arose in the Church, "I use the wise counsel of Vincentius Lirinensis, whom I am sure you will allow; who, giving precepts how the Catholic Church may be, in all schisms and heresies, known, writeth on this manner: 'When,' saith he, 'one part is corrupted with heresies then prefer the whole world before the one part: but if the greatest part be infected then prefer antiquity.'"[8]

Vincent's emphasis on the universal witness of the undivided church as a tool for discernment helped lay the foundation for an Anglican understanding of how Scripture and tradition are connected in the church. Rather than seeing Scripture and tradition as two separate sources of authority, important Anglicans saw them as closely aligned. Scripture records the apostolic deposit of faith, they believed, and early church tradition passed down the interpretation of Scripture as read together by the undivided church. Anglican Reformers believed that these traditions were guidelines for restoring not only apostolic doctrine but also apostolic practice.

Archbishop of Canterbury Matthew Parker (1504–1575), for example, wanted the English Church to be "based upon true scholarship,

---

8.   Charles C. Grafton, "Fond du Lac Tract III: Catholicity and the Vincentian Rule," in *The Works of the Rt. Rev. Charles C. Grafton*, ed. B. Talbot Rogers, vol. 6 (New York: Longman, Green, 1914), 180, anglicanhistory.org/grafton/v6/180.html.

drawing upon the best traditions of the primitive church, faithful to scripture, vital, honest, dignified."[9] As part of that scholarship, he began collecting manuscripts from the Anglo-Saxon church to show that what was "new" in the reformed Church of England was actually "old" and not an innovation at all. It was but a return to the practice of the ancient church in the British Isles before the Norman Conquest, with public worship in the vernacular, Communion in both kinds (bread and wine) for the laity, permission for clergymen to marry, and detachment from obedience to the pope.[10]

John Jewel (1522–1571), bishop of Salisbury, enthusiastically embraced the Patristic church as a model for restoring the church:

> We have searched out of the holy bible, which we are sure cannot deceive, one sure form of religion, and have returned again unto the primitive church of the ancient fathers and apostles, that is to say, to the first ground and beginning of things, as unto the very foundations and head-springs of Christ's church.[11]

In his "Apology of the Church of England," Jewel argued that the English Church was not Roman Catholic but that it was faithful to the ancient primitive catholic church of the apostles and the church fathers—the "mere Christianity" described by Vincent of Lérins: "We, for our parts, have learned these things of Christ, of the apostles, of the devout fathers; and do sincerely and with good faith teach the people of God the same."[12]

The greatest challenge that Jewel and his fellow Reformers faced came from Rome. In his "Apology" he set forth his vision for

---

9. J. R. H. Moorman, *History of the Church in England* (London: Adam & Charles Black, 1961), 213.

10. Michael Ramsey, *The Anglican Spirit* (London: SPCK, 1991), 16.

11. John Jewel, "An Apology, or Answer, in Defence of the Church of England," in *The Works of John Jewel*, ed. John Ayre (Cambridge: Cambridge University Press, 1848), 3:106.

12. Jewel, *The Works of John Jewel*, 3:67.

a reformed church in England by defending Anglicanism against the excesses of Rome and its additions to the apostolic faith that had corrupted the practice of the primitive catholic church.

By the end of the sixteenth century, however, a different challenge had arisen. The danger from Rome was much less than it had been in Jewel's time, while the Puritan presence in England had grown greatly in size and prestige. Puritans wanted to bring the Church of England more into line with the continental Reformers, most notably John Calvin. They sought a church based on Scripture alone in both thought and practice. Anything not expressly commanded in Scripture was to be rejected; therefore a reformed church must be stripped of all things Catholic.

Richard Hooker (1554–1600), a student of John Jewel, took up the task of defending Anglicanism against this Puritan minimalism. His five-volume work *Of the Laws of Ecclesiastical Polity* set out to provide Anglicanism with a principled basis for maintaining its distance from the continental reform. He refuted at length the Puritan argument that every item of worship must be explicitly mentioned in Scripture, and he defended the Church of England's right to make laws for worship so long as they were not contrary to Scripture.[13] Hooker acknowledged the supreme authority of Scripture, but he also recognized the importance of catholic tradition as the interpreting of Scripture when read together under the authority of the whole church.

Herein lies the paradox of Anglicanism: it is *neither* Roman Catholic *nor* Reformed, while at the same time *both* reformed *and* catholic. This interweaving of reformed and catholic elements through its appeal to the ancient fathers, while rejecting the extremes of both Rome and Geneva, became increasingly characteristic of Anglican thought. It also became the point of divergence between Angli-

---

13. Moorman, *History of the Church in England*, 215.

can theology and that of the Lutheran and Calvinist churches of the Continent.[14] At the start of the seventeenth century, Anglicanism found itself established between the excesses of Rome, on one side, and the minimalism of Geneva, on the other, and seeking to avoid the claims of infallibility on both extremes. As Hooker put it bluntly, "Two things there are that trouble these latter times: one is that the Church of Rome can not, another is that Geneva will not, err."[15]

In essence, the reformed catholicism of the Anglican Church has sought to embrace the fullness of God's truth as revealed in Scripture, received in the apostolic deposit of faith and embodied in the practice of the undivided church of the first five centuries. Lancelot Andrewes (1555–1626) summarized it well in his mnemonic outline identifying the foundational core of Anglican belief: "One canon reduced to writing by God himself, two testaments, three creeds, four general councils, five centuries and the Fathers in that period (the three centuries before Constantine and the two after) which determines the boundaries of our faith."[16]

Andrewes's definition of Anglicanism as a Reformation church influenced heavily by the belief and practice of the early church does not have the prescriptive force of the continental Protestant confessions. But it is emblematic of the essence of Anglicanism as a synthesis of both reformed and catholic elements: the supreme authority of the Holy Scriptures and the instructive example of the Patristic tradition, with its emphasis on the ongoing sacramental life of the church and its direct historic connection to the apostolic age.

The concept of the Anglican Church as "reformed catholicism" can be seen in Article 19 of the Thirty-Nine Articles of

---

14. Ramsey, *Anglican Spirit*, 27.
15. Ramsey, *Anglican Spirit*, 19.
16. Stephen Sykes, *The Study of Anglicanism*, ed. Stephen W. Sykes and John Booty (Minneapolis: Fortress, 1990), 237.

Religion, which defines the church of Christ as a congregation of the faithful where "the pure Word of God is preached, and the Sacraments [are] duly ministered according to Christ's ordinance." The reformed catholicism of Anglicanism is indeed embodied in her two great legacies to the English-speaking world: the King James translation of Holy Scripture (the early church's apostolic witness) and the Prayer Book translation of the church's liturgies, sacraments, and holy orders (the early church's apostolic practice). Anglicanism has been compared to the child of the great divorce that was the Reformation, carrying the DNA of both her parents, catholic and reformed. All members of the Anglican family share this same DNA. Some will combine traits from both parents in equal measure, while others will tend to resemble one parent far more than the other. But across the full spectrum of Anglicanism, there has always been an unmistakable family resemblance.

Anglicanism's "both–and"—its being catholic *and* reformed—is a reflection of the dynamic tension of the fullness of God's revealed truth, which at times seems contradictory. Christ is fully God and fully man; the Trinity is one and three; God is transcendent and immanent; the gospel is prophetic and pastoral. The whole truth of God, like Scripture itself, is often uncomfortable. It stretches; it pinches; it has something to offend everyone. And one of the signs of orthodoxy is its ability to hold these competing truths in tension, realizing that both are necessary because both are true. Heresy will not abide tension, so it selects one truth while discarding others that are needed to balance or complete it. The both–and of Anglicanism incorporates this dynamic tension by seeking to embrace the entire truth of God's revelation, stating clearly in Article 20 of the Thirty-Nine Articles: "It is not lawful for the Church to ordain anything that is contrary to God's Word written, neither may it so expound one place of Scripture, that it be repugnant to another."

Thus, the Articles of Religion embrace tension without permitting it to devolve into contradiction.

Contrasting scriptural truths are needed, especially when they seem exact opposites. God is eternally just and righteous; God is forever merciful and forgiving. Both statements are true, though they seem contradictory; and both are necessary. Like tightrope walkers clutching the middle of a long pole to keep their balance, as Christians we hold the theological equivalent of that pole, which has God's justice on one end and his mercy on the other. If we do not hold the pole of justice and mercy in the middle, we will lose our balance and fall off the narrow way that Christ has set before us. If we emphasize justice over mercy, our perception of God may devolve into the celestial equivalent of an authoritarian patriarch with anger issues, who always seems to be having a bad day. Choose mercy over justice, and our perception of God may morph into the image of a doting grandma who desires only to make her grandchildren happy by giving them everything they want, since in her eyes they can do no wrong.

From our human perspective, the way to hold competing truths in balance might seem to be found in maintaining an equal distance between two contradictory truths so as not to emphasize one to the detriment of the other. But in God there are no contradictions: he is fully just *and* fully merciful; he is one *and* three undivided. How are these seemingly contradictory truths to be reconciled and not merely balanced by diminishing one or the other? That is the role of the Holy Spirit of God, who holds all things together and leads us into all truth. He is the *dynamis* in the dynamic tension of Anglicanism: in his light we see light (Ps. 36:9). Justice and mercy are alike with God and there is no distance between them. By the power of the Holy Spirit, the Father's justice and mercy were fully joined in Jesus as the incarnate Word of God. On the cross, divine justice and mercy meet, and are made one in the blood of Jesus shed for us. From their union as one flows our salvation.

The genius of Anglicanism is this reformed catholicism, held in dynamic tension by the power of the Holy Spirit. It is like a suspension bridge upheld by the dynamic tension of being pulled equally in opposite directions—reformed on one end, catholic on the other. Yet, at the same time, we are ever drawn into union together by the Spirit of God. When the faith and practice of the Western church were called into question at the time of the Reformation, the Anglican Reformers settled for nothing less than the truth, the whole truth, and nothing but the truth: the truth of the apostolic witness, the *whole* truth of the catholic witness handed down from the primitive church through the centuries, and the reformed insistence to hold as sacred nothing *but* the truth. In this way the Catholic is pinched by the reformed witness to the truth, and the Puritan is stretched by the catholic witness to the truth, so that the fullness of God's truth may not be divided.

This dynamic tension of Scripture is complementary rather than contradictory. The prophetic call to individual holiness and the pastoral call to corporate mercy are both scriptural. Both are absolutely necessary. The apostles and the early church saw them as complementary and incorporated both equally into the life of the church.

In reading the book of Acts and the Epistles, it is difficult to say which strikes us more forcibly—the earnestness of the exhortations to holiness or the willingness to deal charitably with those who fail to reach that standard.[17] Both are needed and in equal measure, for "the strictness of the Reformed tradition is an admirable balance to the charity of the Catholic."[18] When the prophetic and the pastoral

---

17. Huntington, *Church Idea*, 83.
18. Huntington, *Church Idea*, 91.

of Scripture are integrated in practice, then will the church be able to fully "speak the truth in love" (Eph. 4:15).

The pattern of Anglican worship reflects this same integration of Scripture and practice. Cranmer's revision of the Book of Common Prayer in 1549 was the fruition of his desire for the English Church to have one uniform liturgy that is true to Scripture and consonant with the practice of the early church. This, he believed, would be edifying to the people. In the Anglican tradition, faith and prayer—belief and worship—are inseparably united in the liturgy. Scripture and sacrament are there woven inextricably together according to the principle of *lex orandi lex credendi* (how we are to pray is how we are to believe) as a living expression of the profound union between what we pray and what we believe. Uniting prayer with Scripture invites the presence of God into our human encounter with God's word written as the Holy Spirit weaves scriptural truth into the very fabric of our being.

The structure of the Anglican liturgy as "the pure Word of God . . . preached and the Sacraments duly ministered according to Christ's ordinance" follows early church practice[19] and Scripture's own description of the prototype of our two-part Eucharistic liturgy (Luke 24:13–32). On the road to Emmaus, two of Jesus's disciples have the Scriptures opened and interpreted to them, "beginning with Moses and all the prophets," as prophetic of Jesus the Messiah. Then, at table with his disciples, "he took the bread and blessed and broke it and gave it to them. And their eyes were opened, and they recognized him" as their risen Lord (vv. 30–31). The disciples' hearts burned within them as the Holy Spirit opened the Scriptures and then their eyes to reveal to them the risen Lord Jesus in the breaking of the bread. This was Word and sacrament infused by the Holy Spirit. In this same way, the Word and Table of

---

19. See. for example, Justin Martyr, *First Apology*, 67.

Anglican worship are unified and sanctified by the Holy Spirit, who is still at work opening eyes and establishing in hearts the reality of Jesus Christ crucified and risen, the fulfillment of God's promise of salvation.

Scripture, sacrament, and Spirit are often identified as three separate streams representing Anglicanism's evangelical, sacramental, and charismatic traditions. Yet these are not three independent streams but, rather, three interdependent currents flowing together within the one river of Christ's church, "a river whose streams make glad the city of God" (Ps. 46:4). Together they form the seamless garment of the undivided church: an emphasis on Scripture as read and understood by the church together to establish the Christian rule of faith; an emphasis on the sacraments as means of grace received by the whole church for the initiation, nourishment, and strengthening of all the faithful; and an emphasis on the continuing work of the Spirit, given by Jesus to his church to be actively at work in her and through her as Christ's witness in the world and herald of God's salvation.

Narrowing the Gap

One of the charisms (gifts) of Anglicanism is that it has never claimed to be the one true church to the exclusion of all others, but regards itself as merely that part of the one, holy, catholic, and apostolic church that was brought to England and planted there. As a church that is both reformed and catholic, it is able to hold hands and partner in fellowship with liturgical churches, evangelical churches, and charismatic churches: to be a servant of the wider church and perhaps even a means of fulfilling the prayer of Jesus that we all might be one. As a "both–and" church, Anglicanism has been uniquely gifted to serve as a nucleus for the convergence of the different traditions of the divided church.

That was the vision of Bishop William Reed Huntington (1838–1909), who saw the "mere Christianity" of Anglicanism as a template for bringing the divided church closer together. The Lambeth Quadrilateral of 1888 lays out what Huntington considered the apostolic essentials of the early church, which might serve as the nucleus of convergence for the divided church: Holy Scripture "containing all things necessary to salvation" as the rule and standard of faith; the Apostles' and Nicene Creeds as the sufficient statement of that faith; the sacraments of baptism and the Lord's Supper ordained by Christ himself; and the historic episcopate, locally adapted, to maintain the church's direct link to the apostolic age.

Anglicanism's gift to the wider church of unity by convergence is already at work, for both Rome and Geneva are moving toward the Anglican center. For centuries portions of the Book of Common Prayer have been widely used in English-speaking Protestant circles, and the Prayer Book has played and continues to play a significant role in shaping Protestant worship and practice beyond the jurisdiction of Canterbury. In this way Geneva, symbolizing the reformed churches of Protestantism, is moving toward Anglicanism.

In the 1960s the Anglican Reformation, one could say, arrived in Rome. When the Second Vatican Council accepted liturgy in the vernacular based on early Patristic models, communion in both kinds, and a renewed emphasis on the authority of Scripture—all of which can now be seen in the new Catholic Catechism prepared under John Paul II—Rome signaled a shift toward what is recognizably Anglican. Pope Benedict XVI's 2010 encyclical *Verbum Domini* (*Word of the Lord*) stressed the incorporation of Scripture into the life of the church, emphasized the close connection between Scripture and liturgy, directed clergy to teach and preach Scripture, and called for Bible-based catechesis in Christian formation.[20] This too showed movement toward Anglican norms.

The early twentieth-century East African Revival began in the Anglican Church in Rwanda and spread quickly through the Protestant churches of Africa, influencing Catholic churches as well.[21] There are now Baptists who have incorporated the Prayer of Humble Access into their communion services,[22] evangelical churches that have added Ash Wednesday services,[23] and Catholic parishes with Bible studies based on reading, studying, and understanding Scripture.[24]

Billy Graham, the great unifier of evangelical Protestantism, was asked by a reporter in his later years if he would do anything different, were he starting over. Graham replied that he would be "an evangelical Anglican," for "he saw spiritual beauty in the evangelical order."[25] The great preacher selected an Anglican priest to officiate at his funeral.

When he laid the foundation for what became the Lambeth Quadrilateral (see above, p. 145), Bishop Huntington had no desire to create a united church by making all churches Anglican. He wanted only to provide a practical way to restore apostolic unity to a fractured church. The bishops of the Episcopal Church concluded that to ful-

---

20. Benedict XVI, *Post-Synodal Apostolic Exhortation* Verbum Domini *of the Holy Father Benedict XVI to the Bishops, Clergy, Consecrated Persons and the Lay Faithful on the Word of God in the Life and Mission of the Church* (Vatican City: Libreria Editrice Vaticana, 2010), http://w2.vatican.va/content/benedict-xvi/en/apost_exhortations/documents/hf_ben-xvi_exh_20100930_verbum-domini.html.

21. John Senyonyi, "East African Revival Distinctives," GAFCON address, October 13, 2013; see "The East African Revival: A Brief History, Its Beliefs and Practices" (October 21, 2013), https//www.gafcon.org/sites/gafcon.org/files/news/pdfs/East_African_Revival_Talk_Senyonyi.pdf.

22. See the later chapter by Timothy George.

23. Richard Varra, "More Protestants Are Turning to Ash Wednesday," *Houston Chronicle*, February 6, 2008.

24. St. Michael Catholic Church, Greenfield, Indiana, https://www.stmichaelsgrfld.org/Bible-Studies.

25. Grant Wacker, *America's Pastor* (Cambridge, MA: Harvard University Press, 2014), 184.

fill Huntington's vision of unity, it would require of Anglicanism a willingness to give itself up gladly for the good of the entire church:

> That in all things of human ordering or human choice, relating to modes of worship and discipline, or to traditional customs, this Church is ready in the spirit of love and humility to forego all preferences of her own; That this Church does not seek to absorb other Communions, but rather, co-operating with them on the basis of a common Faith and Order, to discountenance schism, to heal the wounds of the Body of Christ, and to promote the charity which is the chief of Christian graces and the visible manifestation of Christ to the world. But furthermore, we do hereby affirm that the Christian unity . . . can be restored only by the return of all Christian communions to the principles of unity exemplified by the undivided Catholic Church during the first ages of its existence; which principles we believe to be the substantial deposit of Christian Faith and Order committed by Christ and his Apostles to the Church unto the end of the world, and therefore incapable of compromise or surrender by those who have been ordained to be its stewards and trustees for the common and equal benefit of all men.[26]

Their work was picked up by the 1888 Lambeth Conference, and successive Lambeth Conferences "have also declared the provisionality of the Anglican Communion for the cause of, for the sake of the unity of the whole Church."[27] John the Baptist famously said of his relationship to Jesus, "He must increase, but I must decrease" (John

---

26. Bishops of the Protestant Episcopal Church in the United States of America, "Chicago-Lambeth Quadrilateral 1886, 1888," in *The Book of Common Prayer and Administration of the Sacraments and Other Rites and Ceremonies of the Church: Together with the Psalter or Psalms of David; According to the Use of the Episcopal Church* (New York: Seabury, 1979), 876–77.

27. Michael Nazir-Ali, "Jerusalem: GAFCON III: God's Church: An Address Given by Bishop Michael Nazir-Ali," *VirtueOnline*, June 19, 2018, https://www.virtueonline.org /jerusalem-gafcon-iii-gods-church.

3:30); so, too, Anglicans could express their own vision of a reunifed church in similar terms: "She must increase, but we must decrease."

As a child of the church's Reformation "divorce," Anglicanism as "reformed catholicism" was shaped by the Reformers' efforts to restore the faith of the undivided church. Archbishop Michael Ramsey suggests that this desire for apostolic unity in the church might ultimately bring "Anglicanism" to an end:

> If the Anglican Communion disappeared because it was no longer fulfilling a mission, or abandoned its true mission, that would be sad indeed. But if the Anglican Communion were to disappear because of its good and great service in the reconciliation of all Christians, then its disappearance would be something in which we would rejoice. Why? Because in looking at the long term of God's purposes, we have to face this: the very term "Anglicanism" is one produced by the situation of sad Christian disunity and the disappearance of Christian disunity might well mean the disappearance of the word "Anglicanism." Until that happens, we believe that God has given us real work to do.[28]

Expanding the Church's Outreach

The contribution of Anglicanism is not limited to healing the divisions of the past. It also looks forward in mission. Wherever the British Empire went, it brought with it the Church of England and established chaplaincies primarily for the benefit of its expatriates. Anglican missionaries soon followed in its wake: George Whitefield and John Wesley to the British colonies in America, and the Church Missionary Society to Africa and Asia a century later. A serious question then arose: Must Anglicanism outside of England be forever clad in British European vesture, or may it take root and become

---

28. Ramsey, *Anglican Spirit*, 142.

indigenous while still remaining thoroughly Anglican? Is it possible to separate the Anglican *principle* of the Reformers from the
Anglican *system* of the Church of England?[29]

Let me explain. The Anglican principle contains the spiritual
DNA of the Anglican Reformation, which was missional at its core.
It was designed to bring the gospel in its entirety to the common
people of England in their own language and culture. The logi-
cal implication of this is that the gospel can be translated into the
idiom, thought forms, and language of every culture. Our own Anglican formularies give us warrant for doing this. The Book of Common Prayer, with its preface, and the Articles of Religion show us
how the gospel can be rendered into forms of worship with which
we are familiar and that fit our cultural forms.[30]

The Anglican system, on the other hand, incorporates the external trappings of religion, whether cultural or institutional. It
includes various forms of churchmanship, music styles, vestments,
and other cultural ways of expressing the unchanging essence of
the gospel. The Anglican system can also be extended to encompass
human organizational structures created solely for the purpose of
facilitating church administration: commissions, programs, ministries, and institutional bureaucracy.

The principle is spiritual and eternal; the system is external and
temporal. One is essential to the faith, and the other is not. It is
therefore necessary to distinguish the two. The Anglican Communion does not depend upon political and cultural settings, because
it is able to move with so many. In both the last century and the
present one, the Anglican Church has moved into all continents
and among many different races and nationalities. Anglo-Saxons
are now only a minority within the total Anglican population of
the world. The Anglican Communion will fulfill this mission if it

29. Huntington, *Church Idea*, 204.
30. Nazir-Ali, "God's Church."

realizes that it has within itself spiritual treasures that are able to transcend cultural differences and may even be able to unite them.[31]

This spiritual treasure of the Reformers, founded on Scripture and directly connected to the early church, has now become fully inculturated in the Global South. Archbishop Henry Orombi of Uganda recently bore witness to this.

> From Thomas Cranmer to Richard Hooker, from the Thirty-Nine Articles and the 1662 Ordinal to the 1998 Lambeth Conference, the authority of Holy Scripture has always held a central and foundational role in Anglican identity. This is true for the Anglican church in Uganda; and, if it is not true for the entire Anglican Communion, then that communion will cease to be an authentic expression of the Church of Jesus Christ.[32]

> As bishops are successors to the apostles, so our focus through the historic episcopate is on apostolic faith and ministry. A bishop is ordained in apostolic succession to be the apostolic presence in the community. A bishop, therefore, is the ongoing presence and voice of the apostles. He is our link to the early Church, and this link between bishop and apostolicity gives Anglicans our transcultural identity.[33]

The upshot of all this history is that one no longer has to be English to be Anglican. The Anglican principle of the English Reformers is flourishing outside of England and multiplying rapidly. As Archbishop Peter Akinola of the Anglican Church of Nigeria put it, "We don't need to go through Canterbury to get to Jesus."[34]

---

31. Nazir-Ali, "God's Church."
32. Henry Luke Orombi, "What Is Anglicanism?," *First Things*, August 2007, https://www.firstthings.com/article/2007/08/001-what-is-anglicanism.
33. Orombi, "What Is Anglicanism?"
34. Andrew Goddard, *Rowan Williams: His Legacy* (Oxford: Lion, 2013), 161.

Anglicanism in the postmodern Global North, however, is now in decline. Wherever this Northern Anglicanism has allowed itself to be enculturated by secular humanism, it is now verging on collapse. It has become a religion constructed not on the Anglican principle of the Reformers but on an Anglican system of its own invention that sees the church primarily as a sociological institution or a political entity, ever reforming itself to reflect the views and values of the ambient society. It turns away from the church's fountain of living water flowing forth from Scripture and the apostolic church and is busy digging for itself broken cisterns of cultural relevance.

It is no accident that the Anglican Communion finds itself at the epicenter of global Christian realignment and in the forefront of the tectonic shift of apostolic Christianity from the dying established churches of Europe and North America to the vibrant apostolic Christian leadership of Africa and the Global South. Archbishop Orombi boldly proclaimed in 2007: "The younger churches of Anglican Christianity will shape what it means to be Anglican. The long season of British hegemony is over."[35]

Looking Forward

So what is the future of Anglicanism? These "younger churches of Anglican Christianity" have now begun meeting together: Global South Anglicans in 1994 and the Global Anglican Future Conference (GAFCON) in both 2008 and 2018. With significant overlap, both groups are fully committed to working with each other for the renewal and restoration of the Communion in accordance with Scripture and the Anglican principles set forth by the Reformers. Together they represent 80 percent of the world's practicing Anglicans and include in their midst an increasing number of "younger churches" in the Global North.

---

35. Orombi, "What is Anglicanism?"

In the twenty-first century, these two missions of Anglican-ism—to heal the divisions in the body of Christ and to proclaim the gospel to the world—are being brought together as one. In June 2018, international leaders of the Protestant parachurch organiza-tion Cru (Campus Crusade for Christ) came to GAFCON III seeking to partner with the Anglican Church of North America and the Anglican Church of Kenya to plant Lambeth Quadrilateral churches on every college campus in North America and Kenya. That mission partnership has already begun and is starting to bear fruit.[36] It is a part of a global ecumenical net being formed from the strands of different Christian traditions—tied together by the Holy Spirit—to catch men, women, and children for Jesus Christ.

Orthodox Anglicans now find themselves in yet another typi-cally Anglican "both–and" situation: to strengthen the faith of the historic churches and to bear witness to the world by proclaiming Christ to the nations. They call the church to embrace its God-given unity of fellowship in Christ, forever present in his church through time and across cultures. "The credibility of Anglicanism lies not in its own virtues or successes, but in the Lord of the Church . . . and the Lord of the Church is Jesus, crucified and risen, who through his Church still converts sinners and creates saints."[37] He it is who has given to the Anglicans of the present all that they need, to do the work they have been given to do, together as one, for the heal-ing and building up of the church and the redemption of the world in Christ.

---

36. Cornerstone Cru at University of Illinois-Chicago is "a church movement resourced by Cru and the Greenhouse Movement" (ACNA), http://www.cornerstonecru.com.

37. Ramsey, *Anglican Spirit*, 150.

7

AN ANGLICAN HISTORIAN AND THEOLOGIAN

A Church in Search of Its Soul

Gerald Bray

A Nineteenth-Century Invention

Anglicanism, understood as a system of thought and theology comparable to Catholicism, Lutheranism, and Calvinism, was essentially a nineteenth-century invention. Before the 1830s, although the word "Anglican" existed, it was seldom used. When it was, it referred to the *Ecclesia Anglicana*, or the Church of England. The idea that the *Ecclesia Anglicana* represented a distinct form of Christianity was unknown. The English Reformers saw themselves as catholics who were determined to restore the church to its primitive purity. If they were different from Reformers in other countries who shared the same aim, it was for political reasons more than anything else. In Germany and France, the Reformation was a popular movement distinct from the secular state, which eventually had to come to terms with it. In England, on the other hand, the Reformation was an act of state that had almost no popular support, at least in its initial stages. When Henry VIII (1509–1547) broke ties with Rome in 1534, it was in order to annul his marriage, not to reform the church. Henry had no sympathy with Luther and cannot be described as a Protestant in any meaningful sense of the term. What he wanted was catholicism without the papacy, but that was easier said than done. His most dedicated supporters favored a Lutheran-style Reformation and did what they could to secure it, but with limited success. It was not until the king died and Thomas Cranmer, the archbishop of Canterbury, was put in charge of the church during the minority of King Edward VI (1547–1553), that a meaningful reformation became possible. Cranmer and his colleagues were put in charge of a Protestant state that had no Protestants in it, and it was to create them that they constructed what we now call Anglicanism.

A church rests on three fundamental pillars—doctrine, discipline, and devotion. In terms of doctrine, the Church of England adopted a confession of faith that took the form of Forty-Two Articles of belief. These Articles established that the church was rooted both in the catholic consensus of the first five centuries and in the Protestant doctrines of the still recent Reformation on the Continent. The Articles were supplemented by a book of sermons, known as the Homilies, which explained their teaching in greater detail. It is to them that we must turn to discover what the church was expected to believe about such things as the supremacy of Holy Scripture and the centrality of justification by faith alone. To implant these beliefs in the hearts of the people, Cranmer produced a Prayer Book that aimed to express biblical teaching—in particular, justification by faith—in the form of public worship. It was a halfway house toward a more thoroughgoing reformation, which appeared in a revised Prayer Book in 1552. He also edited a book of church discipline, though this failed to get the approval of Parliament, a fatal flaw that was to have serious consequences in the next generation.

Edward VI died before reaching his majority, and was succeeded by his half-sister Mary I, who took the country back to the Roman obedience. Mary met with little opposition at first, but her extremism and her persecuting zeal, coupled with her inability to produce an heir to the throne, discredited her policies. All she really did was produce Protestant martyrs whose bravery and determination in the face of death won the hearts of the public. After only five years on the throne, she was succeeded by her half-sister Elizabeth I, who restored the state of affairs that had obtained at her brother's death, with slight modifications. The 1552 Prayer Book was revised in a somewhat more conservative direction, and the Articles of Religion were overhauled to take account of the most recent theological developments among continental Protestants. A divide had opened between self-proclaimed Lutherans and other reformed people, loosely known nowadays as Calvinists, and the Church of England tried to steer a middle course between them. That proved to be impossible, and in the end it came down on the side of the "Calvinists," where it was to remain. A second book of Homilies was issued in order to expound the church's Protestantism still further, but its discipline remained stubbornly unreformed. The appointment of clergy remained in the hands of lay patrons, many of whom had little interest in providing suitably qualified ministers, and there was no effective way to ensure that the clergy had the required standard of theological education. Bishops remained political appointees whose loyalty to the Crown mattered more than their suitability for the post.

It was the failure to remedy these problems that set the scene for the next hundred years, as increasingly influential groups in the church tried to establish a discipline consistent with reformed doctrine and devotion. They found their greatest support among the gentry class in the House of Commons but were opposed by the Crown and an influential section of the nobility. Queen Elizabeth would countenance no change to her religious settlement, whose somewhat mixed character she regarded as essential for the peace of the realm, and in this she was followed by her immediate successors. Those who wanted to take the Reformation further were dubbed "Puritans," but their views were generally resisted by the state. The Puritans were not theologically distinct from the mainstream of the Church of England, but they stood out because they wanted to see the commonly agreed theology applied more consistently in the life of the church, and in society generally. After Elizabeth's death their pressure increased, but so did resistance to their program. The end result was a civil war in which the king was defeated, but the victorious Puritans, who knew what they were against, could not agree on what they were for. The result was chaos, and in the end the monarchy was restored as the best means of keeping the peace. In 1660 the Elizabethan settlement was reimposed, and two years later disaffected clergy were ejected from their pulpits if they refused to accept the new Prayer Book, which was a slightly revised version of the 1559 one.

Unfortunately, those who left the church included some of its most energetic and gifted theologians. Their places were taken by undistinguished men who often owed their positions to their family connections and loyalty to the king rather than to any serious grasp of theology. The Great Ejection of 1662 has entered the founding mythology of the English dissenting, or nonconformist, tradition, further strengthening the false impression among later generations that those who conformed to the new dispensation were "Anglicans" in a way that those who dissented were not. Most dissenters accepted the Thirty-Nine Articles, and their scruples over the use of the Prayer Book were mostly confined to complaints about the lack of flexibility allowed by the rubrics rather than about its doctrinal content. How many clergymen were ejected has long been a matter of controversy. The dissenters themselves claimed to number up to 20 percent of the total, but that is undoubtedly too high a figure. Recent research has shown that hardcore dissent touched only about 5 percent of the clergy. Many of those who were ejected in 1662 were back in the church's ministry five years later, and there is no sign that their Puritan theological views had changed to any appreciable degree. There was a further attempt to reconcile dissenters to the national church in 1688, when the Catholic king James II was forced to flee, and Protestantism was officially established by a Parliament that was now recognized as the supreme authority in both church and state, but this failed. Dissent was henceforth officially tolerated, though with many restrictions, and from that time onward the Church of England was no longer coterminous with the nation.

The settlement of 1688–1689 remained in place until the great reforms of the early nineteenth century. Most of the traditional or "high" churchmen, who had opposed the Puritans and resisted the deposition of James II, gradually abandoned the Jacobite cause and came to terms with the new reality. They produced catechetical literature, established missionary societies, and did their best to inculcate their view of the church as a divine society among a people that was increasingly subjected to the rationalistic and anti-Christian propaganda that flourished after censorship was abolished in 1695. By 1750 many of the dissenting congregations had either fallen into heresy, like the Presbyterians, who almost all became Unitarians, or declined into insignificance, like the Baptists. The universities had largely succumbed to the deism and open irreligion, if not quite atheism, that we now call the Enlightenment. In this climate, many high churchmen distinguished themselves as defenders of classical orthodoxy. One thinks, for example, of Bishop Joseph Butler (1692–1752), Bishop George Berkeley (1685–1753), and Dean William Paley

(1743–1805), all of whom acquired reputations as apologists for the Christian faith against the attacks of the godless rationalists. Less well known now, but equally important in their own time, were men like Daniel Waterland (1683–1740), David Wilkins (1685–1745), and Bishop Edmund Gibson (1669–1748), whose scholarly endeavors set the Church of England on what seemed to be firm historical ground as an authentic church of the apostles.

But just as this traditional orthodoxy was reasserting itself in intellectual circles, a quite different religious movement was emerging at the grassroåots level. This was the Evangelical Revival, or Great Awakening, as it is usually known in America. Its most prominent leaders were John Wesley (1703–1791) and George Whitefield (1714–1770), both Church of England clergymen but from different ends of the ecclesiastical spectrum. Wesley was a high churchman who disliked Puritans and regarded their theology as unduly restrictive. He did not hesitate to describe himself as an Arminian, something that earlier high churchmen had never done, and he even rewrote the Thirty-Nine Articles to remove what he thought was their Calvinist bias. George Whitefield was the exact opposite— a low churchman of Puritan leanings who supped with dissenters as readily as with members of the established church, and who happily evangelized among them too. In the end, Wesley's followers left the church and became Methodists, but Whitefield's stayed within it and formed what became its evangelical wing.

This was the situation at the time of the great reforms of 1829–1832. During those few years, the civil disabilities imposed on dissenters were largely removed, and non-Anglicans were admitted to Parliament, which until then had functioned as the lay synod of the Church of England. The Evangelical Revival had breathed new life into the old dissenting tradition, which now emerged as nonconformity, a liberalizing element in English life that remained powerful for the next century. Evangelical churchmen happily cooperated with dissenters in ventures like the Bible Society, founded in 1804, and embarked on foreign missionary adventures, sometimes under the aegis of the church and sometimes in nondenominational mission societies. Whether the churches they established in other parts of the world were linked to the Church of England or not was a matter of indifference to most of them. They were happy if they were, but lost little sleep if they were not.

High churchmen, on the other hand, felt that the state was abandoning the church and feared that if it were disestablished, as many nonconformists wanted, it would disappear. Was there something that could hold it together even if the state connection were to be abandoned? The English Church was older than the state it belonged to; could it not survive without it? Overseas expansion was creating a Church of England beyond the national boundaries, not least in settler colonies like Canada and Australia. What was going to happen to them? The need to evangelize the non-Christian world was undeniable, but how could there be a Church of England that was not English? There was a tiny Scottish Episcopal Church, left over from the religious settlement of 1690, when Presbyterianism became the established religion in Scotland, and the remnant of the Church of England in America, which set itself up as an independent Episcopal Church, initially under Scottish auspices. Could the Church of England recognize a body that had repudiated allegiance to its supreme governor, King George III?

The Rise and Fall of Anglo-Catholicism

Before these questions could be given a proper answer, the Church of England was rocked by another religious convulsion, very different from the Evangelical Revival but equally threatening to the traditional establishment. In Oxford, young clergymen were gathering around the charismatic figure of John Henry Newman (1801–1890), seeking a way to revive the fortunes of the church in a world that seemed to have forgotten God. Newman came from an evangelical family—his younger brother Francis was one of the founders of the Plymouth Brethren before he lapsed into agnosticism—but Newman grew increasingly disenchanted with that. He turned instead to a kind of religion that mixed the formality of outward observance with the mystical piety of Counter-Reformation Catholicism, which appealed to his temperament. He wrote a notorious treatise about Luther's doctrine of justification by faith, which he misunderstood and rejected. He also studied the church fathers, coming up with an equally fanciful interpretation of Arius, whom he dismissed, along with Luther, as an arch heretic.

As Newman and his friends reinvented church history, their own beloved Church of England came under their careful scrutiny too. As they saw it, the English Church had fallen on hard times, but although it was unduly subordinated to the state and had a sadly diluted spirituality, its catholic foundations remained solid. In their view, the Church of England could trace its ancestry back to the apostles themselves. British Christianity was therefore not Roman in origin, although it had been in communion with the papacy in ancient times. When the Roman Empire fell, the British church went its own way, and its golden age began. Patrick, the great saint of Ireland, was a British Christian, not a Roman one, and Rome's appropriation of him was inauthentic. Much the same could be said for the later Anglo-Saxon church. According to many Anglo-Catholics, communion with Rome was reestablished, but subordination to the papacy was not. They claimed that, when Henry VIII broke with the pope in 1534, he was doing no more than reasserting the ancient independence of the Church of England. Internally, nothing in that church changed, and there was no Protestant reformation at all. It remained as Catholic as it had always been; no new teachings were introduced (though some corrupt practices were removed); and everything went on as before. It was the Puritans who tried to introduce Protestantism, but that was rejected and the establishment reaffirmed its traditional Catholicism by driving that alien element out.

To get their message across, Newman and his friends started writing tracts. Some of these were highly spiritual in nature and attracted the favorable notice of evangelicals. But the overall tone was one of rejecting the Reformation. Matters came to a head in 1840, when Newman wrote his famous Tract 90. In it, he claimed that the Thirty-Nine Articles, to which all clergymen, including himself, had to subscribe, were perfectly compatible with Catholic teaching and in no way Protestant. The storm of protest against this interpretation was so strong that it alienated Newman from the Church of England and set him on the journey that would soon take him to Rome.

Some of his Tractarian colleagues followed him, but many did not. Men like John Keble (1792–1866) and Edward Pusey (1800–1882) held on to their original vision and claimed that their catholicism was different from that of Rome, which had fallen into error on precisely those points where the Church of England differed from it. Keble and Pusey grounded catholicity not in dependence on the papacy but in the consensus of the early church. They were prodigious scholars, but they were also men with an agenda that was far from scholarly. They, along with a number of like-minded colleagues, were on the committee that produced the *Library of Anglo-Catholic Theology*, a mishmash of post-Reformation English divines who were neither conforming Calvinists nor dissenting Puritans, but who otherwise had little in common with each other. We are not surprised to find the works of Archbishop William Laud and John Overall's *Convocation Book* in this *Library*, but some of the others are more puzzling. Would the late seventeenth-century Bishop John Pearson, for example, have been comfortable with the designation "Anglo-Catholic"? And what about Thomas Wilson, the legendary bishop of Sodor and Man from 1698 to 1755? By string-ing them together and claiming "catholicism" as their common thread, the Anglo-Catholics effectively created "Anglicanism" more or less as we now understand it, though it was not birthed with-out controversy. Far from it! Almost immediately, the defenders of Protestantism in the Church of England came out with their own collection of post-Reformation English divines. The Parker Soci-ety, which these Protestants created, published the works of such sixteenth-century luminaries as Miles Coverdale, Thomas Cran-mer, Edmund Grindal, John Jewel, Hugh Latimer, Matthew Parker, Nicholas Ridley, William Tyndale, and John Whitgift. They made a much more coherent collection and, true to their lack of concern for "Anglicanism," the Parker Society also included the works of the Swiss Reformer Heinrich Bullinger, because of his great impact on the English theologians of his time. The society also reprinted a comprehensive selection of confessional documents—articles of re-ligion, catechisms, prayer books, and so on—which were intended to show that the Anglo-Catholic attempt to downplay the Reforma-tion could not be sustained by the evidence.

Objectively speaking, there can be no doubt that the Protes-tants had a better claim to have represented the spirit of the post-Reformation Church of England, and modern scholarship has almost unanimously supported that view. But the Anglo-Catholics had a romantic streak that their Protestant adversaries lacked, and the Victorian era was given to flights of religious romanticism. They built neo-Gothic churches, dressed in neo-Gothic clerical vestments, and generally tried to resurrect an imaginary medieval "age of faith" as far as they could. It was a con trick, but it had wide appeal, not least in the United States, where Episcopalians tended to be romantic Anglophiles for whom mock medievalism provided a welcome antidote to the crass materialism of modernity and the ungenteel rudeness of frontier society.

From the start, Anglo-Catholicism was unashamedly elitist and clerical, looking back to the Middle Ages and downplaying the impact of the Reformation. Other members of the church combated this with every weapon at their disposal, not least the legislative power of Parliament, but although they usually won their cases, they made martyrs of the romantics and alienated popular opinion.

The consequences of the Anglo-Catholics' success were catastrophic. This became apparent as early as June 30, 1860, when in a famous debate held in Oxford, the high church bishop Samuel Wilberforce clashed with Thomas Huxley and a number of other scientists over Darwin's newly published *The Origin of Species*. The arguments on both sides appear dated now, but it was clear that Wilberforce was relying more on prejudice than on scientific evidence to attack his opponents. Wilberforce was not a card-carrying Anglo-Catholic, but his views were close enough to theirs to confuse the general public, which increasingly identified Anglicanism with obscurantism and distanced itself from it. It took a generation for the full effects of this to be felt, but by the end of the century it was becoming clear that the church had no convincing answer to modernity, and it suffered accordingly. Ordinations, which peaked in 1886, were down to a fraction of their former level by 1900, and the decline continued unabated until after the First World War.

In the more restricted sphere of church politics, the Anglo-Catholics made a greater impact, at least in the longer term. The opening of Parliament to non-Anglicans forced the Church of England to petition for the revival of its own synods, a request that was granted in 1852. At first this was a highly ambiguous gesture. The archbishop of York refused to summon his provincial synod, and some colonial dioceses asked to be included because they saw themselves as part of the Church of England. The first problem was solved when a new archbishop was appointed in 1861, but the second was more difficult. The Judicial Committee of the Privy

Council ruled that colonial bishoprics were not part of the Church of England, and in 1865 Parliament passed the Colonial Clergy Act, which gave effect to that decision. This prompted members of the Canadian church to ask for a pan-Anglican conference that would establish some principles for governing what now appeared to be an evolving Anglican Communion.

The archbishop of Canterbury assented to the request, and the first Lambeth Conference, as this new body became known, met in 1867. All the bishops in communion with Canterbury were invited, and just over half actually attended. They were given a typically chilly English welcome. The archbishop of York and most of his suffragan bishops boycotted it, and the dean of Westminster refused to allow the bishops to use the Abbey for their closing service. Nothing much was decided, and it was assumed that this novelty would soon fade from memory. But the Canadians persisted, and eleven years later another Lambeth Conference was called, attended this time by about two-thirds of the worldwide episcopate. It was then agreed to meet once a decade, and at the third conference in 1888, a statement of common purpose was drawn up and agreed upon. This was the now famous Lambeth Quadrilateral, which had been adopted by the American Episcopal Church two years before with the aim of restoring communion with Rome and the Eastern Orthodox churches.

It proposed that there should be four main elements required as the basis for unity—the Bible, the two main creeds, the two gospel sacraments, and the "historic episcopate." It was, to say the least, a minimalist approach to doctrine, but while the first three items were relatively noncontroversial, the fourth soon became a bone of contention. The Church of England had always been Episcopal, but it had never made that a criterion for communion with other national churches in Europe. When the French Huguenots were expelled, they were received into the English Church without reordination by a bishop, and a bishopric in Jerusalem had been operated jointly by the Church of England and the Prussian State Church from 1842 to 1881. The Prussian bishops were not in the historic succession as the Lambeth Quadrilateral envisaged it, and Anglo-Catholics had objected to this joint venture from the start. In 1888 they got their wish, and their view of episcopacy was accepted as a requirement for being Anglican.

The effects of this were not long in coming. On the one hand, it cut Anglicans off from other Protestant churches, which was what the Anglo-Catholics wanted, but which did great damage to what had otherwise been friendly relations. As for Rome, the pope soon pronounced Anglican orders null and void, closing the door in that direction. The Eastern churches made friendly but noncommittal noises, and nothing came from attempts to unite with them. The Lambeth Quadrilateral thus defined Anglicanism by cutting Anglicans off from other Christians and leaving them with little more than a claim to episcopacy that was rejected by those with whom they wanted to unite.

In the early twentieth century, Anglo-Catholics maintained themselves reasonably well within their own constituency, but as wider society secularized, their eccentricities became ever more apparent. The failure of the Church of England to move decisively in their direction discouraged some of them, who then converted to Rome when they realized that they could never be more than a tolerated minority within their own church. The majority became a kind of church within the church, with institutions and parishes that operated as independently as possible from the mainstream. Today the legacy of Anglo-Catholicism is most apparent in superficial things like the vestments many clergy wear and the deference that is sometimes shown to the clergy, who are often addressed as "father," something that is common in the Unites States but unthinkable in most other parts of the Anglican world. As a creative theological dynamic though, Anglo-Catholicism is dying, even if it is not yet dead. The post–Vatican II modernization of the Roman Church has left it looking strangely old-fashioned, and the ordination of women has effectively relegated it to the sidelines.

A Reformed Catholicism?

The failure of orthodox Anglo-Catholicism reopened the quest for a definition of Anglicanism. If it was not the survival of primitive Christianity, what was it? Liberal voices from within the Anglo-Catholic world had a simple answer—Anglicanism is the fullest realization of the incarnation of Christ. The Son of God took on human flesh, thereby sanctifying humanity and the created order. Christians must therefore embrace the world and develop a fully incarnational spirituality. In their view, evangelicals and Roman Catholics tended to emphasize an otherworldly spirituality, but Anglicans got their hands dirty. They became deeply involved in the affairs of state, sensing a call to bear witness to the transforming power of the gospel in a sinful world. Sometimes, as in South Africa, they did this by opposing the government in power, but more often they were part of the establishment, nourishing and challenging the consciences of those whose job it is to be good stewards of creation. Of course, this emphasis was paralleled by a number of other Protestant churches, as well as the Roman Catholic Church following the Second Vatican Council (1962–1965). Even some evangelicals, stung by the criticism that they have ignored social problems, have embraced it, so it is no longer possible, if indeed it ever was, to identify incarnational theology as a defining hallmark of Anglicanism.

The enduring legacy of liberal Anglo-Catholicism is a church that is traditional in form but not in substance. For those who come to it from a Protestant background, the apparently traditional outward ceremonial is an attractive way to dispose of any orthodox theological convictions they may have brought with them. It is a

hard thing to say, but evangelicals from other denominations cannot become Anglicans merely by donning a chasuble and swinging
incense, and those who think they can must be prepared for a chilly
reception from Anglican evangelicals who put their emphasis on
substance and are relatively indifferent to matters of form.

The failure of Anglo-Catholicism means that Anglicanism is
now a concept in search of content. There is an Anglican Communion, which provides a kind of common reference point, but it is
hard to see what the commonality is. The Church of England is the
mother church and is respected as such, but it is not an appropriate model for the others. The Canterbury trail, as some would-be
Anglicans have dubbed their spiritual pilgrimage, is a road to nowhere. This is because the Church of England remains an established state church, which no other Anglican body now is, and this
acts as a considerable constraint on its activities. The Church of
England cannot submit to the resolutions of an outside regulatory
body like the Anglican Consultative Council, because that would
infringe the sovereignty of Parliament. But it is also true that the
Church of England reaches into the depths of its society in a way
that no other Anglican church does. Its mission field is the whole
country, and in deprived inner-city areas it often provides an important focus for social cohesion. No citizen falls outside its remit,
and even if unbelief is widespread and churchgoing poor, it retains
a place in national life that is unique in the Anglican world.

Elsewhere the local Anglican church is often the ghost of the
British Empire, carrying on the traditions and responsibilities of
its colonial past. The empire was not unpopular, and its beneficial
effects are often missed, especially in Africa, where the new states
have proved to be weak and uninspiring. In those places the Anglican Church is a living reminder of the high standards that ought to
be expected in public life, and its leaders have the unenviable task
of speaking truth to power. It also provides a network that crosses

international boundaries and unites a continent in search of itself, which is one reason why pan-Anglican connections matter more to many Africans than they do to members of Western churches. What happens elsewhere has an impact on them in a way that is much less true of Western Anglicans, who seldom give the wider world much of a glance and are happy to ignore it if its opinions do not suit their agenda.

And then there is the American scene, with the Episcopal Church and its many breakaway groups that vie for recognition. What is the rest of the Anglican world supposed to make of them? Americans tend to be more concerned to define Anglicanism than most others are, but American Anglicanism is eccentric and always has been. A generation ago, many American Episcopal theologians were promoting the idea that a sixteenth-century lawyer called Richard Hooker (1554–1600) was the founder of Anglicanism, even though neither the *Library of Anglo-Catholic Theology* nor the Parker Society showed any awareness of him. That movement seems to have abated now, but it may have been replaced by a cult of C. S. Lewis (1898–1963), which other Anglicans find equally puzzling. They do not belong to the Church of Narnia and find it strange that anyone would think in that way. American Anglicanism also comes across to others as a strange coalition of extremes. Its liberals may be off the wall, but its conservatives can also appear to outsiders to be bizarre and even obnoxious. If the rest of the Anglican Communion is expected to provide an audience for the infighting of its American members, it is unlikely to last long.

A Way Ahead?

Can Anglicanism survive as a coherent concept in the modern world? This is the fundamental issue that underlies the current disagreements over same-sex marriage and the like. This liberal and essentially secular agenda has been pushed in the Western world, but not without opposition, and it is mostly anathema elsewhere. National churches have claimed the right to set their own standards of doctrine, discipline, and devotion, regardless of what the rest of the Anglican world thinks, and when others attempt to impose a common standard, they are shouted down. Some American Episcopalians have even been known to cry "colonialism" when other Anglican churches have tried to restrain them. Not all Anglican churches ordain women, for example, but none of the churches that do has ever thought to consider what other parts of the Anglican Communion think about it, and deferring to them has always been out of the question. It is much the same with same-sex liturgies and so on, though these touch on more fundamental doctrinal issues and have led to divisions that appear to be intractable. But how can two kinds of church walk together if they are not agreed?

Another problem is that we live in an ecumenical age in which Christians of all kinds are working together. Why should we emphasize Anglicanism if all it does is distance us from other Christians? If there is one thing that really does characterize Anglicans over the centuries, it is that they have always been open to welcoming the best from every Christian tradition. Now that the rest of the world is moving closer together, does it really help if we raise boundaries (if not barriers) by emphasizing what makes us different from them? Attempts to define Anglicanism in terms of worship or church order are common, but they fail the test when they are pressed. The so-called "historic episcopate" is both questionable in theory and divisive in practice, making it of little use as a basis for creating a distinctive ecclesiastical identity. The Prayer Book tradition has suffered from liturgical reforms that have created chaos within individual churches and distanced Anglicans from each other. Doctrinal unity is just as elusive. The Thirty-Nine Articles are accorded some recognition but mainly as a historic document. Few Anglicans have studied them, and even most of the clergy know little about them. To propose them as the basis for defining Anglicanism nowadays seems anachronistic and inappropriate in many parts of the world, though no other doctrinal standard has a comparable influence among Anglicans, and none is likely to be forthcoming. Can a theological tradition exist without theology? That often seems to be where we are heading, but if we ever get there, Anglicanism will be as good as dead. Theological renewal is essential if we are to survive, and if it is to be in any way distinctively Anglican, it can only come from, and be rooted in, the formularies that have marked out the Church of England since the Reformation.

And yet, despite all the problems we face, there are still people around the world who want to identify as Anglicans. It is true that some of them have decided in advance what they want that to mean, but there are many who admire the Anglican tradition from outside, perhaps recognizing its virtues more clearly than those within it often do. What is it that attracts them? What do they think when the term "Anglicanism" is mentioned? What should they be looking for and perhaps even be attracted by?

Perhaps the most defining characteristic of Anglicanism is the way that it concentrates on the fundamentals of Christianity and leaves disputed points to one side. That has been true ever since the sixteenth century, when the leaders of the Church of England deliberately sought to find a middle way between what they regarded as the growing extremes of Wittenberg, on the one hand, and Geneva, on the other. Traditionally they have refused to be defined by a form of church government—they are pragmatically Episcopal but not dogmatically Episcopalian. In recent years nonepiscopally ordained clergy have been allowed to minister as if they were Anglicans in some ecumenical contexts, although the Communion itself remains closed to churches that are not episcopally ordered. Nor have Anglicans allowed themselves to be labeled in sacramental terms—they practice infant baptism but do not reject those who disagree with it. All they require is tolerance of others and a sense of perspective when dealing with things indifferent—a tall order, it must be admitted, and one not always realized in practice, but something that is surely essential for ecumenical cooperation in the modern world.

Another defining characteristic of Anglicanism is the centrality of the Bible, not just in theory but in practice. The Anglican liturgical tradition is best described as turning Scripture into prayer, and it cannot be understood otherwise. The first of the Homilies remains one of the best expositions of the doctrine of Scripture and what it ought to mean for the church; it should be read and studied by every Christian concerned to grow in the word of God. At the heart of this Anglican exaltation of the Bible is a devotion to the gospel of Christ and the need to proclaim it. True Anglicanism does not distinguish a ministry of the sacraments from the ministry of the word of God—the sacraments are the ministry of the word by other means. This balance has been severely compromised both by the lingering effects of Anglo-Catholicism and by the ravages of modern liturgical revision, but it must be recovered if the Anglican Church is to be true to itself as an authentic expression of New Testament Christianity, and the 1662 BCP remains a model of what we should be aiming for.

The need to teach Christianity is another thing that is characteristic of authentic Anglicanism. Other Protestant churches emerged from grassroots movements, but in England the reformed faith had to be preached to a nation that was ignorant of it. The Anglican Church's first mission field has always been its own members and the communities they live in. That is why the doctrinal formularies of the Reformation era remain fundamental and must be recovered and adapted to modern circumstances if Anglicanism is to have a future.

Anglicans are not sectarian but appeal beyond the confines of their own Communion and respect the integrity of others whose traditions are different. It is a remarkable fact that two of the most influential exponents of Christianity in the twentieth century were Anglicans—C. S. Lewis in the academic world and John Stott (1921–2011) in the church. Both wrote best-selling books with virtually the same title—*Mere Christianity*, by Lewis, and *Basic Christianity*, by Stott—neither of which so much as mentions Anglicanism, but neither of which would be conceivable without it. Neither man told his audience that they must become Anglicans in order to be saved; they did not even recommend it as their preferred option. At their best, Anglicans try to serve the wider church in an ecumenical spirit rather than steal the sheep that belong to others. They do not put their own leaders on a pedestal; hardly anyone knows who the fathers of the English Reformation were, and almost nobody has read any of their works. The hagiography that surrounds Martin Luther and John Calvin is absent from the Anglican world, and so it should remain—what the Puritans called "the crown rights of Christ the Redeemer" must not be obscured by even the greatest of his human servants. When the supreme governor of the Church of England turned ninety in 2016, a group of Anglicans produced a book in her honor, a book that was composed entirely of her own statements and speeches. Tellingly, it was called *The Servant Queen and the King She Serves*. To be an Anglican is to be a servant of the King of kings, whether we are of high or of low estate here on earth. If Anglicanism is anything, it is a servant church in which every member has a ministry and in which all who believe in Christ are equally welcome.

In 1633, when religious controversy in England was at its height and the church seemed set to divide into rival factions, one of its great pastors and poets, George Herbert, put that spirit of service into verse, in words that still echo in our churches today and that may serve as a fitting summary of what true Anglicanism is and should always be:

> Teach me, my God and King,
>   In all things Thee to see,
> And what I do in anything
>   To do it as for Thee. . . .
>
>   A man that looks on glass,
>   On it may stay his eye;
> Or if he pleaseth, though it pass,
>   And then the heav'n espy.
>
>   All may of Thee partake:
>   Nothing can be so mean,
> Which with [t]his tincture—"for thy sake"—
>   Will not grow bright and clean.
>
>   A servant with this clause
>   Makes drudgery divine:
> Who sweeps a room as for Thy laws,
>   Makes that and th' action fine.
>
>   This is the famous stone
>   That turneth all to gold;
> For that which God doth touch and own
>   Cannot for less be told.[1]

Amen. Come Lord Jesus!

---

1. George Herbert, "The Elixir," Poetry Foundation (website), https://www.poetry foundation.org/poems/44362/the-elixir.

Response to the Vocational Perspectives

Chandler Holder Jones

The three preceding chapters are an exercise in Anglican diversity. John Yates worries that we will lose Anglican essentials, by which he means justification, the Prayer Book, and service to the nation. I regard those as minima rather than what makes Anglicanism distinctive—the fullness of liturgy and sacrament of the first millennium.

Barbara Gauthier is right to focus on that first millennium, for that is when the English Church was closest to the faith once delivered to the saints. If Gerald Bray's definition of Anglicanism is to be followed, there will be no more Anglicanism, which he seems not to regret. Along the way he takes unjustified aim at members of the Oxford Movement as having "an agenda that was far from scholarly" for cosponsoring the *Library of Anglo-Catholic Theology*, which contained noncatholic authors. But the *Oxford Handbook of the Oxford Movement* reports that Newman, Keble, and Pusey were not the original sponsors of this *Library* and were "lukewarm" toward it precisely because of the non-Catholic character of some of the authors. They had already started their own *Library of the Fathers* five years earlier.[1]

Since Anglo-Catholicism has been criticized in some of these chapters, it might be helpful to sketch its history and outlook. Sometimes called the high church movement, or better the "first millennium undivided church faith," this way of seeing Anglicanism possesses a direct and unbroken continuity throughout the history of the English Church—from centuries before the Reformation through the Henrician, Edwardine, Elizabethan, and Stuart periods. It continued in the Caroline divines and Non-Jurors, to the Tractarians of the nineteenth century, to today. No other claimant to Anglicanism's authenticity can demonstrate such a historical continuum. Other movements in Anglicanism started at the Reformation and later. But Anglo-Catholicism is simply the English Church in her givenness—her inherited theological and liturgical patrimony.

This means that Anglicanism is far more than a "system of thought and theology." It is a way of life ordered by worship, doctrine, and practice. Separating worship, doctrine, and practice from one another distorts the essence of the church and her deposit of faith. It misses the fact that dogmatic theology is a mystical theology which lies in Anglican liturgy and sacramental life.

The church is not a sociological entity but the mystical body of Christ endowed with a supernatural reality, a supernatural society of souls effused with divine grace. Anglicanism, at her best, professes a faith that comes from the church's great councils and creeds so that it is part of what the creeds call the one holy, catholic, and apostolic church.

Anglo-Catholicism has been particularly shaped by the seventeenth-century Caroline divines, such as Lancelot Andrewes and

---

1. James Pereiro, "'A Cloud of Witnesses': Tractarians and Tractarian Ventures," in *The Oxford Handbook of the Oxford Movement*, ed. Stewart J. Brown, Peter B. Nockles, and James Pereiro (Oxford: Oxford University Press, 2017), 114–16.

Jeremy Taylor. The Carolines deeply influenced the nineteenth-century Tractarians (principally Newman, Pusey, and Keble). These leaders of the Oxford Movement were not starry-eyed medievalists but romanticists, men of earth and altar who sought a renewed church life based on the incarnation and the sacramental principle. Pusey's *Library of the Fathers* was inspired by the Carolines' conviction that the church will be best renewed by returning to the great fathers of the early church.

Anglo-Catholics see the church as a divine society that divinizes the material world. They restored Anglican monasticism in an effort to engage secular culture directly, by serving the poorest of the poor. For the last two centuries Anglican monks have served the suffering, the outcast, and the underprivileged.

Anglo-Catholicism has also spawned a rebirth of theological and spiritual formation, missionary work and zeal, and Christian culture and civilization. Its members have brought their incarnational vision to art, architecture, music, academic scholarship, and the religious life. Their vision and life are not so much eccentric as ecstatic, reaching beyond themselves to Christ and his creation. They regard the Anglican catholic faith not as mere Christianity but *more* Christianity.

Let me be a bit more specific about the incarnational vision of Anglo-Catholics. We believe, along with the church of the first millennium, that the church lives in and is made by the sacraments, which extend and apply the incarnation. Hence, creation, redemption, and glorification are ontological (matters of being) and sacramental, which means they involve the transformation of the material by the spiritual. As the historic church has taught, grace perfects nature. So the church, which is the prime example of this perfecting, is the great sacrament of Christ. Because Anglo-Catholic churches continue, Anglo-Catholicism is a living and growing reality. It is neither a failure nor a relic of the past.

I agree with Barbara Gauthier that Anglicanism has never claimed to be the one true church. It is a *via media*, but not the sort that she and others have articulated in this book. I see Anglo-Catholicism as the *via media* between Roman Catholicism and Eastern Orthodoxy, not between Rome and Geneva. It is not a compromise between Catholicism and Protestantism but the central mainstream tradition of the undivided church shared by the churches of East and West. It is what all first-millennium Christians believed and lived, and what Rome and Constantinople still possess in common today—the *consensus fidelium* of apostolic tradition. To paraphrase John Henry Newman's original meaning of the term, the *via media* signifies that the Anglican Church lies between Puritanism and popery. So Anglicanism is neither Puritan nor papalist.

But Anglicanism is far from unified. One could say there are three Anglicanisms today. One is that of the first millennium consensus, or Anglo-Catholicism, now mostly found in what are called "continuing churches." Second, there is liberal Anglicanism, now found in the Lambeth Canterbury Communion. And third, there is evangelical Anglicanism, mostly found in those bodies adhering to GAFCON. The Elizabethan Settlement—in other words, a unified church comprehending diverse believers who worship with common prayer—has for all practical purposes collapsed and ceased to exist.

PART 3

ECCLESIASTICAL PERSPECTIVES ON ANGLICANISM

8

AN EPISCOPAL DEAN

Renewed Anglicanism

Andrew C. Pearson Jr.

Anglicanism is the English witness to the biblical convictions of the Reformation. Like those who have gone before us, we must find our answers in the Bible, alongside the Reformers' commitment to the church being formed and re-formed by Scripture. We do not go back naively, believing the sixteenth century was some high-water mark for Anglicanism (as if there ever were one). Instead, we return to its rediscovery of the grace of God in Jesus Christ, for this grace is all too easily lost when man's wisdom supplants the authority of the Bible.

The formularies produced during the English Reformation (whether heeded or not) have been the trust deeds for those of us who are evangelicals—that is, "gospel people." In an Anglican voice, they point to and call us back to fix our hearts, our lives, and our churches on the person and work of Jesus Christ.

Our formularies are the 1662 BCP, the Ordinal, the Thirty-Nine Articles, and the Homilies compiled by Thomas Cranmer.[1] All stand as Anglican expressions of the gospel of Jesus Christ. As our trust documents, they first shaped and formed us as Anglicans. By God's grace, they will continue to do so. Renewal in Anglicanism will require a renewed commitment to the scriptural foundations articulated by these formularies.

I write as a pastor and preacher trained in the evangelical tradition, and as an inheritor of a congregation that has held these commitments. I have seen firsthand the fruits of renewal at the Cathedral Church of the Advent (Birmingham, Alabama). It is a vibrant witness to the biblical faith of our forebears.

Using our formularies as our guide, I pray that in the coming days, as we await the return of the Lord Jesus Christ, we might commit ourselves to following and living more fully into our Anglican identity: a renewed commitment to orthodoxy, a renewed commitment to the gospel, a renewed commitment to preaching, a renewed commitment to the church, a renewed liturgical conviction, a renewed commitment to mission, and a renewed commitment to prayer. To each of these we now turn.

A Renewed Commitment to Orthodoxy

Even those of us in the "orthodox" Anglican camp must ask ourselves, What does it mean to be orthodox?

---

1. The Ordinal provides the services and liturgies for the ordination of bishops, priests, and deacons. Cranmer's first Ordinal appeared in 1550 and was revised—along with the Prayer Book itself—in 1552. In it, Cranmer simplified the ancient ordination services, recognizing only the three main orders, with an increased emphasis on word and sacrament. The Homilies, first appearing in 1547, spell out the Protestant doctrine of justification by faith. Twelve in total, the first six pertain particularly to doctrine, while the latter address other concerns. For further reading on the Articles and Homilies, see Gerald Bray, *The Faith We Confess: An Exposition of the Thirty-Nine Articles* (London: Latimer, 2009), and Bray, *The Books of Homilies: A Critical Edition* (Cambridge: James Clarke, 2016).

Many would say that orthodoxy is defined by the creeds. Indeed, that is a good place to start. But is that enough? In our day and age, we need to have the patience and perseverance to drill down to what we mean when we confess the creeds. We cannot take for granted that we are all saying the same thing.

Anglicans say that the creeds possess an authority as an articulation of what we believe. Article 8 (of our Thirty-Nine Articles) begins, "The Three Creeds, Nicene Creed, Athanasius' Creed, and that which is commonly called the Apostles' Creed, ought thoroughly to be received and believed." But why should they be believed? Because a majority of those at church councils voted for them? Or because they were written early in the life of the faith of the church and therefore merit greater authority than anything written more recently? Article 8 continues and tells us why: "for they may be proved by most certain warrants of holy Scripture." The creeds have authority because they agree with and convey the truths of the Bible.

Orthodoxy is defined ultimately not by the creeds but by the authority of Scripture. Put another way, we are orthodox when we submit to Scripture as set forth in the creeds; we are orthodox insofar as we are in agreement with the Bible. Nigerian archbishop Nicholas Okoh explains it like this:

> Some may object that we should not break fellowship over matters which do not directly go against the ancient creeds of the Church. The Archbishop of Canterbury himself has recently said that the church should not be split by issues that are not, as he puts it, "creedal," but it is important to remember that the authority of the Creeds is derived from the Bible, and it is the Bible which is the Church's supreme teaching authority.[2]

---

2. Archbishop Nicholas Okoh, "Chairman's September 2017 Letter," GAFCON, September 5, 2017, https://www.gafcon.org/news/chairmans-september-2017-letter.

We Anglicans who call ourselves orthodox must allow the Scriptures to guide us in all that we do. The line in the sand must be a willingness to submit oneself to the Bible in all of life.[3] To that end, we should ask, Is the Bible informing all areas of our Anglican life and practice?

A Renewed Commitment to the Gospel

In addition to biblical fidelity, there has been a large-scale loss of the gospel in our churches. It seems like a straightforward question, but what is the gospel that we as Christians are called to preach?

The propensity of the liberal-minded is to subtract from the gospel, whereas the conservative is prone to add. These responses are two sides of the same coin. We must neither subtract from nor add to the gospel of God's grace for sinners. Many ideas masquerade as the gospel. We too often hear it said, "The gospel is loving God with all your heart, soul, mind, and strength, and loving your neighbor as yourself." While both loving God and loving neighbor are biblical admonitions, even corollaries of the gospel, the gospel itself remains obscured when reduced to action steps, and the consequence is a cruel falsity.

Some, fearing that preaching the pure gospel means deemphasizing God's law and commandments, immediately cry "Antinomian!" They wonder about the role of obedience, or fear that grace would be cheapened. As a corrective, intending to uphold the law, they actually lower the commandments of God, making them manageable, approachable, doable. The gospel is not cheap grace, for it cost the Son of God his life for the sins of the world. Though the gospel is not cheap, it is free, for it costs us nothing. (With what would we pay for it, even if we could?)

---

3. There is an understandable tendency currently to define orthodoxy according to one's convictions regarding sexuality. As important as these questions are, merely following biblical guidance on sexuality is not enough to define orthodoxy.

The gospel is not a balance of the law (which requires our obedience) and grace (which forgives when we do not obey). This understanding places the church (usually the priests) in the position of adding a little a bit of the gospel here or taking away some of it there, depending on how people are behaving. By no means! God's law is as different from his gospel as death is from life. The law requires absolute obedience and gives no power to accomplish what it requires; the law of God (which is good, right, and holy) is not the way to salvation. Only the gospel can declare sinners to be righteous; it is the power of God unto our salvation. The gospel is our righteousness, solely because of the work of Jesus Christ. This is the gospel we are to preach:

> For God so loved the world, that he gave his only Son, that whoever believes in him should not perish but have eternal life. (John 3:16)

> For God has done what the law, weakened by the flesh, could not do. By sending his own Son in the likeness of sinful flesh and for sin, he condemned sin in the flesh, in order that the righteous requirement of the law might be fulfilled in us, who walk not according to the flesh but according to the Spirit. (Rom. 8:3–4)

> For our sake he made him to be sin who knew no sin, so that in him we might become the righteousness of God. (2 Cor. 5:21)

> But God shows his love for us in that while we were still sinners, Christ died for us. (Rom. 5:8)

The gospel is God's grace for sinners in Christ Jesus. It is the good news that by his cross and resurrection we have been delivered from sin and death and reconciled to God.

Do we have any other message to preach other than Christ and him crucified? Do we know the gospel? Can we say of our ministry,

"I am not ashamed of the gospel" (Rom. 1:16)? Let us not have a pusillanimous doctrine of the atonement but one that we proclaim to all, for nonbelievers and believers alike need the gospel.

Commandments, even biblical ones, are not the good news of salvation. To see Jesus primarily as a teacher, a social activist, or someone mostly concerned with our moral behavior is to reduce him to a lawgiver and miss him altogether. Thomas Cranmer understood this. The message of the law does not give life but drives us to the cross of Jesus by making known to us our sinfulness.[4] This is why Cranmer has us respond, after the summary of the law in our Holy Communion service, "Lord, have mercy upon us." But though the law is always distinguished from the gospel, it is never separated. After the law has done its work, Jesus's word to us who are reckoned dead in our trespasses and sins is the same as it was to Jairus's daughter who had died: "I say to you, arise" (Mark 5:41).

We cannot afford to be vague about the gospel as souls are on the line. By the proclamation of the gospel, the eyes of hearts are opened, and sinners are turned to the Lord Jesus Christ in newness of life.

A Renewed Commitment to Preaching

As the gospel is to be preached and proclaimed, this understanding ought to have an impact on our preaching. In light of the meaning of orthodoxy and the gospel, what then ought we to preach?

Anglicans pride themselves on the quantity of Scripture that is read at each service, and rightly so. Cranmer insisted on it and was convinced that all the people of God must be able to handle the word of God themselves. As Robert Smith of Beeson Divinity School has put it, "I preach so that you can preach."

---

4. "Through the law comes knowledge of sin" (Rom. 3:20); "If a law had been given that could give life, then righteousness would indeed be by the law" (Gal. 3:21).

But we must not expect the reading of God's word in our gatherings or our biblical liturgy to be enough. Hugh Latimer (echoing Rom. 10:13–14) declared: "We cannot be saved without faith, and faith cometh by hearing of the word. . . . There must be preachers if we look to be saved."[5] Latimer understands preaching to be the efficacious work of God to justify sinners, working faith in them through their hearing. To preach is to proclaim and deliver the gospel to sinners: it is nothing less than the power of God unto salvation for all who believe. Such an understanding of preaching has lost its position of importance in our gathered worship.

While visiting an Anglican theological college, I was able to sit down for coffee and conversation with most of the faculty. One of the questions I asked them was "What is the purpose of preaching?" One faculty member replied, "Its purpose is to inspire, because the liturgy carries so much water." If this division of labor were true, how do we explain our current situation in the Episcopal Church? Liturgy cannot carry the water that the Lord ordains preaching to do.

The marks of the church are not mere possession of the Bible but the preaching of "the pure Word of God" and the faithful administration of the sacraments.[6] It is in preaching that the pastor is being as pastoral as he can possibly be. It is the one time in the week where his entire flock is gathered together. Pastoral work may include visiting hospitals and shut-ins, but the principal work of a pastor is to preach. The saying wrongly attributed to Saint Francis implying that gospel words are often unnecessary has made the rounds long enough;[7] pastors are to preach the gospel at all times, using words.

---

5. P. E. Hughes, *Theology of the English Reformers* (Abington, PA: Horseradish, 1997), 129.

6. See Article 19.

7. Some variation of this saying has for a long time been wrongly attributed to Saint Francis of Assisi: "Preach the gospel at all times. Use words if necessary."

A Renewed Commitment to the Church

The local church is ground zero for the preaching of the gospel. As important as pan-Anglican events are (Lambeth, GAFCON, etc.), the outworking of our Anglican convictions regarding Scripture, the gospel, and preaching needs to take place in the life of the church. And by church, I mean the local gathering of believers as the earthly manifestation of the heavenly gathering of which we are a part right now (Eph. 2). This is how our Article 19 defines the church: "The visible Church of Christ is a congregation of faithful men, in the which the pure Word of God is preached, and the Sacraments be duly ministered according to Christ's ordinance, in all those things that of necessity are requisite to the same."

This is not to deny the use of the word "church" for a collection of assemblies within a geographic area (the Articles use it in this way), but we must recapture the priority of the mission and ministry of the local congregation. Dioceses and denominations must give way to playing the supportive role they are meant to play as the gospel is preached and sacraments are ministered in the specific contexts of local congregations.

This will be hard for Anglicans. In the States, the original expression of Anglicanism identified itself as "The Episcopal Church" and continues to do so. But should we not pause and wonder whether our method and structure of church governance should define who we are? Is polity really the *regula fidei* of Anglicanism?

In a meeting with diocesan leadership, I once asked, "What holds us together as a diocese?" One priest answered, "Money and the canons." Though my heart sank when I heard him say it, I have come to see that he was absolutely right when orthodoxy has given way to confusion and heresy. Though more holds us together within orthodoxy than money and canons, diocesan structure supports the ministry of local congregations through such things as health insurance and any number of administrative tasks that free the congregation for ministry. Fellowship, if fellowship can be had, is an added bonus—but a diocese should not be mistaken for the church. The unity of the church does not depend on common external rules and regulations but is constituted by the word of God preached and the sacraments duly ministered.

The understanding of the church that the Articles offer is not congregational but connectional. This is because the New Testament itself describes both the independence and interdependence of churches, as they neither exist in isolation from one another nor defer to others the proclamation of the gospel in word and sacrament. No doubt is left where the action of ministry occurs: at the local level. Writing in the nineteenth century, Bishop Daniel Wilson of Calcutta said, "We best advance the prosperity of our various bodies, when we seek the honor of our great Master, and the salvation of souls; and make our ecclesiastical platforms entirely subservient to these great aims."[8] Our renewal will follow when our various bodies—whether local parishes, dioceses, or national structures—honor our Master and Lord through faithful ministries of word and sacrament in the local church. A denomination or diocese exists for the parishes; parishes do not exist for a diocese or denomination.

A Renewed Liturgical Conviction

Beyond the local church, one of the things that holds us together is a commitment to common prayer through our liturgy. The Articles allow for differing expressions of this,[9] but by and large, Anglicanism has rooted itself in the theological convictions and

---

8. Iain Murray, *Evangelicalism Divided: A Record of Crucial Change in the Years 1950 to 2000* (Carlisle, PA: Banner of Truth, 2012), 143.

9. Article 20 allows the church to develop its own liturgies and rites, though it cannot ordain anything contrary to Scripture: "The Church hath power to decree Rites or Ceremonies, and authority in Controversies of Faith: and yet it is not lawful for the Church to ordain any thing that is contrary to God's Word written, neither may it so expound one place of Scripture, that it be repugnant to another."

liturgical expression of the 1662 BCP. Its Reformational sensibilities and structure keep us moored as churches to God's saving grace for sinners, and it is this which we must see as our liturgy.

The crafters of the 1979 BCP showed us that the adage *lex orandi lex credendi* (the law of praying shapes believing) has great truth to it, as we now see the fruits of their liturgies. A less penitential prayer book has created a less penitential church. A catechism that reduces sin from a condition to "wrong choices" has become a clarion call for unbounded self-determination and self-actualization in the Episcopal Church. And, most egregiously, a shift away from an emphasis on the atonement has made Jesus something less than what the Bible says he is: a propitiation for our sins (Rom. 3:25; Heb. 2:17; 1 John 2:2; 4:10).[10]

Orthodox Anglican belief, as articulated by our formularies, ought to shape the way we pray. As their principal architect, Cranmer organized our formularies to present clearly Scripture's work on us. Illustrative of this is his emphasis on salvation—on God's justifying activity meeting the sinning human—in his liturgical formulas. With characteristic Reformational orientation, the word of God's law leads us to our need of Christ, while the word of God's gospel delivers Christ to us. To take but one example from the service of Holy Communion: from the convicting word of the law in the confession, our liturgy moves immediately to the freeing word of absolution. Cranmer then goes further, delivering to the convicted and freed sinner the comfortable words: a storehouse of the gospel and its resurrective power.[11] What we have been given to believe and know shapes the way we pray and gather beneath the word of God.

---

10. For more thorough treatment, see Peter Toon and Louis Tarsitano, *Neither Orthodoxy nor a Formulary: The Shape and Content of the 1979 Prayer Book of the Episcopal Church* (Philadelphia: Prayer Book Society of the USA, 2004), and Paul Zahl, *The Protestant Face of Anglicanism* (Grand Rapids, MI: Eerdmans, 1997).

11. See Ashley Null, *Divine Allurement: Cranmer's Comfortable Words*, Latimer Briefing 16 (London: Latimer, 2014).

This is not an argument against revision beyond 1662. As beautiful as Cranmer's Prayer Book is, he would choose content over aesthetics. We love the Prayer Book not because its English is Elizabethan but because it causes us to see ourselves correctly as sinners, finally and completely delivered only by Christ's full and sufficient work. From there, we may properly view our redeemed lives as lived in response only to God's grace.

If the unchanging gospel of Christ is veiled in our worship services, then as a matter of faithfulness we must change and revise our liturgy. Too many evangelicals in both the Episcopal Church and Anglican Church of North America have fallen into the trap of allowing a divide between our theological convictions and our practice: we must do so no longer. On the one hand, we may buy the new and go with the latest fad, whether that be a particular praise song or program; on the other, we may revert to the medieval or ancient practices under the illusion that old is necessarily better or more pristine. Whatever our practice may be, the main aim of our services is to declare to God's people the good news of Jesus Christ. To think we must dress up or—God forbid—add to the gospel is to obscure it or take it away altogether.

Our unity must be more than a commitment to the shape of the liturgy—its form alone will not save us. Our unity must be grounded in what the liturgy is saying. It was doctrinal consideration that motivated the first Books of Common Prayer (1549 and 1552). The 1552 is, by and large, what we have in the 1662 BCP. It should continue to be our guiding light, not for its beautiful form and language but as it proclaims the person and work of Jesus Christ.

A Renewed Commitment to Mission

If you were to search for a record of incorporation for the Episcopal Church, you would not find one under that name. Nor would you find one even for the Protestant Episcopal Church (USA). What you would find as the incorporated name of the Episcopal Church is an entity called the Domestic and Foreign Missionary Society.

Historically speaking, everyone who joined the Episcopal Church was joining a missionary enterprise. That zeal was largely lost in the latter part of the nineteenth century when the denomination was consumed with controversy sparked by the Tractarian movement and subsequent departure of prominent evangelicals in 1873.[12] This zeal has not been recovered, save in some pockets of renewal. A loss of confidence in the gospel leads to a lack of evangelism and mission.

Today, in the Episcopal Church there are no full-time missionaries serving an indefinite term through the denomination. To be sure, there are Episcopalians in the mission field serving through other agencies, and groups exist such as the Young Adult Service Corps and Episcopal Volunteers in Mission, but both are time-limited, and neither has making disciples of Jesus Christ as its main aim.[13]

If one were to look at a map of the Anglican Communion, it would speak volumes about missions. How else would one explain the global growth and reach of Anglicanism? At one time, the Society for the Propagation of the Gospel and the Church Missionary Society worked diligently in their respective fields, but in the Western world, an Anglican urgency for proclamation has largely been lost.

North American Anglicanism must turn once again to the Lord Jesus Christ and make mission and evangelism a priority, both at home and abroad. At home, we must equip our own people with the ability to articulate the gospel and share it with others.

---

12. Bishop David Cummins and others left the Episcopal Church and formed the Reformed Episcopal Church. See http://anglicanhistory.org/usa/rec/cec_dec1873.html.

13. For reference, see https://www.episcopalchurch.org/posts/missionpersonnel/frequently-asked-questions-about-episcopal-volunteers-mission.

We must hold up to our people the invitation to "go," even to the ends of the earth. How many people are coming to Christ through our churches? How many are going into the mission field? If we are honest, we would rather not ask such questions, though they burned in the hearts of our Anglican forebears. May God raise up more Wesleys, Whitefields, Simeons, and Wilberforces!

We should acknowledge as well the great work God is doing among our brothers and sisters in the Global South. They are being used to evangelize the world. One is always struck by their confidence in the gospel: they believe that God will do what he promises to do. In many cases, you see people with very little, materially speaking; and yet when Jesus is all that you have, it turns out he is enough. May we learn from them this confidence and joy in the work God has given us to do.

A Renewed Commitment to Prayer

At the heart of all this is the need to pray. With all that has happened in the Anglican wars of this century, it is easy to develop spiritual *Schadenfreude*, being too ready to delight in the misfortune and demise of others as we proudly believe we are in the right. We are reminded that even those who seek to undermine the gospel in Anglicanism are not the enemy: "for we do not wrestle against flesh and blood, but against the rulers, against the authorities, against the cosmic powers over this present darkness, against the spiritual forces of evil in the heavenly places" (Eph. 6:12). Those on the other side should be the subject of our prayers and compassion, not our anger (righteous as it may be). As John Bradford, English martyr, is often quoted as saying, "There but for the grace of God go I."

If not for God's intervention in our own lives, we would not find ourselves in the ark of salvation. George Whitefield articulated well his compassion rooted in the truth of Christ: "It is not true of all, but the generality of the clergy are fallen from our Articles and do

194 Andrew C. Pearson Jr.

not speak agreeable to them, or to the form of sound words delivered in Scripture; woe be unto such blind leaders of the blind! How can they escape the damnation of hell?"[14] Would any of us delight in seeing another remain in the grasp of damnation? May we all be given the compassion of Bradford and Whitefield, persevering for the saving truth of God's gospel.

At the very heart of our controversies is sin. So it should bring us some comfort that God knows how to deal with sin. Yes, we should stand against the false teaching we encounter from any sector, but we must understand that the battle will be won not politically or legislatively but only through prayer and the conversion of souls to the Lord Jesus Christ.

William Tyndale risked, and ultimately lost, his life so that others might read God's word in a language they could understand. He was forced to live in exile and great fear that he might be taken at any moment. But he persevered. When finally captured and about to be strangled and burned, Tyndale offered one last prayer for Henry VIII: "Lord! Open the king of England's eyes!"[15] He prayed for his greatest enemy. It was an act not just of charity but also of faith, for just three years after Tyndale's death, Henry had the English Bible placed in every parish church.

May we pray with fervent faith, knowing that God alone can deliver us from error. But let us also give thanks that, in his mercy, God would use the Tyndales of the world to open the eyes of the blind. May it be so, Lord Jesus.

If there is to be renewal and a future for our Anglican Communion, especially in the West, it must be by a renewed commitment to the Lord Jesus Christ himself. Renewed structures, resolutions,

---

14. George Whitefield, *Sermons on Important Subjects*, ed. J. Smith (London: Baynes, 1825), 390, cited in Murray, *Evangelicalism Divided*, 161.

15. David Daniell, *William Tyndale: A Biography* (New Haven, CT: Yale University Press, 1994), 383.

and statements at conferences, helpful as they may be, have their limitations. Votes do not change people's hearts, but Jesus does. The great strength of Anglicanism is its commitment to biblical Christianity as articulated by our formularies. They are foundational to what it means to be an Anglican, and are essential if we are to see a renewed Anglicanism. Anglican comprehensiveness must be a principled comprehensiveness, anchored in Scripture.

We must pray for a renewed commitment to this faith that has been handed down to us, and we must steward it as God's faithful people. Even when things seem their darkest, we are a resurrection people and know that

> the LORD [our] God is in [our] midst,
>   a mighty one who will save. (Zeph. 3:17)

9

AN ANGLICAN THEOLOGIAN

An Ancient-Future Anglicanism

Gerald R. McDermott

Anglicanism did not begin in the sixteenth century. There was a distinctive English way of living in fellowship with the triune God for at least a millennium before that. In this chapter I want to chart that English character of Christian worship in four ways: its spirituality, liturgy, sacraments, and theological method. Then I will propose a way forward in this twenty-first century: a way where being evangelical is not enough. At least not as evangelicalism is commonly configured today, where experience is central, and doctrine and church are minimized. This is far removed from the classical evangelicalism of Edwards and Wesley, both of whom prized doctrine, the church, and sacraments.

Anglican liturgy and sacrament help us avoid the Pelagian temptation to show our gratitude to Christ by trying hard enough.

They bypass the frustration of repeated efforts to "worship in spirit and in truth" by our feeling and imagining. Instead, the Anglican tradition provides a way to participate in the Son's worship of the Father.[1] And to grow in "the divine nature" (2 Pet. 1:4) by sharing in Christ's humanity. Sacraments and liturgy provide beauty and power that appeal to all five senses and to people of all capacities, which helps prevent an intellectualism attractive only to the cognitively inclined.[2]

A Distinctive Spirituality

Historians tell us that Christians probably came to England in the first two centuries as England was colonized by Rome. Roman soldiers, administrators, and/or traders brought Christ along as they were deputized to the cold island by the empire. The first mention we have of English Christianity comes from Tertullian, who wrote in 200 that "the haunts of the Britons—inaccessible to the Romans [were] subjugated to Christ."[3] The first English Christian

---

1. This participation is in Christ's humanity rather than his divinity. The divine persons do not worship one another, but the man Jesus worships his divine Father, as he did after the Last Supper (Matt. 26:30; Mark 14:26), and sings his praise now (Heb. 2:12), leading the Gentiles in their worship (Rom. 15:9). See Mark A. Seifrid, "Romans," in *Commentary on the New Testament Use of the Old Testament*, ed. G. K. Beale and D. A. Carson (Grand Rapids, MI: Baker Academic, 2007), 689. See also James B. Torrance, *Worship, Community and the Triune God of Grace* (Downers Grove, IL: InterVarsity Press, 1996), where he criticizes the existential, present-day experience model of faith as too anthropologically centered: "It emphasizes *our* faith, *our* decision, *our* response in an event theology which short-circuits the vicarious humanity of Christ and belittles union with Christ. . . . It fails to see the place of the high priesthood of Jesus Christ as *leitourgos* (Heb 8:2). . . . By his Spirit [God] draws men and women to participate both in [Christ's] life of worship and communion with the Father and in his mission from the Father to the world" (29–31). This participation in the liturgy of the Son by the Spirit to the Father is the meaning of Anglican liturgy and sacrament.

2. A critic could say that my dislike of experience-centered worship contradicts my recommendation of sacraments, which involve sensory experience. True enough at one level, but there is an important difference: sacraments come from the Church *outside* me, while so much of contemporary evangelical worship looks *inside* the self for validation. Critics could also wonder if my esteem for doctrine conflicts with my distaste for intellectualism. Not if the doctrine is taught through liturgy and sacrament as well as sermons.

3. Tertullian, "An Answer to the Jews," chap. 7, in *Ante-Nicene Fathers*, ed. Alexander Roberts and James Donaldson, vol. 3 (Peabody, MA: Hendrickson, 2012).

mentioned by name was Alban, who was martyred at some point in the next century for protecting a priest from execution.[4] Origen wrote around 240 that England was among the places where Christians were found. By 314 there were several English bishops, and the great Athanasius wrote that the results of the Council of Nicaea (325) were "accepted by the British church." In 359, British bishops attended the Council of Rimini.[5]

After Anglo-Saxon invasions in the fifth century forced the Romans to abandon control of the isle, a new Celtic Christianity arrived to replace it. In the next century Columba founded a monastery on the island of Iona, off the Scottish coast (563), which monastery adopted the Celtic pattern of worship and life. This new Celtic brand of English Christianity sent missionaries to Scotland to convert the Druids. Aidan, a monk at Iona, restored the Christianity of northern England through monasteries at Lindisfarne and Whitby. These were the work of the Celtic church, whose spirituality was at once Trinitarian and creational, seeing the natural world and everyday life as filled with the glory of God. This, arguably, is a stream that runs through the long history of Anglican spirituality.

The Celts were also great missionaries, and this is another characteristic of the nascent English Church. Boniface, the eighth-century "Apostle of Germany" and martyr, was a missionary sent by the English Church to bring the gospel to the pagans of Germany. In the tenth century, English missionaries were sent to Scandinavia, resulting in the conversion of Olaf (d. 1000), king of Norway, who turned his people to the church of Jesus Christ. By this time the Celts had given way to the Benedictines, after the evangelist Wilfrid introduced the Benedictine Rule to English monasteries at the end of the seventh century.

---

4. Bede, *Ecclesiastical History of the English People* trans. Leo Shirley-Price (London: Penguin, 1990), 51–54.

5. John R. H. Moorman, *A History of the Church in England*, 3rd ed. (Harrisburg, PA: Morehouse, 1980), 3–5.

So, in the first millennium of Christianity, the English Church was already taking on a distinctive character. It was also challenging Rome from fairly early on. The Celtic church differed with Rome over the date of Easter, tonsure, penance, and Eucharistic consecration. These differences persisted until the Synod of Whitby in 633. But resistance to Rome became more acute in the Middle Ages. Archbishop Lanfranc was passive-aggressive in response to Pope Gregory VII's mandate for priests to be celibate (1074), enforcing it with deliberate unhurriedness. King John, of Magna Carta fame (1215), locked horns with Pope Innocent III over the appointment of Stephen Langton as archbishop of Canterbury. The pope deposed John, who then submitted. But the result was widespread English resentment of Rome. Later in the thirteenth century, that resentment deepened as Rome extracted more money from the English Church to pay for its wars against Islam. When a papal nephew was recommended by Rome for an English canonry, Bishop Robert Grosseteste of Lincoln refused to approve it: "With all filial respect and obedience I will not obey. I resist. I rebel."[6]

In the fourteenth century, King Edward I forbade English Christians from sending money overseas in the Statute of Carlisle (1307), a dig against Rome. This was probably in retaliation against Pope Boniface VIII whose *Clericis laicos* (1296) forbade prelates and monasteries to pay taxes to the state without his permission. When Boniface claimed the power of both swords—the spiritual and the material—in *Unam sanctam* (1302), the English throne struck back in its First and Second Statutes of Praemunire, which stopped appeals to Rome for benefices or legal redress. So it may not have shocked many English Christians when the Oxford philosopher and priest John Wycliffe (1328–1384) called the pope "a poisonous weed" and denied transubstantiation. They probably agreed with the first and

---

6. Moorman, *History of the Church in England*, 93.

accepted the second, since Wycliffe affirmed the real presence of the body and blood of Christ in the Eucharist. He simply refused Rome's philosophical explanation of it.

So when, in the sixteenth century, King Henry VIII made noises about separating the English Church from Rome, this was a radical step, to be sure. But it was also in keeping with a long-standing English skepticism toward Roman authority.

If English distance from Rome had a long history before the Reformation, so did English spirituality. Martin Thornton argues in his *English Spirituality* that, by the fourteenth century, England had developed its own spirituality.[7] This was the first golden age of what he calls the "English School" of spirituality, which was only elaborated but not fundamentally changed in the second golden age of the seventeenth century. It was an "ascetical theology," which means that it was a disciplined growth into holiness. Thornton says this approach was rooted in the synthesis of doctrine and prayer taught by two Christian greats: Augustine of Hippo, the great theologian whose *Confessions* is an extended prayer, and Benedict of Nursia, whose monasteries modeled the Christian life as work amid liturgical prayer. Already by the twelfth century, England was known as the "Benedictine land" because of the dominance of its Benedictine monasteries and their influence on English church life. By the fourteenth century, English Christianity had long been influenced by both Augustine's "pessimistic" emphasis on sin and Benedict's "optimistic" stress on joy in common life.

According to Thornton, Anselm was the father-founder of a peculiarly English spiritual synthesis that developed six characteristics by the fourteenth century. Thornton claims it was then instantiated in the Book of Common Prayer and refined by the Caroline divines.

---

7. Martin Thornton, *English Spirituality: An Outline of Ascetical Theology according to the English Pastoral Tradition* (1986; repr., Eugene, OR: Wipf and Stock, 2012).

1. *A speculative-affective synthesis.* This was the refusal to accept a false dichotomy between theology and piety, which is why the English embraced theology as prayer and accepted only that piety which was grounded in church doctrine. It is "the insistence that prayer, worship, and life itself, are grounded upon dogmatic fact, that in everyday religious experience head and heart are wedded."[8] We see this spiritual harmony in Anselm's treatises, such as the *Prosologion* and *Cur Deus homo*, offered as prayerful dialogues between himself and God. "In Anselm, there is neither rationalism nor arrogant humanism, but a respect for human reason as the ally of faith and the promoter of love."[9] The same synthesis can be seen in Julian of Norwich (1342–ca. 1416) whose reflections as a vernacular theologian were remote from the scholastic mediations of Anselm. Yet, in her *Revelations of Divine Love*, where "every distressing detail of the Passion [is related to] almost a treatise on the doctrine of the Atonement," one can see the same conjunction of intellection and affection.[10]

2. *Unity of the church militant.* This is the deep, "family" relationship between prominent church leaders and their most humble parishioners. Benedict was famous for seeing the Christian community not as an army but as a family. This helped the English Church avoid the extremes of clericalism seen elsewhere in Europe. In his *Scale of Perfection*, Walter Hilton (ca. 1343–1396) wrote that active laymen could be just as spiritual as, or even more spiritual than, priests or monks or nuns. Margery Kempe (ca. 1373–ca. 1439), the weeping mystic, was not afraid to disobey priests and bishops if she felt their directives were opposed to church doctrine or biblical teaching. Long before Luther's teaching of the priesthood of every

---

8. Thornton, *English Spirituality*, 49.
9. Thornton, *English Spirituality*, 159.
10. Thornton, *English Spirituality*, 49.

believer, Anglicans were convinced that ordinary believers, and not just clergy, make up the real church.

3. *A unique humanism and optimism.* This is the biblical virtue of hope in the midst of the perplexing details of everyday life. It maintains cheerfulness despite setbacks because it knows that God loves his people and will bring them to victory in the end. Kempe's pilgrimages to Jerusalem and Europe were marked by her tears for Christ's passion, but she shared Julian of Norwich's all-conquering hope: "All shall be well, and all shall be well, and all manner of thing shall be well."[11] Julian's joy went back to Benedictine optimism, rooted in the vision of life as God's family worshiping together and enjoying the beauties of creation.

The Christian humanism of the English spiritual tradition comes out of its Celtic roots. The Celtic church stressed the need for every Christian to receive spiritual direction, and regular private confession was integral to that. But according to Thornton, Celtic confession was different from the Roman penitential tradition. While the latter was juridical and taught that a mortal sin would cut a believer off from God entirely, the Celtic church treated confession and penance as steps on a pilgrimage of love. Sins were not venial or mortal, but from malice or weakness. Rather than final breaks with eternal life, serious sin was treated as an obstacle to progress that needed repentance and remediation. Instead of seeing the confessional as providing legal return to grace, the Anglican tradition treats it as "an expression of penitential love."[12]

---

11. Julian of Norwich, *Showings*, chap. 15 in the short text, ed. Edmund Colledge OSA and James Walsh SJ (New York: Paulist, 1978), 151.

12. Julian, *Showings*, 103. It has long been known that private penance with its concomitant handbooks originated in Ireland, Wales, and Cornwall (Rob Meens, "The Historiography of Early Medieval Penance," in *A New History of Penance*, ed. Abigail Firey [Leiden: Brill, 2008], 74). Kate Dooley argues that the Celtic contribution to the sacrament of penance was to change the focus from penance to confession (Dooley, "From Penance to Confession: The Celtic Contribution," *International Journal for Philosophy and Theology* 43, no. 4 [1982]:

4. *Liturgy as the foundation of Christian life.* Thomas Cranmer is justly recognized as a liturgical genius. His marriage of beauty and adoration in corporate prayer is one of the sparkling jewels that have attracted millions to the Anglican tradition. But Cranmer did not start from scratch. He adopted much of the medieval prayer services—"the same canticles, the same prayers, the same dialogues [call and response between leader and people]."[13] He affirmed the purpose of the services—to soak Scripture in the corporate prayer of the church—while taking them outside the monastery to the congregation.[14] The result was what a liturgical scholar has called "one of the purest forms of Christian common prayer to be found anywhere in the world."[15]

Already in the fourteenth and fifteenth centuries the great English spiritual writers—Rolle, Hilton, Kempe, and Julian—were convinced that church liturgy, both in the Daily Office and in the Sunday Eucharist, was foundational to spirituality. They taught Spirit-inspired prayer throughout the day, but all insisted that the best individual prayer arose from contemplation on Scripture in the liturgy and that corporate liturgical worship was an indispensable means of grace, apart from which individual prayer would go astray.[16]

390–411). For a fuller account of the history of penance, see O. D. Watkins, *A History of Penance* (London: Longmans, Green, 1920).

13. Jesse D. Billett, "A Spirituality of the Word: The Medieval Roots of Traditional Anglican Worship," *Pro Ecclesia* 27, no. 2 (Spring 2018): 159. Billett argues that a "spirituality of the Word" in which Scripture is received as God's word in the midst of the worship of the church goes back to the Gregorian chants of the sixth century and that these chants are "ultimately, the origin of the harmonized recitation tones of Anglican chant." Billett, "A Spirituality of the Word," 163.

14. Billett, "A Spirituality of the Word," 174.

15. Louis Bouyer, *Liturgical Piety* (Notre Dame, IN: University of Notre Dame Press, 1955), 47. By this, Bouyer seems to mean that the services are performed not by specialists but by the people, and the whole Bible is read in an accessible way "in its traditional context of praise and prayer" (46–47).

16. The contrast between individual and corporate prayer was not seen as sharply as it is today in our individualistic era, but they repeatedly referred individual spiritual concerns

In the seventeenth century, which Thornton calls the golden age of Anglican preaching, there was new attention to Scripture. Lancelot Andrewes (1555–1626) was responsible for the production of a major part of the Old Testament in the King James Bible: Genesis to 2 Kings. The beauty of diction in the creation and the fall, Abraham and Isaac, the exodus, David's laments for Saul and Jonathan and Absalom, Elijah and the still small voice—all were his. Andrewes's sermons did not have the emotional impact of Jeremy Taylor's or the drama of John Donne's, but they were prized for their meticulous use of Scripture. As T. S. Eliot described them, "[In his sermons we see Andrewes] squeezing and squeezing the word until it yields a full juice of meaning."[17]

Yet, for all these Anglican thinkers, Scripture apart from liturgy and sacrament lacked a certain power. Of course Scripture by itself has power, but when read in the midst of corporate praise and prayer, it displays *more* of its meaning and power. This stands to reason because Scripture was written for and by the church (both Jewish and Christian), and has always taken its primary meaning and use from the church's worship. As Jeremy Taylor (1613–1667) put it, liturgy that reads Scripture amid worship is "the most excellent instrument, and act, and ligament of the Communion of saints."[18] When later Puritan critics complained that liturgy forced Anglicans to pray in words that don't always correspond to their own lives, as in the canticles of Zechariah, Mary, and Simeon, Richard Hooker (1554–1600), who was almost an exact contemporary of Andrewes, replied that biblical words can transform us no matter our situation: when we recite them "our minds are daily more and more inured

back to church liturgies. They could not imagine a spiritual life apart from regular participation in the church's liturgy and sacraments.

17. T. S. Eliot, "Lancelot Andrewes," in *Selected Prose*, ed. Frank Kermode (London: Faber, 1975), 184.

18. Jeremy Taylor, *An Apology for Authorized and Set Forms of Liturgie: Against the Pretence of the Spirit* (London: R. Royston, 1649), 32, http://anglicanhistory.org/taylor/apology.html.

with their affections."[19] In other words, Scripture read in the midst of corporate prayer and praise takes on new meaning and power.

5. *Habitual recollection*. This means reflecting during the day on the Scripture portions from the daily or weekly liturgies. Julian wrote that prayer is founded on facts, not moods. It should spring from meditation on the great stories of the Bible and doctrines of the church.[20] Margery Kempe was continually reflecting on scenes from the Gospels as she walked the streets of Lynn and Norwich, traveled the roads of England and Europe, and sailed on ships as a pilgrim. It was this habitual recollection that provided the fodder for visions that reduced her to tears. Her weeping was often directed heavenward as intercessory prayer, which was repeatedly and remarkably answered in visible ways.[21]

6. *Spiritual direction*. This is the English tradition of getting spiritual guidance from an individual who is further along the pilgrim road. This tradition began with the Celtic days of English Christianity and continued under Benedictine influence. Anselm was a renowned spiritual guide. So were Kempe, Julian, and all the Caroline divines. Thornton himself was a famous spiritual director, known for leading retreats and personally guiding many Anglicans.

This combination of characteristics, collectively called "English spirituality" by Thornton, was developing in the English isles centuries before the Reformation gave it further refinement.

The Most Beautiful Liturgy in the English Language

If the Anglican tradition developed its own spirituality, it is perhaps best known for its liturgy. The "sombrely magnificent prose" of the Book of Common Prayer has attracted legions of admirers all

19. LEP, 5.40.3.
20. Julian, *Showings*, chap. 42 in the long text, 252.
21. Anthony Bale, ed. *The Book of Margery Kempe* (Oxford: Oxford University Press, 2015).

around the world.[22] It reflects the liturgical genius of Thomas Cranmer, but it also provides moderns access to the worship of the early church. Cranmer and the many other hands that produced the BCP were adapting a basic catholic pattern of worship derived from the first few centuries of the church and then developed over the course of the Middle Ages. So if Cranmer and later bishops produced a way of worshiping in the "beauty of holiness," it was because they were refining and reforming a great tradition of worship that had been delivered into their hands from the early church and even before.

The origins of this historic liturgy go back to what Jonathan Edwards called "the Jewish church."[23] For example, there was an entrance rite in the temple liturgies, based on Psalm 122:1:

> I was glad when they said to me,
>   "Let us go to the house of the LORD!"

Temple prayer services three times a day (not to mention Torah reading and preaching in the synagogue) provided patterns for early Christian prayer and preaching. Temple worship that was focused on daily sacrifices, culminating in the Passover sacrifice, was the fundamental background for the Last Supper and the later Eucharistic celebrations.

The two basic parts of Christian liturgy—the liturgy of the word and the liturgy of the Table—are based on these two fundamental features of Jewish worship: synagogue worship focused on Torah and prayer, and temple services centered in sacrifice.[24]

Soon after the closure of the New Testament, a pattern of worship was developing that has been refined but not replaced in the

---

22. Eamon Duffy, *The Stripping of the Altars: Traditional Religion in England 1400–1580* (New Haven, CT: Yale University Press, 1992), 593.

23. Jonathan Edwards, *A History of the Work of Redemption*, ed. John F. Wilson, vol. 9 of *The Works of Jonathan Edwards* (New Haven, CT: Yale University Press, 1989), 192, 226–28.

24. Hans Boersma and Matthew Levering, eds., *The Oxford Handbook of Sacramental Theology* (Oxford: Oxford University Press, 2015), 7–82.

last two thousand years. What we see in Justin Martyr's description of worship in word and sacrament (AD 150) is remarkably similar to what can be seen in the 1662 BCP—still the only official Anglican Prayer Book in the Church of England, the mother church for the Anglican Communion—and in most, if not all, Anglican churches today.[25]

What did the fathers believe was happening in this liturgy? Why did they think it was necessary? At one level, they saw it as the church's Spirit-guided answer to the disciples' request of Jesus "Lord teach us to pray." It was the Lord's solution to the problem stated by Paul in Romans 8:26: "We do not know what to pray for as we ought."

The liturgy helped explain why God struck down Nadab and Abihu when they offered unholy fire (Lev. 10:1–2). These young men presumed they could figure out on their own how to worship, rather than recognizing that God had already given precise instruction on how Israel was to worship. David drew the same conclusion after he tried to bring the ark to Jerusalem and Uzzah was struck dead for touching the ark, which had been forbidden (Num. 4:15): "The LORD our God broke out against us, because we did not seek him according to the rule" (1 Chron. 15:13).

But the fathers, of course, added a Christological dimension to liturgy. They conceived of the early church's liturgy as worship that joins in Christ's human worship of his Father, since the Son is the only perfect worshiper of the Father. But it is also the *church's* worship, and so our *participation* with Christ, by the Spirit, in his offering himself and his body (the church) to the Father in adoration.[26] The letter to the Hebrews tells us that the Messiah is still ("now")

---

25. For Justin's descriptions in his *First Apology* and *Dialogue with Trypho*, see Maxell E. Johnson, ed., *Sacraments and Worship: The Sources of Christian Theology* (Louisville: Westminster John Knox, 2012), 184–86.

26. Boersma and Levering, *Oxford Handbook of Sacramental Theology*, 130–33, 151–53, 158–62, 171–79.

offering his own blood before the throne of the Father (9:14, 24), not like the high priest who offered himself repeatedly "with blood not his own" (9:25). And the book of Revelation suggests that we, the body of the Messiah, are joined with him as he offers his once-for-all Calvary sacrifice to the Father in the presence of the saints and angels in their celestial worship (Rev. 4–5).[27]

By the late medieval period the church's liturgy, especially in its understanding of the Eucharist, came to be seen as something Christians contributed to their own salvation. Some thought the priest was resacrificing Christ on the altar. Cranmer and other Reformers rightly protested.

Cranmer also objected to the gradual disappearance of the Bible from daily liturgy. In his preface to the first Prayer Book (1549), Cranmer wrote that the fathers had intended for most of the Bible to be read through in church each year, but this was not happening. So many "uncertain stories, Legendes" and others things were being recited that books of the Bible such as Isaiah and Genesis were only started and "never read thorow." Besides, he wrote, Saint Paul wanted people to be spoken to in their own language, but because Latin was used so widely, they "have not been edified thereby." And only a few of the Psalms were being used in the English churches at the beginning of the sixteenth century.[28]

Cranmer's principal purpose was to make the prayers and Scriptures "plain and easy to be understanded." Rather than many liturgical books being used—usually in ways hard to understand—one book would be used with "few rules." And rather

---

27. E. L. Mascall explains that because Christ's manhood was taken into heaven and, as John saw, the Lamb as it was slain is before the throne of the Father, that perfect act of human worship has not ceased. Christ united our human nature to his so that we may participate in that worship by being his body, which means in turn that he offers his offering in and through us. Mascall, *Christ, the Christian and the Church* (1946; repr., Peabody, MA: Hendrickson, 2017), 160–62.

28. Thomas Cranmer, preface to *The First and Second Prayer Books of King Edward the Sixth* (London: Dent, 1910), 3.

than different regions of England using different liturgies (Sarum [Salisbury], Bangor, Yorke, etc.), now all would use the same "common" prayer.[29]

Cranmer was also concerned for comprehensiveness, yet deliberately ambiguous on controversial issues so that those with different views could feel included. According to Gordon Jeanes, Cranmer's language was a "verbal incense that offered an attractive religious haze but no clarity of meaning."[30] In the Communion prayer, for example, there are commendations for "the departed": "Grant them thy mercy," which could be understood in two ways. It was either a prayer to help those who have died or a proclamation that God would apply his mercy at the end of a life.[31] The prayer of consecration was also carefully worded: The "sacrifice" was "once offered" and so was not on the altar.[32] Another concession to new Protestant influences were the rubrics (instructions) that the priest was not to show the sacrament to the people or to elevate the host.[33] But as a concession to those who appreciated more traditional understandings, the priest was to pray that the people "maye worthely receive the most precious body and bloude of thy sonne Jesus Christe . . . and bee . . . made one bodye with thy sonne Jesu Christe."[34]

Another sign of accommodation to previous practice was the burial of the dead. It avoids any mention of purgatory and so leans toward a Protestant inclination; but, in a nod to the tradition, the priest prays that the departed's sins not be imputed to him, that he may escape "the gates of hell and paynes of eternall derkenes . . .

29. Cranmer, preface, 4

30. Gordon Jeanes, "Cranmer and Common Prayer," in *The Oxford Guide to the Book of Common Prayer*, ed. Charles Hefling and Cynthia Shattuck (New York: Oxford University Press, 2006), 28.

31. 1549 BCP, 30.

32. 1549 BCP, 30.

33. 1549 BCP, 31.

34. 1549 BCP, 31.

[and] ryse also with the just and righteous . . . [and that God might] set him on the right hand of thy sonne Jesus Christ."[35]

Riots broke out in certain parts of the country after this first prayer book was imposed on the parishes throughout the land. The disorders were led by conservatives who resented these changes. Among other things, they wanted "prayers for the souls in purgatory by name, 'as our forefathers dyd.'"[36] But there were also political motivations for people outside London who had long resented taxes and other changes legislated from afar. This was a match that lit a long-smoldering tinderbox.

A More Protestant Prayer Book in 1552

Martin Bucer, the continental Reformer, analyzed the 1549 BCP in print and was displeased by what he took to be "the benediction of material objects."[37] He thought it placed too much spiritual value on things of matter such as bread and wine. Cranmer was influenced by this critique, and the 1552 revision was the result.

The 1552 edition of the BCP was substantially more Protestant by being more verbal and less visual, marked by "an aversion to sacramental and ritual elements."[38] It placed more emphasis on repentance and thanksgiving. Its famous "black rubric" (added at the last minute and therefore in black rather than red ink) allowed kneeling but forbade adoration of the host and an understanding of a "real and essential presence" of the body and blood in the sacrament. All references to the saints and departed were removed. The 1549 words of administration for the sacrament ("The body of our Lord Jesus Christ which was given for thee . . .") were dropped and replaced by

---

35. 1549 BCP, 88.

36. Introduction to The Book of Common Prayer: The Texts of 1549, 1559, and 1662, ed. Brian Cummings (Oxford: Oxford University Press, 2011), xxxi.

37. F. Procter and W. H. Frere, A New History of the Book of Common Prayer (London: Macmillan, 1901), 573, quoted by Cummings, introduction to The Book of Common Prayer, xxxii.

38. Cummings, introduction to The Book of Common Prayer, xxxiii.

"Take and eat this, in remembrance that Christ died for thee, and feed on him in your heart by faith, with thanksgiving."

The new Communion liturgy made clear that the presence of Christ is not in the sacrament but only in the heart of the believer. There were no manual acts by the priest, no fraction or elevation. Music was virtually abolished. The rest of this BCP was stripped of other Catholic practices. There was no allowance for private confessions. Nor was there any hint of prayer for the dead in the burial office.[39]

Apparently, Canterbury was moving faster than the conservative populace. The 1552 BCP was unpopular everywhere. It was in use only eight months when young Edward VI died and Mary assumed the throne in 1553.[40]

Almost immediately Mary deauthorized the Book of Common Prayer and reinstituted the Sarum Rite, which was the Catholic liturgy in use before Cranmer's first Prayer Book. For five years she tried to return England to its pre-Reformation Catholic state. But her death in 1558 brought to the throne her sister Elizabeth, who liked much of what she had seen in Cranmer's Prayer Book.

Elizabeth's Attempt at Balance in 1559

Elizabeth's revision of the Prayer Book a year after her accession was more conservative, rejecting many of the most Protestant elements of the 1552 BCP. For example, the words of administration of the Eucharist combined those of 1549 ("the body of our Lord Jesus Christ") and 1552 ("Take and eat in remembrance . . ."). The black rubric was dropped, and music was officially encouraged during Communion.

The Puritans had advocated for the "regulative principle," that nothing should be included in Christian worship that cannot be

---

39. William Sydnor, *The Prayer Book through the Ages*, rev. ed. (Harrisburg, PA: Morehouse, 1997), 20–22.

40. Sydnor, *Prayer Book through the Ages*, 23.

found explicitly in Scripture.[41] The Puritans also wanted the removal of anything that resembled Roman practice, even if it might be found in Scripture, such as the use of wafer (unleavened) bread. They campaigned against the surplice (a white linen vestment worn by clergy), the sign of the cross in baptism, kneeling at Communion, the ring in marriage, the veil in churching, bowing at the name of Jesus, and the use of organs and "over-refined" music.[42] Because these were either spelled out in the new Prayer Book or employed in churches that used it, the Puritans were unhappy with the 1559 BCP. They also objected to the new translation of the Bible (KJV) when it was proposed to King James I in 1604. They had grown attached to the Geneva Bible of 1560 with its Calvinist notes.

The Only Official Anglican Prayer Book for England: 1662

After the death of Cromwell (1658) and the restoration of Charles II in 1660, the Presbyterians tried to get rid of the Prayer Book altogether. In 1661 the new king called a conference at Savoy to try to resolve the conflict, appointing twelve Presbyterians and twelve bishops. The Presbyterians lobbied for many changes, but the bishops accepted very few of them. In the new Prayer Book that was approved in 1662, the "priest" and not the "minister" gives absolution in both Morning Prayer and Evening Prayer, and petition is made for "bishops, priests, and deacons" rather than for "bishops, pastours [sic], and ministers." The black rubric was restored but changed. Instead of saying that kneeling is not intended to imply

---

41. Some might object that when Anglicans point to the deaths of Nadab, Abihu, and Uzzah as warnings against worship innovation, as I suggested above, they practice their own kind of regulative principle. But while reformed use of the regulative principle insists on explicit biblical precept or precedent, traditional Anglicanism allows for development. David, for example, introduced music to the mostly silent sacrifices in Mosaic law. Traditional Anglicans also worship according to the historic liturgical tradition, which allows for development beyond New Testament proof texts. For David going beyond Mosaic practice, see Peter Leithart, *From Silence to Song: The Davidic Liturgical Revolution* (Moscow, ID: Canon, 2003), esp. 11–30.

42. Sydnor, *Prayer Book through the Ages*, 32.

a doctrine of "real and essential presence there being of Christ's natural flesh and blood," it now read that "no adoration is intended . . . unto any Corporal Presence of Christ's natural Flesh and Blood." In other words, the Eucharist did not contain the real presence of his *earthly* preresurrection body, but this did not rule out a real *sacramental* presence of Christ's body and blood.

Other changes to the 1662 BCP restored traditional understandings. Throughout the book "congregation" is changed to "church." The usages to which the Puritans had most vociferously objected were retained: use of the Apocrypha (intertestamental books such as Wisdom and Sirach) in the Daily Offices; a traditional form of the Litany (petitions at special times of the year); vestments; kneeling at Communion; the sign of the cross at baptism; the giving of a ring at marriage; a prayer of absolution for the sick "if he feel his conscience troubled" and makes confession; and the declaration in the baptismal liturgy for infants that God regenerates the infant "with thy holy Spirit." A strong view of the real presence of Christ's body and blood in the Eucharist can be seen in the Prayer of Humble Access ("Grant us therefore . . . so to eat the flesh of thy dear Son . . . and to drink his blood"), the words of administration ("The body of our Lord Jesus Christ, which was given for thee" and "The bloud of our Lord Jesus Christ, which was shed for thee"), and the post-Communion prayer ("We most heartily thank thee, for . . . the spiritual food of the most precious body and bloud of thy Son our Savior Jesus Christ").

A Realist Sacramental Theology

This version of the Prayer Book is "still the official Book of the Church of England."[43] It set both Presbyterianism and Roman

---

43. Sydnor, *Prayer Book through the Ages*, 51. Rowan Williams calls it "the touchstone for the ethos and even, for hundreds of years, the unity of a whole church." Williams, foreword to Hefling and Shattuck, *Oxford Guide to the Book of Common Prayer*, xiii.

Catholicism outside the bounds of mainstream Anglicanism.[44] Though reset more than a century after Cranmer's martyrdom, its cadence is still Cranmerian in its spiritual profundity and literary artistry. But while its sacramental theology is sharply non-Roman, its catholicity goes beyond what Cranmer allowed. In this higher view of the sacraments, the 1662 BCP is consistent with the Thirty-Nine Articles. The sacraments, we are told in Article 25, are "not only badges or tokens of Christian men's profession" but also "effectual signs of grace . . . by the which [God] doth work invisibly in us." Baptism is

> a sign of regeneration or New Birth, whereby, as by an instrument, they that receive Baptism rightly are grafted into the Church; the promises of the forgiveness of sin, and of our adoption to be the sons of God by the Holy Ghost, are visibly signed and sealed. . . . The Baptism of young children is in any wise to be retained in the Church, as most agreeable with the institution of Christ. (Art. 27)

Transubstantiation is rejected, but the real presence of the humanity of Christ, "after an heavenly and spiritual manner," is not. Communion for those who receive "rightly, worthily, and with faith . . . is a partaking of the Body of Christ; and . . . a partaking of the Blood of Christ. . . . The Body of Christ is given, taken, and eaten, in the Supper" (Art. 28).

Cranmer, then, gave the Anglican tradition a liturgy that is the envy of the Christian world in its beauty and profundity. The bishops who gave the Communion its standard version of the BCP and the convocation that produced the final version of the Articles in 1571 delivered to the English Church a sacramental

---

44. Sydnor, *Prayer Book through the Ages*, 50–51. The Act of Uniformity was issued on August 24, 1662, which dissenters called Black Bartholomew's Day because it resulted in the ejection of perhaps twenty-five hundred ministers from their pulpits.

theology that is not Roman but is closer than earlier versions of the Prayer Book to what was common among the fathers in the church's first five centuries.

A Distinctive Theological Method

How did this happen? The biggest clue can be found in Anglicanism's most foundational theologian, Richard Hooker, and his most characteristic method: to read the Bible and understand the tradition while sitting at the feet of the fathers.[45] In his classic *Of the Laws of Ecclesiastical Polity*, which has justly been called Anglicanism's *Summa*, Hooker principally battled Puritans who thought the Anglican way had imported too much extrabiblical baggage from Catholic worship. Over and over again Hooker appeals to the fathers of the church to support Anglican liturgical worship. For example, in book 5 he cites Jerome's defense of special vestments for ministers and their ceremonies against Pelagius's complaint that "the glory of clothes and ornaments was a thing contrary to God and godliness." Jerome asked, "If a Bishop, a Priest, a Deacon, and the rest of the ecclesiastical order come to administer the usual sacrifice in a white garment, are they hereby God's adversaries?" Hooker adds, "By which words of Jerome we may take it [that he meant Pelagius was] condemning by so general a speech even the neatness of that very garment itself, wherein the clergy did then use to administer publicly the holy Sacrament of Christ's most blessed Body and Blood."[46]

Puritans also criticized the reading of long passages of different Scriptures in the same Anglican worship service, sometimes without a sermon or with only a short sermon. Hooker went, for

---

45. In one sense, the fathers *are* the best of tradition. But when Hooker, for example, argued with the Puritans about the tradition of using set prayers and the sacramental traditions that the Prayer Book mediated, he went to the fathers often for support and interpretation. In that sense he read both the Bible and the tradition at the feet of the fathers.

46. LEP, 5.29.2.

justification, to Cyprian's observation that people are blessed simply by hearing God's word read.[47]

Hooker turned to the fathers 774 times in his *Laws*, as often to the Latin as to the Greek and African fathers, but Tertullian and Augustine were his favorites. He appealed to the great bishop of Hippo ninety-nine times, either to justify an Anglican practice or to interpret a controverted passage of Scripture.[48] In one of his most important arguments against Puritans, for example, Hooker argued against the regulative principle that everything in church government and worship must have an explicit biblical—preferably New Testament—command. Augustine recognized, according to Hooker, that while the most important Christian doctrine is clear in Scripture to those willing to see, many matters of church polity and worship are either unclear or not addressed. Therefore, church leaders are free to use reason and charity to keep traditional practice that does not violate the clear teaching of Scripture. Hooker quotes Augustine, "The custom of the people of God and the decrees of our forefathers are to be kept, touching those things whereof the Scripture hath neither one way or other given us any charge." Then Hooker offers this interpretation: "St. Augustine's speech therefore doth import, that where we have no divine precept, if yet we have the custom of the people of God or a decree of our forefathers, this is a law and must be kept." This is not, for Hooker, tradition simply for the sake of tradition—keeping what was done in the past because change is anathema. No, it is a recognition of what could be called the providential ordering of Christian faith and worship, and a sense that there was a divine rationality in the ways that worship unfolded over the centuries, even if there was also need for continual attention to how Scripture and reason should guide that unfolding.

---

47. LEP, 5.22.13.

48. John K. Luoma, "Who Owns the Fathers? Hooker and Cartwright on the Authority of the Primitive Church," *Sixteenth Century Journal* 8, no. 3 (1977): 57.

According to Nigel Atkinson, two things convinced Hooker that God had ordered the gradual unfolding of Christian tradition. First, humility:

> For Hooker . . . it is presumptuous to think that God would reveal unto a few what he has not revealed unto many. Again and again Hooker writes in this vein, insisting that Christians should not "lightly esteem what hath been allowed as fit in the judgment of antiquity, and by the long continued practice of the whole Church; from which unnecessarily to swerve, experience hath never as yet found it safe."[49]

Second, Hooker's deep "historical sense." His "refusal to concede that the Church had utterly fallen and become totally corrupt enables [sic] Hooker to regard the Church's development as being directed, controlled and under the hand of God."[50] The Anglican theologian saw the development of both liturgy and the church over a millennium and a half and believed there was a divine impetus behind much, if not all, of it. This made it all the more important to listen to the wisdom of the fathers in its first critical centuries.

The fathers were necessary for Hooker because he saw Scripture operating at different levels. At its highest are the things that "Scripture plainly doth deliver." Then there are deductions made from Scripture by "force of reason." But "after these the voice of the Church succeedeth" because there are many things in church life that Scripture does not explicitly address (LEP, 4.14.5). Here, as C. S. Lewis put it, "it is in Hooker's nature to listen to this voice very lovingly—to 'uniform practice throughout the whole world' (7.9.2), 'the use of the people of God' or 'ordinances of our fathers' (3.11.15)

49. Nigel Atkinson, *Richard Hooker and the Authority of Scripture, Tradition and Reason* (Carlisle, UK: Paternoster, 1997), 53; the Hooker quote is from the *Laws*, 5.7.1.

50. Atkinson, *Richard Hooker and the Authority of Scripture*, 53.

which it would be 'heathenish petulancy' to 'trample under foot' (5.65.9)."[51]

Now, Hooker did not accept every tradition, nor did he agree with the primitivist conviction that the earliest is always the best (LEP, 5.20.4). For circumstances change, and the shape of tradition sometimes must be adjusted to accommodate new contingencies. But, as Lewis saw, Hooker would countenance adjustment "only of order not doctrine, the one mutable, the other not, because truth does not change and convenience does (5.8.2)."[52]

Hooker set a pattern that the best Anglican thinking has followed ever since—interpreting Scripture and church tradition with the help of the fathers. He recognized that there is no such thing as Scripture without tradition, that every person reads Scripture through some tradition or other, whether she or he realizes it or not. Even Jehovah's Witnesses, proud proclaimers of *sola Scriptura*, use a hermeneutical tradition—in their case, one that interprets Christological passages in an Arian framework. So the question is not *whether* we use tradition to understand Scripture but *which* tradition has informed our interpretation. Hooker used sixteen hundred years of Patristic, medieval, and Reformation tradition for his interpretation but privileged the Patristic tradition.

Lewis points out that while previous English controversialists used tactics, Hooker was the first to add strategy.[53] His principal Puritan opponent, Thomas Cartwright, claimed to find only Puritan worship in the New Testament, but Hooker showed that Cartwright was cherry-picking the New Testament and advocating worship

---

51. C. S. Lewis, *English Literature in the Sixteenth Century* (Oxford: Oxford University Press, 1973), 456.

52. Lewis, *English Literature in the Sixteenth Century*, 455.

53. Lewis, *English Literature in the Sixteenth Century*, 459. By this he means that long before he fights the Puritans in close quarters in book 5, he has already undermined their position in books 1 and 2 by asking and answering questions they never considered, but which "are fatal to their narrow scripturalism." The result is that his final refutation of their position is "a very small thing, a by-product" of what was a long-developing argument.

practices that could not be found there. In other words, Cartwright was using Puritan tradition, not Scripture alone, to draw Puritan conclusions about worship. The Puritans who criticized Anglicans for using tradition to interpret Scripture and order worship were using their own tradition to read the Bible and order their worship. Hooker turned the tables on them and established a method that many later Anglican thinkers used to great profit: interpreting the Bible and ordering their lives and worship after Patristic patterns.

To sum up the descriptive portion of this chapter, Anglicans have a distinctive spirituality, a unique liturgy, a robust sacramental theology, and a traditional method of interpreting the Bible and church. So, what shall orthodox Anglicans do with these? How ought they move into the future?

Tendencies within Modern Evangelicalism

Anglicanism is reformed catholicism, where the second word means not Roman Catholicism but the undivided universal (hence catholic) church of the first millennium. "Reformed" refers to the Reformation emphasis on Scripture to correct, principally but not solely, semi-Pelagian tendencies in the late medieval period. We have just seen that the greatest Anglican theologian of the sixteenth century, Richard Hooker, read Scripture and tradition at the feet of the fathers. Likewise, Martin Luther, the most famous progenitor of *sola Scriptura* as a theological method, appealed to Augustine and other fathers, especially against late medieval theology.

When Luther used the term *sola Scriptura*, he meant something quite different from what many evangelicals mean today. For those with an individualistic bent, the term means something closer to *solo Scriptura* or *nuda Scriptura*: reading the Bible not only *for* themselves but *by* themselves, stripped of theological tradition as if learning from the ancient creeds and fathers were methodologically wrong and necessarily corrupting. Many believers today assume that all they need is the Holy Spirit guiding their minds to understand and apply the word of God. Who needs tradition?

The problem is that they use tradition every bit as much as Hooker and Luther did, but often without realizing it. They read the Bible through the lens of their own recent traditions, which often conflict with what Luther or Calvin or even Edwards and Wesley—the founders of classical evangelicalism—taught. Unaware of the influence of their own pasts, many evangelicals are equally unaware of how twenty-first-century Western culture slants their readings of Scripture. For example, many are convinced that God opposes all hierarchies because they are also sure that equality in Christ (Gal. 3:28) means what Western culture means by "equality" today. But it is clear that New Testament authors considered hierarchies in church and society to be part of the way God lovingly orders the world and his people.

The same individualistic tendency can truncate one's notion of having a "personal relationship with Jesus." Jesus told us that eternal life is knowing him and his Father, and Paul said that faith involves knowing God as our Father—as *abba*. Evangelicals have rightly interpreted this as an affective experience of knowing that we are forgiven and loved in an ongoing way by the Creator of the universe. That is a stupendous message, one that reflects the teaching of the fathers, as well as the Reformers and classical evangelical theologians. But starting (principally) with Schleiermacher, who came from an evangelical pietist tradition, this experience of personal relationship started to be seen as the only necessary ingredient in a proper knowledge of God. Specific, even creedal, doctrine about God and his Son was considered nonessential. So was connection to the church. Of course, Schleiermacher granted that knowledge of Christ was principally mediated by the church, but at the end of the day what really counted was having warm fuzzies for Jesus. Church membership and particular beliefs did not—finally—matter. Ironically, this is core *doctrine* for legions of evangelicals today: that only a personal relationship with Jesus matters. Everything else is manmade and therefore negotiable.

If a personal relationship is all that matters for millions of evangelicals, that relationship is often seen as *casual*: Jesus called his disciples "friends" and came from heaven to relate to us as someone "closer than a brother," so he must be like us, someone to treat like a buddy. The formality and reverence of traditional worship seem inauthentic and off-putting. Worship services begin to have a nightclub atmosphere, featuring the latest music styles, a charismatic personality up front, low lighting, and the latest trends in contemporary culture. Sermons are therapeutic, teaching their audiences how to cope with problems or succeed in life.

The gospel preached in many churches differs from that preached by Wesley and Edwards. For the two eighteenth-century evangelical progenitors, the good news is salvation from sin, death, and the devil by the life, death, and resurrection of Jesus Christ, accessible to sinners through the church's word and sacrament.[54] Where there is no steady diet of word and sacrament, a believer is left with a distant memory of a conversion experience and a fading sense of gratitude in the face of ongoing temptation. But what if I find that I cannot break free from a serious sinful habit? What if I no longer *feel* forgiven? Is my faith saving faith or only historical faith? The result can be either a Pelagian striving to prove my gratitude or hopelessness and despair when I repeatedly fail. Feeling condemned, some resort to a new antinomianism that preaches cheap grace without the cost of discipleship. Others jump to a new universalism that says discipleship is unnecessary because all will be saved.

---

54. Edwards was less sacramentally and liturgically inclined than Wesley, but both were far more concerned for church and sacrament than the kind of evangelicalism-lite that is prevalent today.

Some take a more sophisticated approach to the gospel, proclaiming a gospel message similar to that of Wesley or Edwards, but without those divines' use of liturgy and sacrament. They tend to make the sermon the center of worship, and it is often long and complex. Those with keen theological interest and training revel in this approach. But worshipers who are not intellectually inclined—the young and many older believers—have a difficult time. The risk is a new intellectualism that appeals only to the head and the ear. Where is the recognition that the gospel is made for all five senses, and for those who are not cognitively gifted? For the mentally impaired? Can the gospel be offered to them if they cannot follow a sermon crafted for the learned? What about the *drama* of the gospel? Can it be *shown* to those who cannot understand much intellectually? Can it be presented in ways they can see and smell and taste—and act out? Can they take the gospel into themselves in a material way and not just observe it or understand it from a distance? Can it fill their bodies and souls and not just their heads?

The Anglican Alternative

Good answers to all these questions are provided in the historic Anglican tradition. It testifies that the gospel comes to all senses: to the eye, by watching the drama of salvation as enacted by the whole church—clergy and laity—in the liturgy; to the ear, by hearing the whole biblical word read in a multiyear cycle and preached every week; to the nose, by smelling both the fermented grape that captures the blood of Christ and the incense, representing prayers offered up; to the touch, by feeling the ashes on the forehead on Ash Wednesday and the rough wood of the cross on Good Friday; and to the taste of wine and bread every Eucharist.

This is how the gospel comes to children who cannot understand adult sermons, and to the Down syndrome Anglicans and grandmothers with Alzheimer's. They watch sacred actions and beautiful vestments that convey not information but beauty and power. They too can taste and process and recess and call out and bend down in reverence. They too can be marked with ashes in quiet one day in the church year, and kneel and stand and sit on every day in that year, and shout for joy at Easter. They can join the clergy in confessing sins and proclaiming creedal faith, and reply to clergy, who need their response for proper worship. In other words, they too participate in the adoration of the Son before the Father by the Spirit. They are not spectators watching the "real" actors, the clergy, but are part of the people of God whose every member participates in the great thanksgiving of body and soul and matter that Christ uses to enact his redemption of the world.

This means that Anglicans have a unique tradition that frees them to pursue that "holiness apart from which no one will see the Lord" without feeling guilty of works righteousness. It enables them to join worship imbued with a sense of awe and mystery that is absent from so many churches. It gives them a Eucharist in which they are given not only the divinity of Christ but also his risen humanity—the whole Jesus Christ—which fills them with more of the divine nature (2 Pet. 1:4), helps unite the body of Christ around the world, and contributes to the Messiah's ongoing redemption of the world. Its liturgy frees them from ignorance and futility in prayer by joining them to the Son's prayer by the Spirit in the historic church's adoration of God. Finally, it provides Anglicans the fullness of the gospel in all its beauty and power.

Power

Saint Paul wrote, "We do not know what to pray for as we ought" (Rom. 8:26). We all have times when we don't know what to pray, either because we don't know others' needs or we don't know how to express our own thoughts. Then there are those times when our prayers seem to bounce off the ceiling. The power of Anglican prayer in the Daily Office and Sunday liturgy is that it distills the best of the early church's prayers as they developed over time, and, more importantly, it shares the traditional conviction that these prayers participate in the prayers of the Son to the Father. After all, it is the prayer of the church, which is the body of the Son. So, no matter how we feel, we can know that we are praying profoundly biblical and majestic prayers that are purified by participating in the Son's intercession before the Father's throne (Heb. 7:25). That is power for us in our weakness.

The sacraments, especially the Eucharist, convey power. What can be more powerful than sharing in the body and blood of Christ (1 Cor. 10:16)? On those days when we feel especially vulnerable and powerless, it is great comfort to know that in taking Communion we are taking in the risen Christ's very humanity and thereby growing as "partakers of the divine nature" (2 Pet. 1:4). This helps combat the hopelessness and despair of Christians who try to muster up holiness from within. In the sacrament Christ comes to them from *outside* them in a material, tangible way. It is a great comfort.

There is another kind of power in the Eucharist—that of being lifted up out of linear time and entering sacramental time as we become contemporaries of Jesus in his passion and resurrection. Just as Jews in their Passover liturgy refer to the present, not the past— "We *are* passing through the Red Sea"—so too in the sacrament we participate in Christ's present offering of his own life (Rom. 5:10) and passion to the Father for the sake of the church. This is why the letter to the Hebrews speaks of Christ "now" appearing "in the presence of God on our behalf" (9:24) with his once-for-all blood sacrifice of himself (9:14, 26).

The sacrament of baptism displays yet another kind of power. What a thrill to see a new baby who has just come into this frightening world, absolutely helpless, a few days later receiving the Holy Spirit in baptism to transform its tiny little soul! This baptism by the Holy Spirit does not guarantee that this baby will later embrace this divine inheritance by faith, but it confers powerful advantages to the baby nonetheless—nothing less than being "born of water and the Spirit" (John 3:6)! That is power.

Beauty

But there is also beauty in Anglican liturgy and sacrament. The colors of the church change throughout the church year. Clerical vestments, including multicolored chasubles, are designed to represent the beauty of God in all of his attributes, especially in the work of redemption. The drama of redemption is enacted every week as the church processes in from the world to listen to Jesus speak and to be fed by his sacramental body and blood. In the Eucharistic rite the church recalls the history of salvation as it prepares to feast at the Lord's Table. Then the church recesses back out into the world, newly filled and inspired to bear witness in the world. The gospel is not only heard in the reading and preaching of the Word but also seen and enacted in the sacrament. In the enacted drama of the liturgy and pageantry of sacrament, the church not merely remembers God's past redemptive acts but also mysteriously participates in their enactment. The past becomes present.

The Bible speaks of "the beauty of holiness" (Ps. 96:9 KJV). There is beauty in the holy sacraments and the story of salvation. But there is also a sense of holiness and mystery in Anglican liturgy and sacrament. There is the palpable recognition of a special divine presence when the church joins the prayers of the ages in the liturgy and participates in the Messiah's own body and blood. Worshipers know this is the time to "be still, and know that I am God" (Ps. 46:10). They see and sense beauty in this holy awe.

Conclusion

Anglicanism without the beauty and power of its liturgy and sacraments will become just another evangelical alternative. It might continue to use the "Anglican" moniker, but it will be indistinguishable from many nondenominational networks that are denominations by another name. It will not be able to compete with its flashy competitors on the other side of town with more exciting youth programs and sermons tied more directly to the latest cultural trends. People will wonder why they should be Anglican when they can get pretty much the same thing elsewhere without the name.

But if Anglicans retrieve their ancient heritage of liturgy and sacrament, they will have something unique to offer this new century when the "beauty of holiness" is resonant in ways it has not been for centuries. And catholic Anglicanism that retrieves the best of Catholic worship with the best of the Protestant preaching tradition will be attractive to Romans who are now looking elsewhere.

10

A BAPTIST THEOLOGIAN

Reflections on Anglicanism

Timothy George

My task is to write about Anglicanism and the Baptist way, but I want to begin with a question of context: Why is this book coming out of a conference that took place at Beeson Divinity School? Beeson is not an Anglican seminary. Our charter documents call for us to be Christian, Protestant, evangelical, and interdenominational. We also like the words "catholic," "orthodox," "Reformational," and "ecumenical." Beeson is a place where Baptists and Anglicans alike, along with believers from many other denominations, have been able to find koinōnia in our core commitment to Jesus Christ and in our love for his body, the church—the one, holy, catholic, and apostolic church. Furthermore, I am not an Anglican. I have been called an Anglo-Baptist, a label not always intended as a compliment. In fact, I am a Baptist—indeed, a Southern Baptist (the worst kind, according to some!).

Still, look around Beeson and you will find Anglicans every-where—not only among students and faculty, including the An-glican Chair of Divinity, and in the Institute for Anglican Studies, which organized that conference, but also in our curriculum and especially in the art and iconography of Hodges Chapel. Among the six martyrs memorialized here in statuary, one from each of the six inhabited continents, there are two Anglicans, Archbishop Janani Luwum from Uganda and the missionary nurse May Haman from Australia. Among the four preachers staring out at confer-ence attendees from our pulpit is George Whitefield, an Anglican who was at once an evangelist and a Calvinist. And if you tilt your head upward into the dome of our chapel, you will find portrayed there on the mural a very interesting array of sixteen saints—our students call them the "Sweet Sixteen." There you will find Martin Luther standing right next to Thomas Aquinas, the only painting I know of where the definitive theologian of medieval Catholicism and the seminal Reformer of magisterial Protestantism are depicted standing shoulder to shoulder. Just one niche over on the mural is Thomas Cranmer. He stands not between Luther and Aquinas, so he does not represent a true *via media*, but is nonetheless close enough to both the Reformer and the Schoolman to signify that all three hold something in common. Close by in the dome is yet another Anglican, John Wesley, who for all the formative influence he wielded as the founder of the Methodist church, remained a priest of the Church of England until the day he died, as did his brother Charles.

At Beeson we practice an ecumenism of conviction, not an ecu-menism of accommodation. There are various ways to think about this approach to Christian unity. One was offered by Count Ludwig von Zinzendorf, the founder of the Moravians. He compared the worldwide Christian community to different "tropes" or tropical zones, at various latitudes and diverse climates, which nonetheless constitute one single globe.[1] Others have found an analogy for the unity we seek in the diverse religious orders within Roman Catholicism, very different and sometimes at odds with one another—Benedictines, Augustinians, Franciscans—each order with a unique charism to offer the entire Christian community.

Anglicans and Baptists can best contribute to the renewal of the church in our time not by downplaying or negotiating away our real differences in the interest of a bland, shallow togetherness but rather by drilling down deep within each of our traditions, until at last we come to that common font of Christian life and spiritual wisdom which Richard Hooker—I think he coined this term—referred to as "the essence of Christianity."[2] Whatever Hooker meant by this expression, it echoes the epistle of Jude's counsel to the early Christians when the writer urged them "to contend for the faith that was once for all delivered to the saints" (Jude 3). This principle also resonates in an important question posed by Anglican bishop and theologian Stephen Sykes: "Have we got to the point where theologians have a greater concern for nice denominational distinctions than for the very faith itself?"[3] But can two groups, Anglicans and Baptists, which seem to be at opposite ends of the ecclesial spectrum, talk meaningfully about "the faith" once delivered, or indeed about "the essence of Christianity"?

Some have thought not, including D. Michael Doty, who in 1995 published an essay in the *Sewanee Theological Review* titled "The Episcopal Church and the Baptist Tradition: A Comparison of Faith Perspectives."[4] Using as his template the four principles found in

1. John Joseph Stroudt, "Count Zinzendorf and the Pennsylvania Congregation of God in the Spirit: The First American Oecumenical Movement," *Church History* 9, no. 4 (December 1940): 378.

2. LEP, 3.1.4.

3. Stephen Sykes, *Unashamed Anglicanism* (Nashville: Abingdon, 1995), ix.

4. D. Michael Doty, "The Episcopal Church and the Baptist Tradition: A Comparison of Faith Perspectives," *Sewanee Theological Review* 38, no. 2 (1995): 137–54.

the Chicago-Lambeth Quadrilateral of 1888—the Bible, the creeds, the sacraments, and episcopacy—Doty presents Baptists and Anglicans as polar opposites.

According to Doty, Baptist adherence to the Bible is filtered through the twin principles of soul competency and the priesthood of the individual believer. This leaves no room for the corporate understanding of scriptural authority, nor for the creation of a "common mind" in the context of Christian community. Interpretation of the Bible is left entirely to the individual. On the second point, Baptists, Doty claims, are not a creedal people, and so the classic creeds of the church have no purchase as expressions of the church's faith. Third, there are no sacraments in the Baptist tradition; baptism and the Lord's Supper are reduced to memorial rites. Finally, since Baptists have no bishops, any discussion of apostolic authority or the historic episcopate is a nonstarter. However, Doty's essay reflects a thin, even superficial reading of the Baptist tradition and must be set over against more balanced, robust, and historically nuanced tellings of the Baptist story across time. To this must be added two developments that have become more prominent in the quarter century since Doty wrote his essay.

The first of these involves serious ecumenical conversations between Anglicans and Baptists that have resulted in surprising convergence in key areas. In addition to a number of local and national conversations that have occurred, an international bilateral dialogue between the Anglican Communion and the Baptist World Alliance took place between 2000 and 2005. The results of this dialogue are recorded in the report *Conversations around the World*.[5]

---

5. The Anglican Consultative Council and the Baptist World Alliance, *Conversations around the World 2000–2005: The Report of the International Conversations between the Anglican Communion and the Baptist World Alliance* (Falls Church, VA: Baptist World Alliance, 2005), https://www.bwanet.org/images/pdf/baptist-anglican-dialogue.pdf. See also *Pushing at the Boundaries of Unity: Anglicans and Baptists in Conversation* (London: Church House, 2005).

The second development is a reclaiming of Baptist tradition, especially its catholicity, seen in the writings and work of a number of younger theologians. Of special note here is the Center for Baptist Renewal, whose principal participants identify as Southern Baptists. They hold to a high view of biblical inspiration and authority and also clearly affirm traditional Baptist distinctives, such as the necessity of personal conversion, regenerate church membership, believers' baptism, congregational church governance, and religious freedom. But they also promote the ongoing affirmation, confession, and catechetical use of the three ecumenical creeds and the doctrinal insights of the first seven ecumenical councils. Liturgical worship is important to this group, and they propose incorporating historic practices such as lectionary readings, the liturgical calendar, the corporate confession of sin, the assurance of pardon, and both public and personal use of confessions and creeds. They also recognize the use of sacramental language in early Baptist history to refer to both baptism and the Lord's Supper (more often called "ordinances"), which they define as signs and seals of God's grace, not *nuda signa* or bare symbols but rather tangible demonstrations of "our union with the risen Christ and with his Body, the church." They also commit themselves to what might be called a chastened ecumenism, seeking Christian unity across ecclesial and denominational lines. They encourage "a critical but charitable engagement with the whole church of the Lord Jesus Christ, both past and present."[6] Both of these trends—serious bilateral theological dialogue at the level of world Christian communions and a deliberate retrieval for the sake of renewal—offer an opportunity for Baptist and Anglican engagement seldom if ever seen before in the more than four hundred years of our shared but contested history.

---

6. R. Lucas Stamps and Matthew Y. Emerson, "Evangelical Baptist Catholicity: A Manifesto," Center for Baptist Renewal, accessed August 21, 2018, http://www.centerforbaptist renewal.com/evangelical-baptist-catholicity-a-manifesto/.

At this point, we must introduce the elephant in the room—intraconfessional fragmentation within both Anglican and Baptist traditions. A generation ago, Princeton sociologist of religion Robert Wuthnow pointed out that differences *within* denominations are more pressing, more critical, and often more church-dividing than historic differences *between* denominations.[7] Michael Doty's 1995 portrayal of the Baptist tradition was thus not entirely off the mark. He was reporting what he had seen and heard within his limited circle of Baptist acquaintances, a Baptist ethos characterized by modern rugged individualism and accommodated to the consumerist culture of postmodern America, but sadly out of touch with the deeper wellsprings of historic Baptist church life. The Baptist divide, no less than the Anglican one, is deep and wide. I can introduce you to Baptists who would make Bishop Spong look like a traditionalist, and to others who would make the Reverend Ian Paisley seem like an untethered progressivist!

In his book *The Identity of Anglicanism*, the noted ecclesiologist Paul Avis told the story of two of his friends from England who spent the weekend with some business associates in America. On Sunday morning, their hosts invited them to church. "We're Episcopalians," the host family explained. "How about you?" "Oh, we're Church of England," they replied. "That's all right," was the response. "We may be different religions but I guess we both worship the same God."[8] In our present ecclesial moment, however, it may be necessary to reverse that statement: "We may be the same religion, but do we worship the same God? Do we follow the same Jesus Christ? Do we proclaim the same gospel?"

---

7. Robert Wuthnow, *The Struggle for America's Soul: Evangelicals, Liberals, and Secularism* (Grand Rapids, MI: Eerdmans, 1989), 24.

8. Paul Avis, *The Identity on Anglicanism: Essentials of Anglican Ecclesiology* (London: Bloomsbury T&T Clark, 2007), 1.

In our official Anglican-Baptist dialogues, we have assumed that the answer to those questions is yes. Based on that assumption, we have pushed at the boundaries of ecclesial identity in four major areas, *faith, liturgy, mission,* and *unity,* corresponding to the four Nicene attributes of the church, *one, holy, catholic,* and *apostolic.*

The Faith Once Delivered

It is important to note that the Baptist movement, no less than Methodism, although at an earlier time and in a different way, emerged from the womb of Anglicanism. In the early seventeenth century, both General and Particular Baptists—that is to say, those who leaned toward Arminianism in their view of salvation and others who were Calvinistic in their soteriology—arose over against, and in opposition to, the established Church of England.[9] Thus, Baptists have rightly been seen as nonconformists, a part of the tradition of dissent. This fact accounts for the virulence of our controversies at times, but also for the underlying commonality in the strand of our ecclesial DNA. It was Lancelot Andrewes who summed up the position of the Anglican Church as holding to one canon, two testaments, three creeds, four general councils, and five centuries.[10] While this is an Anglican rather than a Baptist way of putting it, it is clear that early Baptist pastors and teachers, some of whom had been former Anglican priests, affirmed *ex animo* the Trinitarian and Christological consensus of the early church, as well as the normative authority of Holy Scripture, which William Perkins, a Puritan who never left the Church of England, called "our rule and

---

9. For a good overview of Baptist history, see David Bebbington, *Baptists through the Centuries: A History of a Global People,* 2nd ed. (Waco, TX: Baylor University Press, 2018); Anthony Chute, Nathan Finn, and Michael Haykin, *The Baptist Story: From English Sect to Global Movement* (Nashville: B&H Academic, 2015); H. Leon McBeth, *The Baptist Heritage: Four Centuries of Baptist Witness* (Nashville: Broadman, 1987).

10. "*Nobis Canon unus in Scripta relatus a Deo, Duo Testamenta, Tria Symbola, Quatuor Priora Concilia, Quinque saecula. . . .*" Lancelot Andrewes, *Opuscula quaedam posthuma,* Library of Anglo-Catholic Theology (London: Parker, 1850), 91.

square where by we are to frame and fashion all our actions."[11] Likewise, Baptists confessed justification by faith alone as the central soteriological doctrine of the Bible. These teachings are enshrined in the Thirty-Nine Articles of Religion, reduced by Queen Elizabeth from Cranmer's original forty-two. The Thirty-Nine Articles are still published in the Book of Common Prayer, though seemingly in increasingly smaller print with each successive edition. The Thirty-Nine Articles have been called "conscientiously eclectic,"[12] and that might be true, but they still bear up well in comparison to other Reformation confessions. The Articles have no official standing in the Baptist tradition, but they can be read as a progenitor of seventeenth-century Baptist statements of faith, especially the First London Confession of 1644 and the Second of 1677/1689.

While some Anglicans claim to be creedal but not confessional, and some Baptists want to be neither creedal nor confessional, pointing to the Bible alone as the sufficient witness to the gospel of Jesus Christ, the fact is that both traditions have confessed the faith—the faith once delivered to the saints—in the classic words of the Great Tradition. Even those Baptists who eschew creeds still use the language of the creeds when they refer to the triune nature of God, or to the person and work of Jesus Christ.[13] On occasion, Baptists have made explicit reference to the historic creeds. For example, the 1678 Orthodox Creed, a General Baptist confession of faith, not only affirmed but actually incorporated the entire texts of the Apostles', Nicene, and Athanasian Creeds. This confession declared that these historic standards should be "thoroughly received

---

11. William Perkins, *The Work of William Perkins*, ed. Ian Breward, Courtenay Library of Reformation Classics (Abingdon, UK: Sutton Courtenay, 1970), 464.

12. Marion J. Hatchett, "Prayer Books," in *The Study of Anglicanism*, rev. ed., ed. Stephen Sykes, John Booty, and Jonathan Knight (Minneapolis: Fortress, 1998), 137.

13. See, for example, Steven R. Harmon, *Towards Baptist Catholicity: Essays on Tradition and the Baptist Vision*, Studies in Baptist History and Thought (Eugene, OR: Wipf and Stock, 2006). See also Curtis W. Freeman, *Contesting Catholicity: Theology for Other Baptists* (Waco, TX: Baylor University Press, 2014).

and believed, for we believe that they may be proved by most un-doubted authority of Holy Scripture and are necessary to be under-stood of all Christians."[14] Likewise, in 1905, at the inaugural meeting of the Baptist World Congress in London, the entire assembly arose and recited the Apostles' Creed "as a simple acknowledgement of where we stand and what we believe."[15] This same act was repeated one hundred years later at the centennial of the Baptist World Alli-ance in Birmingham, England.

So, are Baptists a creedal people? Insofar as Baptists have writ-ten and promulgated numerous confessions of faith using the construals of the historic creeds (whether acknowledged or not), and have on occasion declared their faith in the very words of the classic creeds, and have even spoken in an affirming way of "the Baptist Creed" (a phrase used by Andrew Fuller, B. H. Carroll, and E. Y. Mullins, among others), they can rightly be called creedal.[16] In another sense, however, Baptist have never advocated *creedalism*. As good Protestants, Baptists invariably declare that the Bible alone remains the *norma normans* for all teaching and instruction, "the su-preme standard by which all human conduct, creeds, and religious opinion should be tried."[17] Baptists have never "canonized" any of their confessions, but rather have held them all to be revisable in the light of the Bible, God's definitive, unchanging revelation. Baptists have also forged a distinctive witness as advocates of unfet-tered religious freedom. Thus Baptists of all theological persuasions have opposed state-imposed religious conformity and the atten-dant civil sanctions associated therewith. God alone is the Lord of

---

14. "The Orthodox Creed," in *Baptist Confessions, Covenants, and Catechisms*, ed. Timothy George and Denise George (Nashville: Broadman and Holman, 1996), 120.

15. Harmon, *Towards Baptist Catholicity*, 9.

16. Steve Harmon, "Baptist Confessions of Faith and the Patristic Tradition," *Perspectives in Religious Studies* 29, no. 4 (Winter 2002): 349–58.

17. "The 2000 Baptist Faith and Message," Southern Baptist Convention (website), http://www.sbc.net/bfm2000/bfm2000.asp.

the conscience, Baptists have confessed, echoing the Westminster Confession of Faith, and thus civil magistrates have no legitimate authority to regulate or coerce the internal religious life of the people of God. With this very important caveat about the improper use of creeds, however, the idea that voluntary conscientious adherence to an explicit doctrinal standard is somehow foreign to the Baptist tradition is a notion not borne out by careful examination of the Baptist heritage.[18]

The Worship of God in the Beauty of Holiness

One of the great gifts of the Anglican tradition to the worldwide body of Christ is the practice of ordered worship and liturgical life expressed so beautifully in the Book of Common Prayer. Today, more and more Baptists are finding rich resources for devotion and praise in this classic text. One of the features I most admire about the Book of Common Prayer is the note of compunction and penitence that pervades its litanies and supplications. My friend Frank Limehouse, the former dean of the Cathedral Church of the Advent in Birmingham, Alabama, used to always sign his letters to me, "miserable offender." The first time I received such a letter, I wondered what horrible thing he had done to offend me so! But when I saw this refrain at the end of all his letters, I realized that this is exactly the posture we should bring before God every day of our lives. We are miserable offenders against the holiness and majesty of the God who dwells in light inaccessible. "Against you, you only, have I sinned," said the psalmist (Ps. 51:4).

Nowhere is this perspective better seen than in the Prayer of Humble Access. Some years ago, I was a part of a Eucharistic service of worship in Norwich Cathedral. I noted in the service that the

---

18. Timothy George, in *Southern Baptists Observed: Multiple Perspectives on a Changing Denomination*, ed. Nancy Tatom Ammerman (Knoxville: University of Tennessee Press, 1993), 288.

Prayer of Humble Access had been omitted. Afterward, I asked the Anglican bishop who was with me what this meant, and he replied, "Oh, we are trying to get rid of all that groveling!" Well, perhaps a little groveling is just what we need these days, especially when we consider the gravity of our sin and the holiness of the God with whom we have to do. But the Book of Common Prayer does not leave us in the pit of abject groveling. It directs us instead to the God "whose property is always to have mercy," the God of abundant love and amazing grace, the God who spared not his own Son but freely gave him up for us all on the cross (Rom. 8:32). In the remarkable words of Archbishop Cranmer, God provided there "(by his one oblation of himself once offered) a full, perfect, and sufficient sacrifice, oblation and satisfaction for the sins of the whole world."[19] This is why the Eucharist is called "the most comfortable Sacrament of the body and blood of Christ."[20]

Now, Baptists in the seventeenth century opposed the Book of Common Prayer for three reasons: (1) the inclusion of infant baptism, which they did not find in the Bible; (2) the imposition of what they call "stinted" prayers, prefabricated prayers that did not come from the heart and that seemed to quench the spontaneous moving of the Holy Spirit; and (3) the assumption that civil magistrates—the monarch and Parliament—should be the ones to mandate legally and enforce such prayers for the people. However, today, all three of those objections have to be qualified for, in some ways, they have become antiquated.

Infant baptism is still not practiced by Baptists, and we cannot easily speak of a "common baptism" because, as Baptists see it, what happens in the baptism of an infant and what happens in the baptism of a person who has repented and believed are not the same. But Baptists, no less than Anglicans, do want to claim the Pauline

---

19. 1662 BCP, 402.
20. 1549 BCP, 24.

triad: *one* Lord, *one* faith, *one* baptism. Not a common baptism, but *one* baptism. And that *one* baptism is in the name of the Father, and the Son, and the Holy Spirit. When baptism in the name of the holy Trinity happens, a new ontological space is created. A new situation arises, one that allows us as brothers and sisters in the Lord, across this denominational divide, to recognize one another as members together in the body of Christ. On this same basis we may even identify our churches as faithful believing communities of faith.

As to the second objection about the free flowing of the Spirit and no stinted prayers, it is important to consider the charismatic movement's influence on worship in both Anglicanism and the Baptist tradition.[21]

And, finally, Baptists are still committed to religious freedom. It is one of the steady constants in our tradition and is more relevant today than ever before, but it is a freedom not only *from* but also a freedom *for*—freedom for faithful discipleship and mission. For example, Baptists fight for the freedom of Christians (many of whom are Anglicans) to live and worship in the face of Muslim persecution in countries like Nigeria. That is the way forward on the path of Christian unity.

Into All the World

Both Baptists and Anglicans are missionary peoples. Today's thriving Anglican churches in the Global South, especially those affiliated with provinces connected to GAFCON, trace their origin to the Protestant missionary movement that marked the "long" nineteenth century (1789–1914). At the headwaters of this age of intense evangelization, church planting, and mission was the remarkable English Baptist shoemaker-pastor William Carey. Baptized as an

---

21. On "free worship" as practiced in Baptist churches, see Christopher J. Ellis, *Gathering: A Theology and Spirituality of Worship in the Free Church Tradition* (London: SCM, 2004).

infant in the Church of England, Carey was converted under the ministry of a Congregationalist pastor but embraced the Baptist cause and was baptized in the river Nene at the age of eighteen. In 1792, Carey published *An Enquiry into the Obligation of Christians to Use Means for the Conversion of the Heathen*. In this manifesto, he challenged his fellow Baptists, as well as believers of other denominations, to carry the gospel into every corner of the world, especially to those who had never heard the name of Christ. The following year, Carey and his family, which included a nursing infant, set sail for India, where he would stay for the rest of his life (d. 1834), forging a remarkable career as educator, reformer, journalist, evangelist, horticulturalist, and Bible translator. Carey is often called "the father of modern missions," though he was well aware that others had blazed the trail before him. In his *Enquiry*, Carey placed his own work in the worthy succession of many other missionary pioneers, including Saint Patrick, the Protestant Reformers of the sixteenth century, and the Moravians, whose work he particularly admired.

The missionary awakening under Carey, as remarkable as it was, did not occur in isolation. Carey's worldwide vision was supported with great vigor by Anglican leaders who, no less than the Baptists, were inspired by the Evangelical Revival in England. In 1799, the Church Missionary Society was founded. Anglicans and Baptists, while still differing on important matters, collaborated closely in efforts to translate the Scriptures, plant churches, and proclaim the gospel throughout the world. Charles Simeon, Anglican vicar of Holy Trinity, Cambridge, strongly supported Carey's mission and distributed widely his letters and journal entries. Simeon himself also inspired an entire generation of missionary adventurers, chief among whom was Henry Martyn, an Anglican priest who traveled to the East, where he met Carey in India. Of his friendship with Martyn, Carey wrote that "as the image or shadow of bigotry is not known among us here, we take sweet counsel together, and go to the house of God as friends."[22] Although he died at the age of thirty-one, Martyn completed a translation of the New Testament in Urdu and did significant work on the New Testament in Persian and Arabic as well.

One of the first Anglican bishops to arrive in India was Reginald Heber, remembered today as a great hymn writer. He too forged a close friendship with Carey and longed for the union of Anglican and Baptist churches.

> Would to God, my honoured brethren, the time were arrived when not only in heart and hope, but visibly, we shall be one fold, as well as under one shepherd! . . . If a reunion of our churches could be effected, the harvest of the heathen would ere long be reaped, and the work of the Lord would advance among them with a celerity of which we have now no experience.[23]

William Wilberforce, legendary Anglican member of Parliament, was another key figure in the Anglican-Baptist alliance. Baptists in England supported Wilberforce's campaign to abolish the British slave trade. They gathered signatures for him to present to Parliament. At his behest, Baptists also joined in the boycott of sugar and other West Indian products that depended on slave labor. For his part, Wilberforce met with Carey before the latter's departure for India and maintained a cordial correspondence with him across the years. Of great importance was Wilberforce's support of the 1813 parliamentary act to remove the legal sanctions against the sending of missionaries to British India. In making his case for the India Bill, Wilberforce spoke in praise of Carey's

---

22. Stephen Neill, *A History of Christian Missions*, vol. 6 of *The Penguin History of the Church* (New York: Penguin, 1991), 266.

23. Reginald Heber, in George Smith, *Bishop Heber, Poet and Chief Missionary to the East: Second Lord Bishop of Calcutta, 1783–1826* (London: John Murray, 1895), 255–56.

"beneficent labors" in bringing Christianity to India.[24] Wilberforce remained a convinced Anglican and did not always side with Baptists and other nonconformists in matters of public dispute. However, he, like Simeon, embodied an ecumenical spirit that valued cooperation over competition. This enabled them to give hearty support to the work of missions around the world. This ecumenical spirit is evident in a letter of 1824 addressed by Wilberforce to another prominent Baptist leader, John Ryland:

> I must indulge the strong disposition I feel to thank you for your last friendly letter and to express the cordial gratification with which I welcome and I trust I can truly say, I return, your Catholic Christian sentiments and feelings—I cannot tell you how much I delight in them. They seem to unite us more closely than if our opinions were on all points the same and so they are on all points of any importance—for I cannot think that those about which Churchmen and Dissenters differ are *in themselves* of any *essential* value.[25]

On the Foundation of the Apostles

The church is not only one, holy, and catholic; it is also apostolic, a word added to the Nicene description of the church in 381 but clearly expressed already in Paul's metaphor of the church as "the household of God, built on the foundation of the apostles and prophets, Christ Jesus himself being the cornerstone" (Eph. 2:19–20). That church is apostolic which stands under the direction and normative authority of the apostles, whom Jesus chose and sent forth in his name. Baptists, no less

---

24. Timothy George, *Faithful Witness: The Life and Mission of William Carey* (Birmingham, AL: New Hope, 1991), 1.

25. William Wilberforce to John Rylands, 1824, quoted in "An Evangelical Anglican Interaction with Baptist Missionary Society Strategy: William Wilberforce and John Ryland, 1807–1824," in *Interfaces. Baptists and Others: International Baptist Studies*, ed. David Bebbington and Martin Sutherland (Milton Keynes, UK: Paternoster, 2013), 82.

than Anglicans, claim to be apostolic in this sense, but the two traditions have differed sharply on the way in which they understand the transmission of the apostolic witness from the first century until now.

In an essay titled "Why Baptist and Not Episcopalian," published in the year 1900, Baptist pastor J. J. Taylor identified "the historic episcopate" as a major point of contention between the two denominations.[26] One hundred and twenty years later, the issue remains unresolved despite significant progress and much ecumenical goodwill on both sides. This impasse stems from the fact that Baptists do not define apostolicity in terms of a literal lineal succession of duly ordained bishops who alone have authority to ordain other ministers. Instead, Baptists define apostolicity in terms of the primordial character of the gospel, the inscripturated witness of the apostles, and the succession of apostolic proclamation. For most Baptists, the New Testament word *episkopos* refers to the pastor of a local congregation, raised up by the Holy Spirit and duly called and ordained by the believing community to serve the people of God.[27]

If Anglicanism can be described as catholicism without the pope, Baptists might be said to embody *episkopē* without episcopacy. Ruth Gouldbourne has argued that when early English Baptists repudiated bishops in their day, what they rejected was not oversight as such but rather episcopacy as an arm of state power. Baptist advocacy for religious freedom stood over against a theology

26. J. J. Taylor, "Why Baptist and Not Episcopalian," in *Baptist Why and Why Not*, ed. J. M. Frost (Nashville: Sunday School Board of the Southern Baptist Convention, 1900), 81–108.

27. It is nonetheless true that some Baptists in the world, especially in Eastern Europe, have used the word "bishop" to designate a person who supervises Baptist work in a given translocal region or country. For example, in Latvia and Moldova there are Baptist bishops, and in Georgia (in the Caucasus) there are both Baptist bishops and a Baptist archbishop. But these are the exceptions that prove the rule overall. See Ruth Gouldbourne, "Episcope without Episcopacy: Baptist Attitudes to Bishops in Seventeenth-Century England," in Bebbington and Sutherland, *Interfaces. Baptists and Others*, 29–46.

of establishment with bishops as instruments of persecution and harassment.[28]

Baptists rejected the church-state nexus as it was established in seventeenth-century England (no bishop, no king), but they did not repudiate the theological idea of oversight as useful and necessary in the life of the church. For Baptists, the church is a covenanted community of baptized disciples who, led by the Holy Spirit, agree to walk together in love, to watch over one another, and to seek the mind of Christ together. Jesus Christ himself is Prophet, Priest, and King, not only over the entire body of Christ extended through time as well as space (what some have called the "invisible church") but also within each local community of believers. Pastors, elders, and deacons have a distinctive role to play in the oversight of God's people, as indeed does the entire gathered assembly as it meets together in prayer to seek the mind of Christ. Beyond this, *episkopē* among Baptists is also recognized in the wider spheres of associations, and regional gatherings in districts or states, and conventions and unions at the national level.

Anglicans and Baptists have different church structures reflecting our different understandings of both Scripture and tradition. But is it possible to recognize a genuine spiritual concern for oversight despite our differing polities and church structures?

One of the most hopeful exchanges between Anglicans and Baptists on this issue took place in Great Britain in the dialogue between the Faith and Unity Executive Committee of the Baptist Union of Great Britain and the Council for Christian Unity of the Church of England. Out of this ecumenical dialogue came the report *Pushing at the Boundaries of Unity: Anglicans and Baptists in Conversation*. After reviewing questions of apostolic succession, church governance, and ordination, the report offered this hopeful conclusion:

---

28. Gouldbourne, "Episcope without Episcopacy."

Despite the differences in structure and theology, there is a growing convergence in theological reflections on ministry and oversight. This offers the hope that it might be possible to recognize the authenticity of each other's forms of ministry in the same way as recognizing each other's processes of initiation into the Christian life: that is, within the concept of a common pattern rather than looking for symmetry in structure and practice.[29]

Conclusion

At the end of his well-known study of Anglicanism, Bishop Stephen Neill expressed his hope that Anglican churches will not "unduly or selfishly cling to their Anglican life in separation." At the same time, he acknowledged that the path to full visible unity among various Christian denominations is slow and arduous and cannot be accomplished in haste. Neill wrote,

> It seems plain that for a long time yet, the Anglican Communion will have to continue to be, since God still has work for it to do in separation, with a view to that blessed union of all Christian people, which all the Anglican churches firmly believe to be the will of God for the Church which is the body of his Son.[30]

What Neill declared about Anglican churches is equally true of Baptist ones. Throughout their history, Baptists have been far less engaged in ecumenical plans and initiatives than have their Anglican brothers and sisters, but we long for the day when we see fulfilled the prayer of Jesus that his disciples will be one as he and the heavenly Father are one (John 17:21). In the meantime, the ecumenical principle set forth by the 1952 Faith and Order Conference of the

---

29. *Pushing at the Boundaries of Unity*, 86.
30. Stephen Neill, *Anglicanism* (London: Mowbray, 1977), 406.

World Council of Churches held in Lund, Sweden, offers good guidance to both Baptist and Anglican communities of faith. The Lund Principle calls on all believers united in faith to Jesus Christ to act together in concert "in all matters except those in which deep differences of conviction or church order compel us to act separately."[31]

---

31. *An Episcopal Dictionary of the Church*, ed. Don S. Armentrout and Robert Boak Slocum (New York: Church Publishing, n.d.), https://www.episcopalchurch.org/library/glossary /lund-principle.

11

A CATHOLIC THEOLOGIAN

Reflections on Anglicanism

R. R. Reno

The classical definition of Anglicanism as a *via media* between Protestantism and Catholicism suits well. It captures the best of Anglicanism and its potential as a template for the future of Christianity after Christendom. It also evokes the worst aspects of Anglicanism: the spineless, muddling middle way that encourages a managerial mentality and gives rise to a false peace without principles. But let's leave the failures aside. I want to talk about the promising aspects of the Anglican genius, not its flaws and failures.

The Protestant principle in Anglicanism is not theoretical, as is often the case for other forms of Protestantism, especially Calvinism. Anglicanism does not frame a theory of church corruption (alleged Catholic teachings of works righteousness, idolatry, etc.), and then work back to a rigorous program for purifying and re-

newing the church. There are no normative theologians or special
doctrines in Anglicanism. Some point to Richard Hooker, but his
example actually reinforces my observation. The *Laws* amount to an
ad hoc restatement of basic doctrine and analysis of specific church
issues conducted with Calvinist concepts detached from Calvinist
theology. It's unimaginable for an Anglican to proceed as some Lutherans do, proposing the doctrine of justification as the church's
central and organizing affirmation. In a word, the Protestant aspect
of Anglicanism is not "theological," which is why Anglicanism, although rich in theological reflection, has produced no systematic
theologians of note.

The Protestant aspect of Anglicanism is best understood, therefore, in twofold fashion. The first concerns the susceptibility of
the church to corruption, even in her most basic functions. This is
expressed in Article 21 of the Thirty-Nine Articles, which states that
the general councils of the church can err. The church tradition
is therefore subject to reform, which, given fallen human nature,
must be ongoing. *Ecclesia semper reformanda est*—the church must always be reformed—as Karl Barth put it. This theological judgment
underwrites an activist sensibility, one dedicated to renovation and
renewal.

Anglicanism lacks an authoritative theological system. It lacks
even focusing, identity-defining dogmas. Combined with the
Protestant principle of ongoing reform, this relative absence of an
authoritative theology (very uncharacteristic of Protestantism in
general) has made Anglicanism a uniquely vibrant, creative (and
diffuse) form of Protestant Christianity. Anglicanism has a well-
earned reputation for complacency. This is the flaccid, all-things-
to-all-people *via media*. But that is only part of the story. It also
spawned modern Christian revivalism (Baptist movements, John
Wesley, and Methodism), and modern Protestant ritualism (the Oxford Movement and its legacy).

The practice of returning to the apostolic sources, *ad fontes*, constitutes the second Protestant dimension of Anglicanism. Although the Bible looms large, apostolic authority in Anglicanism cannot be reduced to the principle of *sola Scriptura*. Instead, Anglicanism is characterized by a prejudice in favor of the old. This preference for "what came before" is not undifferentiated. Lancelot Andrewes drew up a general statement of the multiple layers of the apostolic deposit: "One canon reduced to writing by God himself, two testaments, three creeds, four general councils, five centuries, and the series of fathers in the period—the centuries, that is, before Constantine, and two after, determine the boundary of our faith."[1]

This enlarged view of apostolic authority protected Anglicanism from vulnerability to modern historical criticism, at least in large part, and thus also from the reactions to that vulnerability as found in biblical literalism and other forms of conservative Christian modernism. It also stimulated a rich tradition of learned churchmanship informed by deep knowledge of the church fathers. Today, many Protestant churches seeking a postliberal or postmodern form of biblical authority are following in the paths long trod by Anglican divines.

A differentiated acceptance of the authority of "what came before" is also manifest in the Book of Common Prayer, which, after the Bible, has been the single most influential document in Anglicanism. The Prayer Book adopts the principle of reform. Cranmer was genuinely Protestant in his effort to provide a vernacular and theologically purified language for common worship. But his apostolic loyalty had an elongated character. The Prayer Book's adaptation of medieval liturgies indicates a conviction that the charisma of the apostolic age remains living and active down the centuries of Christian practice. The Bible's authority is magnified, not dimin-

---

1. Lancelot Andrewes, *Opuscula quaedam posthuma*, Library of Anglo-Catholic Theology (Oxford: Parker, 1852), 91.

ished, by its historical embodiments. They are to be reformed, yes, but also preserved. Today, this Anglican sentiment of honoring the sacred character of "what came before" has become normative for many Protestants who hail from historically austere and iconoclastic traditions as they seek a density of language and worship in our post-Christian age.

Many observers confuse the Anglican deference to "what came before" with the Catholic side of the *via media*. This misconstrues what "catholic" means after the Reformation. At first glance, the Roman Church contrasts with the Protestant churches on questions of authority. There is truth in this, but it misleads, not looking deeply enough into the Catholic reaction to the Reformation. The Council of Trent turns on vigorous affirmations of the visible, this-worldly efficacy of salvation in Christ. These affirmations reflect a worry that the Protestant *sola fide* and iconoclasm reflect an undue pessimism about what God can accomplish in this world to sanctify those born again in Christ. Whether or not the Tridentine-era Catholic judgments about Protestantism are accurate or not can be debated. What's indisputable is the fact that the Church of Rome responded to the Reformation by doubling down on affirmations of the this-worldly efficacy of grace.

Put simply, the Catholic principle stipulates that after the apostolic age God "takes territory," not just in the hearts of believers, but in the affairs of men. This has implications for church polity and authority. The Church of Rome insists that we undersell the power of salvation in Christ if we deny that he has the power to establish indefectible traditions and authoritative deputies after his ascension into heaven. But this is not the main thrust. More importantly, the Catholic principle affirms that the church on earth stewards unpolluted, sacred things. The City of God has an earthly footprint, as it were. Thus, it is not papal infallibility or other matters of authority that express the essence of the Catholic principle but rather *ex opere operato*, a Latin phrase that literally means "out of the working of the work" and that means the ongoing work of the church, especially its sacramental actions, are fully freighted with God's saving and sanctifying grace, no matter how grievous the defects of the church's leaders and members. In short, *ex opera operato* expresses the belief that no amount of human sinfulness can destroy the this-worldly efficacy of God's grace. He can make men saints, even in spite of our failures. And the Lord can establish a supernatural community that partakes of his unchanging, everlasting truth. For this reason the many abuses so evident in the church tend not to unsettle the Catholic sensibility.

The liturgy is an obvious instance of the Anglican *ex opere operato*, as is the Anglican loyalty to her liturgical tradition. The same holds for the Anglican loyalty to the threefold ministry. Both reflect the Anglican conviction, sometimes implicit rather than articulated, that Christ's authority is intermixed with the efforts of fallen men to guide and govern the church over time. The church's constitution is contingent, but it is nevertheless sacred. The finite is capable of the infinite, not just in the person of Jesus Christ, but in his living body, the church, as well.

The Catholic principle influences Anglican piety. Unlike evangelicalism, which emphasizes warm preaching and personal witness, an Anglican sensibility relies on slow conversion wrought by regular participation in an orderly worship steeped in the apostolic tradition. This can lead to faithless formalism, a danger especially evident in Anglo-Catholicism, which by the late twentieth century had become weakened and less influential. At its best, however, the catholic side of Anglicanism trusts in the efficacy of outward forms. The "doing" of church is in itself an evangelical and catechetical act. This Catholic principle can lead to complacency, as if preserving the church's sacred inheritance is sufficient, excusing us from the task of bold preaching and missionary zeal. But the Catholic principle, at its best, encourages a liturgical formation of the soul that deepens the hold of the gospel on the lives of believers. It also establishes a steady, visible form of life and regular, public language of worship that stands as an embodied witness against the world's false claim to sovereignty over our earthly lives.

The Catholic principle has made Anglicanism capacious, not the *via media*, which, when turned into a principle of mere balancing of extremes, actually narrows the church. When the power of the sacred is invested in outward forms, when we trust in what I call the "objectivity of grace," we need not do bed checks, nor need we compulsively take our spiritual temperatures in order to assure ourselves we're under the influence of God's saving power. At its best, Anglicanism has a clear, visible life of sacred worship. A clear, well-defined form of life, which is to say the visible form of Christ present in a community at worship has allowed Anglicanism to maintain relatively porous borders, just as the Torah-observant synagogues of Saint Paul's day could be a place where God-fearing "seekers" could enter into the presence of the one true God. The recession of the Catholic side of the *via media* has been a source of crisis in the American Episcopal Church just as much as a betrayal of the Protestant side. A weakened sense that church governance is first and foremost a stewardship of divine things leads to an invasion of a pietistic sensibility that insists that worship must reflect subjective convictions, and subjective convictions must reshape worship. This has turned Anglicanism into a progressive sect.

In these first decades of the twenty-first century we are becoming aware that a great deal is ending. The collapse of the Soviet Union exposed the failure of Enlightenment utopianism, a utopianism in which all modern political ideologies participate, including our own liberal ideologies. The sense of things coming to an end is not just political and cultural. We also feel it in our churches. To a great extent, the Reformation era is ending.

The Protestant denominational system has lost is cogency and salience. Even the distinctions between Protestants and Catholics have blurred. The causes are manifold, but the most powerful is the de-Christianization of the West. It is forcing our churches toward a more primitive condition in which simple biblical literacy (the Protestant minimum) and a visible form of life independent of secular culture (the Catholic minimum) have become fragile achievements.

In the post-Christian context, the churches in the West that are descended from the Church of England may die of self-inflicted wounds. Nevertheless, I'm increasingly convinced that an enlarged, differentiated vision of apostolic authority (the Protestant side of the *via media*) and something of Anglicanism's modest but tenacious loyalty to outward forms (the Catholic side) will characterize our shared future as Christians. It is my hope that as we are drawn into a broad, tacit movement toward the Anglican gestalt, we will recapitulate its strengths while avoiding its perversions.

Response to the
Ecclesiastical Perspectives

Ray R. Sutton

These last four chapters introduce us to an ecumenical facet of the Anglican way that has not yet been addressed but uniquely touches both Anglicanism's essence and distinction. In short, we often forget that Anglicanism died twice only to be resurrected with renewed vigor each time.

It first died in the sixteenth century with the death of the young King Edward VI. His sister Mary came to power, took the country back to the bishop of Rome, and killed the archbishop of Canterbury, two other bishops, and hundreds of other clergy and laity. Mary's reign did not last long. After Mary's death, her sister Elizabeth I became queen and restored the Anglican way in England. The Church of England regained new life with the appointment of godly bishops to the historic sees, the reinstatement of the Book of Common Prayer for worship, and the approval of the theological statement the Thirty-Nine Articles of Religion.

Anglicanism died again in the seventeenth century during the reign of Oliver Cromwell. He was involved in the Puritan movement that eventuated in a war. This resulted in the deaths of King Charles I and the archbishop of Canterbury, William Laud. For well over a decade, the Anglican Church as an ecclesial entity disappeared. Bishoprics became vacant, reaching a nadir of only thirteen English bishops, most of whom fled to Europe. A substitute church became the state church. Iconoclasts abounded, tearing the fabric of the Anglican way and doing great physical damage to beautiful historic churches. Happily, not long after this second death, overnight the Cromwellian era ended. The nation of England called the Anglican Church back. Anglicanism reappeared.

Each resurgence of life after death left Anglicanism with a greater capacity to become a more unifying church. To cite the great Roman Catholic writer Henri Nouwen, out of the wounds came an ability to heal: a wounded healer. Anglicanism emerged with greater comprehensiveness, bringing in more branches of God's vine.

Why did Anglicanism repeatedly come back? One reason is the ecumenical value of this portion of God's people. The previous chapters demonstrate this: two of the writers are not Anglican. One is a Roman Catholic; the other is a Baptist. At one level, the presence of our brothers demonstrates what has been called the larger realignment of Christendom. At another level, though not typically mentioned as a characteristic of the Anglican way, in this book we see the capacity of the Anglican way to work with and draw together other branches of Christ's church on the Catholic and Protestant sides of Christendom.

But before I comment on the previous chapters, I think two ecumenical presumptions should be understood. First, by interacting with other branches of the Lord's church, we are not overlooking important differences. For example, biblical Anglicans are convicted that the Bible is the final authority for faith and life. In addition, even though much progress has been made in ecumenical dialogues with Roman Catholics in their conversations with Anglicans and Lutherans on the matter of Christ's death on the cross as the only basis for forgiveness, Anglicans still hold to the material center of justification by faith in ways that many Catholics would not. Anglicans insist that God saves us by grace through faith in Christ's finished work and not because of our works. That is not to say that for Anglicans works are irrelevant. For, in the words of James's epistle, "Faith by itself, if it does not have works, is dead" (James 2:17). Salvation by faith alone never stands alone. It always issues in biblical repentance and obedience. But while Catholics will sometimes talk about being saved by the sacraments, Anglicans will insist that without saving faith, the sacraments do not save. And although Anglicans have respect for the bishop of Rome as a major leader among Christians in the world, they do not believe in papal supremacy or infallibility.

A second important principle of ecumenical dialogue is that in this time when there is so much antagonism to Christianity, it is crucial to acknowledge common ground with other orthodox Christians for the purpose of speaking truth to a lost and dying world. We should acknowledge that while we disagree with Rome on a number of important issues, we rejoice when our Roman Catholic friends proclaim Jesus Christ as the true way to God, confess the truths of the Nicene and Apostles' Creeds, affirm the inspiration of the Holy Scriptures, and seek to live out biblical morality as summarized in the Ten Commandments, including agreement on the nature of biblical marriage.

In a preceding chapter, our Roman Catholic brother Rusty Reno astutely refers to a similarity between Roman Catholics and Anglicans: both go *ad fontes*. This Latin phrase means "to the beginnings or sources." For Roman Catholics and Anglicans these sources are the Holy Scriptures and the church fathers. Here there is tremendous common ground on which to forge a new relationship in our work to spread the gospel.

My brother in Christ and Baptist theologian Timothy George in his chapter summarizes much of the significant dialogue that has transpired between Anglicans and Baptists. He sheds important light on the common ground that has been found between these two great traditions regarding the "essence of the faith," a phrase used by the renowned post-Reformation Anglican theologian Richard Hooker. Dr. George also notes that most of the original reasons for the Baptist rejection of Anglican liturgical worship in the Book of Common Prayer no longer exist. Today many Baptists appreciate and use aspects of Anglican liturgy. They enjoy the same beauty of holiness. Finally, George points to the common missional DNA within Anglicans and Baptists. Both participated in and were influenced by the significant missionary movement of the last two and a half centuries. William Carey, the great Baptist missionary to India, was friends with and influenced numerous Anglican leaders of his day. For these reasons, Anglicans and Baptists have much potential for future ecumenical work together to advance the proclamation of the gospel.

The two other chapters touch on additional aspects of the way in which Anglicanism contributes and appeals to the larger body of Christ. Dean Pearson concentrates in his chapter largely on the foundational importance of the gospel and the authority of Scripture in forming a biblical Anglican model that appeals across all denominational boundaries.

The chapter by Gerald McDermott helps us grasp the broad appeal of the Anglican way. He notes that not only did the Reformation restore to the church the word of God written, but it also recovered, in the English Reformation, the beauty of holiness in the liturgy and sacraments. He refers to these two as the verbal and the visual. Together they form a truly balanced Christian life. There is need for both to reshape us into the image of Jesus Christ. I would add that this balance reflects the left-brain–right-brain dual reality required of a mature Christian life. Anglicanism appeals to left-brain and right-brain traditions of spirituality, standing at the intersection of both.

I started with the near-death experiences of the Anglican way. The larger and more urgent death to address is that of Western Christianity. The culture of the West is dying. I am reminded of the line in Tolkien's *Two Towers* in his *Lord of the Rings* trilogy. King Theoden bemoans the sad condition of the West of his country: "The days have gone down in the West behind the hills into shadow."[1] Tolkien clearly is alluding to another West: the Western world of Europe and North America. Just as in Tolkien's stories it took the unification of peoples to resist the enemies, Christendom today will need to stand together for its own survival. No one church is powerful enough to overcome secular, pagan thought and practice by itself. It will take all of us confessing true faith in Christ—the faith once delivered to the saints—to spread the gospel. May Anglicans help the "one holy, catholic [universal], and apostolic church" (Nicene Creed) answer the prayer of Jesus Christ that we may be one so that the world might believe (John 17:21)!

---

1. J. R. R. Tolkien, "The King of the Golden Hall," in *The Lord of the Rings*, part 2, *The Two Towers* (New York: Ballantine, 1965), 143.

CONCLUSION

Where Is Orthodox Anglicanism Headed?

Gerald R. McDermott

The center of gravity of Christianity has moved in the last fifty years from the Global North to the Global South. The year 2018 was the first in which Africa had more Christians than any other continent.[1] Significantly, Nigeria has more Anglicans than any other country on the globe, and Nigeria is poised to become the third most populous nation on the planet by 2050, surpassing the United States.[2] These facts are all the more significant because Anglicanism is growing around the world, but especially in Africa. And in Nigeria, which is the biggest country in Africa, Anglicanism has been—and continues to be—disproportionately influential among the Christian churches, and even in Muslim-Christian relations.[3]

---

1. "Global Christianity: A Look at the Status of Christianity in 2018," Center for the Study of Global Christianity, accessed January 2, 2019, https://www.gordonconwell.edu /ockenga/research/documents/GlobalChristianityinfographic.pdf?g1.pdf.

2. Niall McCarthy, "The World's Most Populous Nations in 2050," *Forbes*, June 22, 2017, https://www.forbes.com/sites/niallmccarthy/2017/06/22/the-worlds-most-populous -nations-in-2050-infographic/#2c21d1e639f6.

3. Kevin Ward, *A History of Global Anglicanism* (Cambridge: Cambridge University Press, 2006), 132–33.

Nigeria is the epicenter of global Anglicanism and so perhaps a harbinger of the future of orthodox Anglicanism. By itself, it tells us that future Anglicanism will be largely nonwhite, vibrant in mission, and a suffering church. Nigerian Anglicans, like other Christians in Nigeria, face unrelenting persecution from radical Islam. It is estimated that since 2001, between twenty thousand and fifty thousand Nigerian Christians have been massacred by Muslims. Another two million have been displaced from their homes.

What else can we learn from the preceding chapters about the future of Anglicanism? Do Anglicans face a diminished future, as Radner and Bray suggest? Radner points realistically to disunity in confession and doctrine, the absence of any common Anglican "attitude," and the intractability of disagreement on major issues in ecclesial disputes. He speaks of polarization and paralysis, both of which have been on display in meetings that pit liberals in the United States and England against conservatives in the Global South. Of course, there are Northern conservatives and Southern liberals, but generally the South has rejected liberal overtures coming from leaders in the North.

Bray is also struck by this division among the leaders of the Communion. He asks how two kinds of church can walk together if they are not agreed. He recommends that Anglicans embrace their calling to be servants, drop their distinctives in this new ecumenical climate, and join a "merely Christian" movement devoted to biblical and theological literacy. Like Radner, he sees little Anglican soul left at the end of Anglicanism's first five hundred years—little enough to have a distinctive identity.

Radner and Bray speak from within Anglicanism in the Global North, and from Anglican churches (the Anglican Church of Canada and the Episcopal Church) that have been taken over by soul-killing liberalism. They speak accurately and helpfully, but from an ecclesial location not shared by other authors.

All of the other authors are optimistic about the future of orthodox Anglicanism. As Bishop Sutton observes, Anglicanism has appeared to be in its death throes several times before. Sixteenth-century Anglicans were justified in thinking the Anglican Church was dying under Queen Mary, and seventeenth-century Anglicans had good reason to think it would die again under Oliver Cromwell. So too today. There are signs of death all over the Global North.

But the Global South sings a different tune. Kenyan archbishop Wabukala thinks the Anglican movement is on the verge of new global growth, and that through its recovery of its reformed catholicity it will bring life to the world. Egyptian archbishop Anis is also optimistic. He agrees with Wabukala that Anglicans have a peculiar ability to minister the gospel in a holistic way, and that their theology can bridge divides between Catholics and Orthodox on one side and Protestants on the other. His churches in North Africa are growing, and he anticipates more growth to come. Nigerian Anglicanism has been growing for decades and is full of initiative and creativity. GAFCON 2018, at which "the African presence was strong,"[4] showcased this Southern vitality.

Our authors range from high to broad to low church. All emphasize the low church insistence on the centrality of the written and preached word of Holy Scripture. They all urge mission to the lost and unevangelized. All point to the cross and the crucial doctrine of justification by grace through faith. Yates rightly warns that without attention to these essentials, Anglicans risk losing the center of the gospel message. Pearson reminds us that the church

---

4. Esau McCaulley, "Why GAFCON Matters: Thoughts on the Opening of GAFCON 2018," *The Living Church*, June 19, 2018, https://livingchurch.org/covenant/2018/06/19/why-gafcon-matters-thoughts-on-the-opening-of-gafcon-2018/.

with liturgy and sacrament is intended to bring us to the person of Jesus, and that we can never know him apart from Scripture.

Yet one also finds in these essays a growing conviction that at the heart of historic Anglicanism is catholic substance sharpened by reformed critique. By this I mean ancient liturgy and sacraments tempered by Reformation criticism of semi-Pelagianism. Wabukala speaks of the need to recover our reformed catholicity. Anis prizes Anglican tradition that enables him to speak with Egyptian Copts, and says that Egyptian Anglicans see their roots in the North African fathers of the first centuries of the church. Gauthier writes of a reformed catholicism that goes back to the undivided church of the first five centuries. She testifies that this retrieval of ancient practices is invigorating Anglican churches in the Upper Midwest of the United States. In my chapter I speak of the beauty and power that come from ancient liturgy and sacraments. These will save us from an intellectualized gospel that appeals only to the cerebral hearer. They capture the one transcendental reality that is particularly resonant with the "nones"—those claiming no religion—and other lost souls of this century: the beauty of God.

Several writers suggest that these Anglican distinctives will help rather than hurt ecumenical relations. Wabukala calls on African Anglicans to retrieve their historic reformed catholicity, and at the same time encourages Anglican partnership with non-Anglicans. Early African Anglicans were known for their ecumenism, and Anglicans should continue in that, he says. Anis points to Anglican cultural centers in Egypt that foster good relations with Egyptian Muslims. Timothy George relates how the Prayer Book and Anglican sacraments have attracted Baptists to more catholic sensibilities. Nineteenth-century Anglican distinctives, he suggests, did not prevent Anglican-Baptist cooperation in social reform and missions. The Catholic thinker Rusty Reno applauds both Anglican faith in slow conversion[5] and Anglican belief that God works objectively through liturgy and sacrament. He says that this catholic way of being Christian combined with an enlarged view of apostolic authority (a more Protestant approach) might be a template for the future of orthodox Christianity.

In sum, what can we expect of the orthodox Anglican future? It will be mostly nonwhite, led by the Global South, and devoted to Scripture. Because of its non-English and non-American majority, it will insist on different ways of choosing its overall archbishop and different ways of governing the Communion. The growth of GAFCON and ACNA will ensure that it resists the call to overturn the marriage of one man and one woman. It will aggressively evangelize and missionize, even under persecution. More will attend to catholic substance, finding in ancient liturgy and sacraments the beauty of holiness and the power of the gospel.

---

5. By this Reno means Anglican belief that one is gradually formed into Christ (Gal. 4:19) through the church's liturgy and sacraments. Regeneration may be instantaneous, but conversion from a self-centered life to a God-centered one may take an entire lifetime.

CONTRIBUTORS

The Most Reverend Mouneer Hanna Anis is bishop of the Diocese of Egypt with North Africa and the Horn of Africa, and chairman of the Global South Fellowship of the Anglican Communion. He studied theology at Moore College, Australia, and at Nashotah House Theological Seminary.

The Most Reverend Foley Beach (DMin, Gordon-Conwell Theological Seminary) is archbishop of the Anglican Church in North America, chairman of the Global Anglican Future Conference (GAFCON), and teacher on *A Word from the Lord*, a radio and Internet Bible teaching ministry.

Gerald Bray (DLitt, University of Paris-Sorbonne) is a Church of England clergyman, director of research for the Latimer Trust (London), and research professor of divinity at Beeson Divinity School.

Barbara Gauthier (PhD, Vanderbilt University) is an Anglican journalist and teaches Latin and Greek. She is married to the canon theologian of the Diocese of the Upper Midwest (ACNA) and serves as a lay leader with Church of the Resurrection and the Greenhouse Movement.

Timothy George (ThD, Harvard University) is research professor at Beeson Divinity School and general editor of the *Reformation Com-*

mentary on Scripture. He served as the dean of Beeson Divinity School 1988–2019.

The Right Reverend Chandler Holder Jones, SSC (MDiv, Duke University Divinity School), is bishop coadjutor of the Diocese of the Eastern United States of the Anglican Province of America and rector of Saint Barnabas Anglican Church in Dunwoody (Atlanta), Georgia.

Gerald R. McDermott (PhD, University of Iowa) is Anglican chair of divinity at Beeson Divinity School. He is the author, coauthor, or editor of more than twenty books.

Stephen F. Noll (PhD, University of Manchester) is professor emeritus at Trinity School for Ministry in Ambridge, Pennsylvania. He served as vice chancellor of Uganda Christian University 2000–2010.

The Very Reverend Andrew C. Pearson Jr. (BD, University of Oxford) is dean and rector of the Cathedral Church of the Advent in Birmingham, Alabama.

Ephraim Radner (PhD, Yale University) is professor of historical theology, Wycliffe College, University of Toronto. An ordained Anglican priest, he is the author of books on pneumatology, ecclesiology, and Scripture.

R. R. Reno (PhD, Yale University) is the editor of *First Things* magazine, author of five books, and the general editor of the *Brazos Theological Commentary on the Bible*. Baptized as an Episcopalian, he was active in the Episcopal Church until he was received into the Catholic Church in 2004.

The Most Reverend Ray R. Sutton (PhD, University of Oxford) is presiding bishop of the Reformed Episcopal Church and dean of the province and ecumenical affairs in the Anglican Church in North America.

The Most Reverend Eliud Wabukala (DD, Wycliffe College, University of Toronto) is archbishop emeritus of the Anglican Church of Kenya. He is currently chairman of the Ethics and Anti-Corruption Commission of Kenya.

John W. Yates III (PhD, New Testament, Cambridge University) is rector of Holy Trinity Anglican Church in Raleigh, North Carolina. Among his previous positions, he served as study assistant to John R. W. Stott.

GENERAL INDEX

SCRIPTURE INDEX